CW01497628

KING STEPHEN'S REIGN

(1135–1154)

KING STEPHEN'S REIGN
(1135–1154)

EDITED BY

Paul Dalton and Graeme J. White

THE BOYDELL PRESS

First published 2008
The Boydell Press, Woodbridge

ISBN 978–1–84383–361–1

The Boydell Press is an imprint of Boydell & Brewer Ltd
PO Box 9, Woodbridge, Suffolk IP12 3DF, UK
and of Boydell & Brewer Inc.
668 Mt Hope Avenue, Rochester, NY 14620, USA
website: www.boydellandbrewer.com

A CIP record for this book is available
from the British Library

This publication is printed on acid-free paper

Typeset by Pru Harrison, Hacheston, Suffolk
Printed in Great Britain by
Antony Rowe Ltd, Chippenham, Wiltshire

Contents

Maps

Preface

This volume represents the proceedings of a conference convened by the editors and held at Liverpool Hope University from 6 to 8 September 2005. With the exception of the Introduction, all of the chapters were read as papers at the conference. We are delighted that our plans to hold the conference, originally discussed in the early 1990s, came to fruition and wish to express our gratitude to all those who helped to make the conference a success. These include the scholars who gave papers at the conference and Dr Marjorie Chibnall whose presence in Liverpool graced the proceedings and who very kindly wrote the Introduction to this volume. We would like to thank them all for their contributions and their patience and understanding during the editorial process. We also wish to thank colleagues, including Dr Chris Lewis, who chaired sessions of the conference, Professor Edmund King for reading the paper of Professor Thomas N. Bisson (who was unable to attend the conference), and all who came to hear the papers and contribute to the discussions. Our thanks also go out to Liverpool Hope University for hosting and supporting the conference, in particular the Vice Chancellor and Rector, Professor Gerald Pillay, Mrs Anne Kermode for her impeccable, extensive and gracious administrative assistance, Dr John Appleby and Dr Fiona Pogson, the Research Committee for the award of a grant, and the conference office, catering, cleaning and portering staff who helped in a variety of ways. We are also grateful to Mrs Brenda Davies of Chester University for some of the work in preparing the text for the publishers, including the abbreviations page; to Mrs Catherine Rising of Canterbury Christ Church University and Ms Lynn Westwood for their assistance; to Caroline Palmer and all at Boydell & Brewer Ltd for agreeing to publish the volume and for their help and efficiency in doing so; to Boydell's anonymous referees for recommending publication; and to Oxford University Press for free permission to use quotations from the editions of the *Regesta Regum Anglo-Normannorum* (volume III), the *Gesta Stephani* and the *Historia Novella*.

Paul Dalton and Graeme J. White
Canterbury and Chester, April 2007

Abbreviations

ANS	*Anglo-Norman Studies*
ASC	*Anglo-Saxon Chronicle*, ed. D. Whitelock et al. (London, 1969)
BL	British Library
Cal. Docs France	*Calendar of Documents preserved in France* ..., i, *918–1216*, ed. J. H. Round (HMSO, 1899)
Chibnall, *Empress Matilda*	M. Chibnall, *The Empress Matilda: Queen Consort, Queen Mother and Lady of the English* (Oxford, 1993)
Complete Peerage	*The Complete Peerage of England, Scotland, Ireland, Great Britain and the United Kingdom*, 13 vols. in 14 (London, 1910–59)
Councils & Synods	*Councils & Synods with other Documents relating to the English Church, I: A.D. 871–1204*, ed. D. Whitelock, M. Brett and C. N. L. Brooke, 2 vols. (Oxford, 1981)
Crouch, *Reign of Stephen*	D. Crouch, *The Reign of King Stephen, 1135–1154* (Harlow, 2000)
Curia Regis Rolls	*Curia Regis Rolls of the Reigns of Richard I and John, preserved in the Public Record Office*, 7 vols. (HMSO, 1922–35); *Curia Regis Rolls of the Reign of Henry III, preserved in the Public Record Office*, 12 vols. (HMSO and PRO, 1938–2002)
Davis, *King Stephen*	R. H. C. Davis, *King Stephen 1135–1154* (3rd edn, London, 1990)
Diceto	*Radulphi de Diceto, Opera Historica. The Historical Works of Master Ralph de Diceto, Dean of London*, ed. W. Stubbs, 2 vols. (RS, 1876)
Domesday Book	*Domesday Book, seu liber censualis* ..., i, ii, ed. A. Farley (Record Commission, 1783); iii, iv, ed. H. Ellis (1816)
EEA	*English Episcopal Acta*
EHR	*English Historical Review*
EYC	*Early Yorkshire Charters*, i–iii, ed. W. Farrer (Edinburgh, 1914–16), and iv–xii, ed. C. T. Clay, Yorkshire Archaeological Society, Record Series, extra series I–X (Wakefield, 1935–65)
Gesta Guillelmi	*The Gesta Guillelmi of William of Poitiers*, ed. R. H. C. Davis and M. Chibnall (Oxford, 1998)
Gesta Regum	William of Malmesbury, *Gesta Regum Anglorum*, ed. R. A. B. Mynors, R. M. Thomson and M. Winterbottom, 2 vols. (Oxford, 1998–9)
Gesta Stephani	*Gesta Stephani*, ed. and trans. K. R. Potter and R. H. C. Davis (Oxford, 1976)

Historia Novella	William of Malmesbury, *Historia Novella: The Contemporary History*, ed. E. King, trans. K. R. Potter (Oxford, 1998)
HMSO	Her Majesty's Stationery Office
Howden, *Chronica*	*Chronica Rogeri de Houedene*, ed. W. Stubbs. 4 vols. (RS, 1889–71)
Howden, *Gesta Regis*	*Gesta Regis Henrici Secundi et Ricardi Primi*, ed. W. Stubbs, 2 vols. (RS, 1867)
Howlett, *Chronicles*	*Chronicles of the Reigns of Stephen, Henry II and Richard I*, ed. R. Howlett, 4 vols. (RS, 1884–9)
HSJ	*Haskins Society Journal*
Huntingdon	Henry, *Archdeacon of Huntingdon: 'Historia Anglorum'*, ed. D. Greenway (Oxford, 1996)
John of Worcester	The Chronicle of John of Worcester, ii–iii, ed. R. R. Darlington and P. McGurk (Oxford, 1995–8)
Jumièges	*Gesta Normannorum Ducum of William of Jumièges, Orderic Vitalis and Robert of Torigni*, ed. E. M. C. van Houts, 2 vols. (Oxford, 1992–5)
King, *Anarchy*	*The Anarchy of King Stephen's Reign*, ed. E. King (Oxford, 1994)
Matthew, *King Stephen*	D. Matthew, *King Stephen* (London, 2002)
MGH	Monumenta Germaniae Historica
Monasticon	W. Dugdale, *Monasticon Anglicanum*, ed. J. Caley, H. Ellis and B. Bandinel, 6 vols. in 8 (London, 1817–30)
Newburgh	*Historia Rerum Anglicarum of William of Newburgh*, in Howlett, *Chronicles*, vols. 1 and 2
ns	new series
Orderic	Orderic Vitalis, *Historia Ecclesiastica*, ed. M. Chibnall (Oxford, 1969–80)
PL	*Patrologiae cursus completus, series Latina*, ed. J. P. Migne (Paris, 1841–64)
PR	*Pipe Roll* (as published by Pipe Roll Society)
PRO	Public Record Office
Regesta	*Regesta Regum Anglo-Normannorum*, i, ed. H. W. C. Davis (Oxford, 1913); ii, ed. C. Johnson and H. A. Cronne (Oxford, 1956); iii, ed. H. A. Cronne and R. H. C. Davis (Oxford, 1968)
RS	Rolls Series, London
ser.	series
Torigni	*The Chronicle of Robert de Torigni*, in Howlett, *Chronicles*, vol. 4
TRHS	*Transactions of the Royal Historical Society*
VCH	*Victoria County History*
Waltham	*The Waltham Chronicle*, ed. and trans. L. Watkiss and M. Chibnall (Oxford, 1994)

The Family Connections of King Stephen

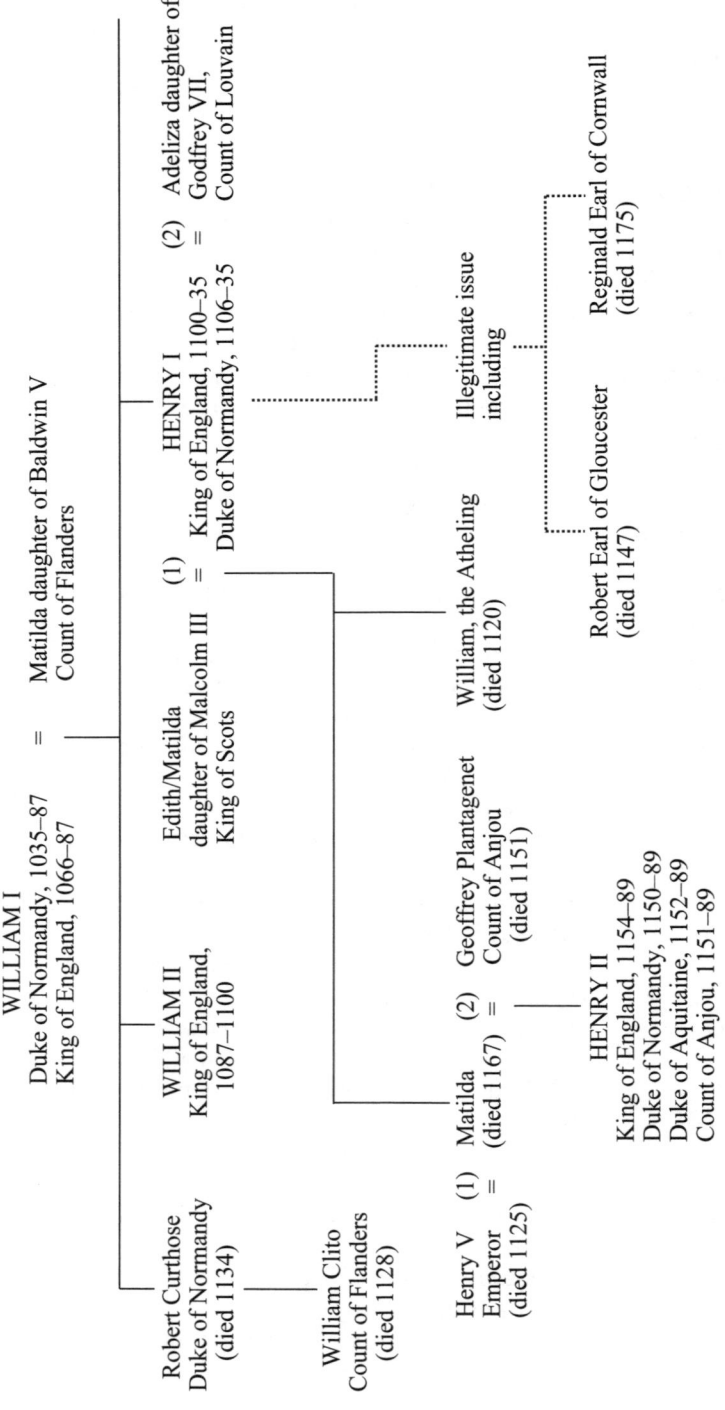

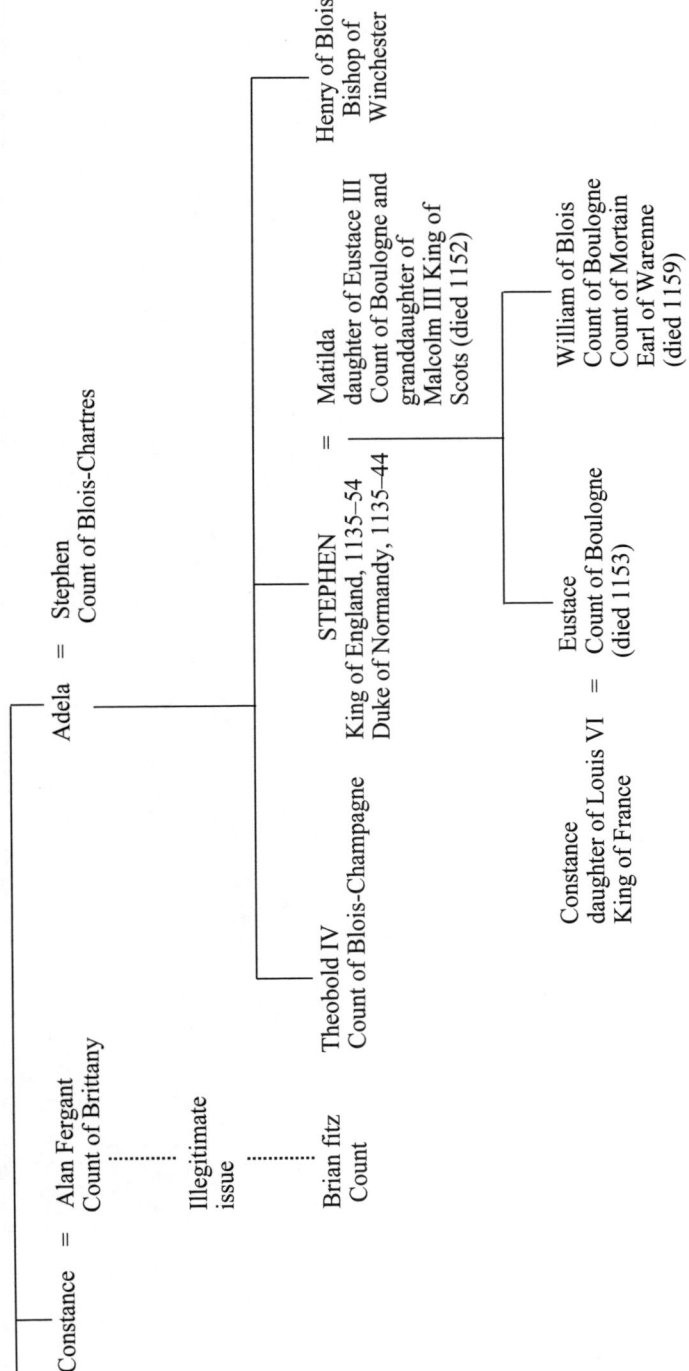

Introduction

MARJORIE CHIBNALL

THE REIGN OF Stephen invites and receives frequent attention from historians. Although it lasted a mere nineteen years it was rich in historical sources, both chronicle and charter. Moreover the charters, whether produced in monasteries or in secular writing offices, were far from stereotyped and frequently contained passages of narrative. Henry I died in December 1135 without any surviving legitimate son; the seizure of the throne by his nephew Stephen before his daughter Matilda was able to reach England occurred at a critical time for the development of the Anglo-Norman realm. Changes were taking place both in royal government and in the relations between lords and vassals, as well as in customary law, regional organisation and relations with other powers. The abundant sources focus a somewhat erratic spotlight on the events of the reign, and the effect is sometimes to illuminate short periods in unusual detail and sometimes to dazzle and invite exaggeration. The importance of the charters granted in Stephen's reign tempted J. H. Round (who might almost be said to have seen historical writing as the interpretation of charters) to produce his nearest approach to a volume of narrative history. Not surprisingly in recent years, when historiography has frequently taken the form of revising specific periods, much work on the reign has consisted of a revision of Round.[1] Most recently, however, historians have preferred to approach the subject from new and different standpoints. In particular it has been seen from a longer perspective and considered in relation to historical changes in Europe as a whole and in the position of the papacy.

If Henry could have chosen the date of his death he would not have chosen December 1135. His efforts after the death in 1120 of his only legitimate son had been directed towards either producing a son by a second marriage or, failing that, securing support for the succession of his daughter Matilda and her heirs.[2] Matilda, widowed in 1125, had been provided with a second husband, young Geoffrey of Anjou, in order to further her father's political ambitions. The

---

[1] King, *Anarchy*.
[2] See below, J. Green, 'Henry I and the Origins of the Civil War'.

marriage had started badly, and not until March 1133 was her first son, Henry, born. Her father needed to live for another fifteen or sixteen years if the boy was to succeed him without a minority. Although the Anglo-Norman baronage might be persuaded to accept Matilda as legitimate 'successor', her father never clarified before death overtook him what the position of her husband Geoffrey would be and there was conflict about the control of the Norman castles that were nominally her dower.[3] The way was open for Henry's nephew Stephen of Blois, whose wife Matilda was the heiress of Boulogne, to cross rapidly to England and win acceptance as king from the Londoners and a handful of bishops and magnates before Matilda, who entered Normandy immediately with her household troops, could make her way beyond Falaise. There she was warned by her half-brother, Robert earl of Gloucester, of the powerful position of her adversary Stephen, and was persuaded to retreat as far as her strong castle of Argentan and wait for a more propitious moment to stake her claim to the kingdom. There is no evidence to support the allegation, casually made and too often repeated even by reputable historians, that she remained passively in Anjou.[4]

The struggles that followed were influenced by new personalities as well as by the changing conditions in north-western Europe as a whole. As David Crouch points out, neither Stephen nor Louis VII had the political ability of Henry I and Louis VI.[5] King Henry had succeeded in preventing the rivalry of the houses of Anjou and Blois from disrupting the southern frontier of Normandy. Even his successful negotiation of the marriage of Geoffrey of Anjou and his daughter Matilda did not result in the alienation of his ally, Theobald of Blois. There was, admittedly, a latent danger, since the favour he had shown to his nephews Stephen and Henry of Blois meant that Stephen controlled Boulogne through his wife Matilda, and Henry, as bishop of Winchester, was strongly placed to influence the English church and the Cluniacs.

Stephen, together with the other English magnates, had sworn fealty to Matilda, but there was considerable ambiguity in the oaths. The various pretexts put forward by those who changed their allegiance after King Henry's death revealed the uncertainties.[6] What kind of pressure justified the renunciation of a solemn oath? Some of the disaffected claimed to have been intimidated, but as yet there was no established legal formula such as the later 'fear that might fall on the constant man' to justify failure to keep an oath. Guarantees of a different kind had to be found, and they usually included the offer of hostages. In the weeks

---

[3] *Historia Novella*, 24–5, 'When he was asked … about his succession, he assigned all his lands on both sides of the sea to his daughter in lawful and lasting succession, being somewhat angry with her husband because he had vexed the king by not a few threats and insults'.

[4] *Orderic*, vi, 454–6; *Torigni*, 128; M. Chibnall, 'The Empress Matilda as a Subject for Biography', in *Writing Medieval Biography, 750–1250: Essays in Honour of Professor Frank Barlow*, ed. D. Bates, J. Crick and S. Hamilton (Woodbridge, 2006), ch. 12, 190–2.

[5] See below, D. Crouch, 'King Stephen and Northern France', 44–57.

[6] See below, P. Dalton, 'Allegiance and Intelligence in King Stephen's Reign', 81–93.

immediately following the king's death his carefully laid plans were shattered by Stephen's speed in securing coronation before Matilda could even reach the Channel coast. From that time her problem was a different one: what could legalise the removal of a crowned and anointed king? Matilda's earlier career as the wife of the Emperor Henry V had taken her into the heart of European politics; she knew Rome and had experienced the difficulties that could result from excommunication. Moreover she was believed in some quarters (perhaps without justification) to have influence on politics in the papal curia.[7] No sooner was Stephen crowned than he sent envoys to Rome to secure papal support.

Matilda also sent an envoy to mount a challenge. Though unsuccessful in invalidating Stephen's claim she was at least able to persuade Pope Innocent II to make his recognition provisional, so opening a loophole for future attempts either to remove Stephen or to prevent his son being accepted as a rightful heir to the throne. In the long run she prevailed, but initially she was impotent. Stephen had two or three years to secure his position before she could mount an effective challenge. Recent work on charters has shown that even in the years she remained under siege in Argentan she was actively building up support.[8] In this she was helped by Stephen's failure to assess the importance of Normandy in preserving his power. He paid one visit to the duchy in 1137 and received the recognition of King Louis, to whom his son Eustace did homage. But trouble broke out among his own followers, and those who had given him merely token allegiance were ready to break away. In particular Robert earl of Gloucester, the ablest of Henry's illegitimate sons, who had secured his position in Bristol and could count on the loyalty of his vassals, renounced his homage in the spring of 1138 and joined Matilda in Argentan. At the same time he was actively securing promises of support from other magnates. There were some negotiations at Domfront, and a *conventio* was agreed by representatives of the empress, in which Miles of Gloucester promised to help whenever she might be able to come to England and claim her rights.[9] Stephen returned to England to deal with disturbances there and never again visited Normandy. He appears, in the words of David Crouch, to have 'let Normandy go'.[10]

To Matilda, on the other hand, Normandy was the essential link between her husband's county of Anjou and England, where Robert of Gloucester was able to provide a safe base for her whenever she could succeed in crossing the sea. The Anglo-Norman realm was a reality to powerful magnates like the Beaumont twins, who had wealthy estates on both sides of the Channel.[11] Their interests helped to ensure the survival of the realm throughout the reign. Besides this,

---

7 John of Salisbury, *Historia Pontificalis*, ed. M. Chibnall (Oxford, 1986), 85.
8 I am grateful to Nicholas Vincent for reference to the fuller version of BL Sloane MS 1301, fo. 422r–v.
9 BL Sloane MS 1301, fo. 422r–v.
10 See Crouch, below, 53.
11 D. Crouch, *The Beaumont Twins: The Roots and Branches of Power in the Twelfth Century* (Cambridge, 1986), 51–2.

economically and culturally Normandy continued to have strong links with Paris, and it had prosperous citizens capable of providing loans to finance the war.[12] And at a time of vigorous rebuilding, before and after the hostilities, the style sometimes described as Norman Romanesque still predominated. Only after the middle of the century, particularly after 1160, did the gothic style that was triumphing in the region of Paris captivate architects and patrons and transform the new cathedrals and other great churches of Normandy.[13] Matilda was guided by the conviction she held, until she was forced to abandon it in1141, that she was here father's heir, not merely his successor, and therefore enjoyed whatever regal power he may have enjoyed.[14] So, during the first phase of the struggle for power, she worked with her husband to secure Normandy as a springboard for further advance. Her husband always regarded the province as the most important part of her inheritance.

Once Matilda had succeeded in crossing the Channel and reaching the secure base of Bristol Count Geoffrey was able to take over the whole struggle in Normandy, while she concentrated on building up her strength in England. Half a century later, when Ralph Diceto looked back on Stephen's reign, he expressed surprise that the final settlement did not follow a victory in battle.[15] Matilda's supporters, led by Robert of Gloucester and Ranulf of Chester, did in fact win a victory at Lincoln. But whereas in 1066, when a disputed succession was decided by the battle of Hastings, Harold Godwinson had been killed and William of Normandy had triumphed, Stephen was merely captured at Lincoln and remained in prison to be a focus of resistance for some months. Henry of Blois, bishop of Winchester, was prepared at first to accept Matilda and recognise her as 'lady of the English'; this gave her regnal status. She could then receive the liege homage of any of Stephen's vassals who came to her individually. There was, however, no 'community of the realm' to speak for them collectively. The support of the church, both of the bishops in England and of the papal curia, was essential. And her position was not helped when, immediately after the election of Theobald of Bec as archbishop of Canterbury, Innocent II granted the office of papal legate not to him but to Henry of Blois. The Londoners, who had been the first to recognize Stephen's claim to the throne, still needed to be persuaded. And Stephen's wealthy and influential kinsmen would not accept disinheritance quietly; they would expect compensation in any settlement. In 1141 Matilda's thoughts were not on pacification but on coronation and the realm was divided. Stephen's wife

---

[12] See D. Bates, 'Rouen from 900 to 1204. From Scandinavian Settlement to Angevin Capital', *The British Archaeological Association Conference Transactions*, 12 (1993), 1–11; R. B. Patterson, 'Robert fitz Harding of Bristol', *HSJ*, 1 (1989), 109–22; M. Chibnall, 'Normandy', in King, *Anarchy*, ch. 3, 114–15.

[13] See L. Grant, *Architecture and Society in Normandy 1120–1270* (New Haven, 2005), esp. chs. 5, 6.

[14] C. W. Hollister, 'Normandy, France and the Anglo-Norman Regnum', in idem, *Monarchy, Magnates* and *Institutions in the Anglo-Norman World* (London, 1986), 17–57, at 47–9.

[15] *Diceto*, i, 296.

Matilda actively collected forces, particularly of Flemings, to support her in an attempt to recover the initiative.

The result was that Empress Matilda was driven back before she could enter London to be crowned. Temporarily established in Oxford, she made a desperate attempt in the summer of 1141 to secure her position by distributing honours and favours to her supporters. The charters issued in July make it possible to pin-point the moment when she recognized that she could never be more than the 'successor' of her father, and that she must concentrate on bringing her son Henry into the struggle as the lawful heir to the throne.[16] Too young to lead forces in battle, he could at least be associated with his mother in promising favours. This clear change in the terms of the struggle increased her chances of ultimate victory, provided her material and military resources were sufficient to secure her position in both England and Normandy.

Once again Normandy emerged as the most significant region in the struggle. Here, as in England, the Angevin supporters were becoming bogged down in sieges and skirmishes; but in Normandy the problem was more manageable, and Count Geoffrey of Anjou took the initiative. He refused an appeal to send knights to help his wife in England on the grounds that he must first subdue the Norman cities he was besieging, and Robert of Gloucester was persuaded to bring a force of knights to help him.[17] The result was that Matilda, besieged in Oxford, had to bear the brunt of Stephen's attack and was forced to escape and abandon the city. Her husband still refused to provide any help, but he allowed their eldest son, Henry, to travel to England when Robert of Gloucester returned. Ultimately he proved justified, for he was able to complete the conquest of Normandy, win recognition from King Louis as duke of Normandy, and establish a safe capital in the now thriving city of Rouen.

After his death in 1151, King Louis was prepared to receive young Henry's homage as duke of Normandy in Paris. When Matilda left England in 1148 she was able to settle in Rouen, and even though Henry forfeited the king's friendship by his marriage to the former queen, Eleanor, in 1152, he was able to fight off renewed attacks on the duchy.

Meanwhile in England both parties were compelled to keep armed forces permanently in strong castles, if necessary building new castles or increasing the fortifications of old ones. Because of the inevitable falling off in the royal and ducal revenues they were reduced to ravaging and extortion to keep their castles permanently on a war footing.[18] There was no doubt about the decline in revenues; Graeme White's analysis of the early Pipe Rolls of Henry II's reign shows that there was a shortfall in the first years of the new reign that was only gradually made up by an increase in the profits of royal justice.[19] Moreover between 1140 and 1153 neither party controlled the whole of the country. The ravaging and

---

16 See E. King, 'A Week in Politics: Oxford, late July 1141', below, 74–5.
17 Davis, *King Stephen*, 75–6.
18 C. Coulson, 'The Castles of the Anarchy', in King, *Anarchy*, 66–92.
19 See G. White, 'Royal Income and Regional Trends', below, 29–43.

brutality of war was made worse by prolonged hostilities. New arbitrary exactions appeared for the first time; of these the most conspicuous was 'tenserie', a form of protection money.[20] This had not previously existed in either England or Normandy; the word was of Flemish origin and indicated the special burden due to the maintenance of permanent garrisons of landless men in castles. The laments of the Anglo-Saxon chronicler were certainly justified in some regions. Many individuals tried with varying success to find sanctuary in churches and chapels. The action of the clerks of Waltham Abbey in 'humiliating the relics' during the ravaging of Geoffrey de Mandeville illustrates the desperation that might be caused by the disorders.[21]

The position of monasteries and parish churches was precarious and the bishops, as both spiritual and temporal lords, came in for some very bitter criticism. When John of Salisbury looked back on events some twenty years later he could attempt the generalisation that the whole English church followed Stephen by papal decree, 'for although individual dignitaries followed different lords, the church as a whole recognised only one'.[22] Individual chroniclers, writing nearer the time, were far from consistent in their praise and blame. The author of the *Gesta Stephani* in one place denounced the bishops collectively as 'reeds shaken by the wind' who took part like laymen in ravaging the country. More specifically, he blamed the bishops of Winchester, Lincoln and Chester but had a good word for Robert of Bethune, the saintly bishop of Hereford, who pronounced sentence of excommunication on Miles of Gloucester and laid Hereford under an interdict.[23] For the archbishop of Canterbury to have taken a strong lead in this time of war papal support would have been necessary. Unfortunately during Stephen's reign there were no less than five popes, and popes were frequently on the road because of disputed papal elections and a revolution in Rome in 1148.[24] Nevertheless, in spite of challenges to Stephen's authority, once he had been provisionally accepted as king he was regarded as the lawful king by most of the bishops. Analysis of charters relating to the dioceses of Chester, Hereford and Lincoln has shown that most of the bishops carried on their normal routine work in royal and shire government in the king's name; there were exceptions elsewhere, particularly in Oxfordshire where Angevin influence was strong. Some bishops were accused of using their knights and archers as much for plunder as for protection. There is as yet, however, no known evidence that they used them in their personal interests even if they contributed little if anything to lessen disorder.[25]

---

20 See T. N. Bisson, 'The Lure of Stephen's England: *Tenserie*, Flemings, and a Crisis of Circumstance', below, 171–81.

21 See below, H. M. Thomas, 'Violent Disorder in King Stephen's England: A Maximum Argument', 139–70; *Waltham*, 78–80.

22 *Historia Pontificalis*, 47–8.

23 *Gesta Stephani*, 154–9; S. Marritt, 'Reeds Shaken by the Wind? Bishops in Local and Regional Politics in King Stephen's Reign', below, 115–16, 120–1.

24 C. Holdsworth, 'The Church', in King, *Anarchy*, 207–39, at 207–9.

25 See below, Marritt, 'Reeds Shaken by the Wind?', 115–38.

Monastic endowments certainly increased considerably during Stephen's reign, as they tended to do in all times of disturbance and in frontier regions. Not that monks could count on immunity from violence for their lands, and some certainly suffered from the depredations of their own tenants,[26] but they could hope for some measure of respect at least some of the time. Moreover the constant danger of violent death facing all landholders caused many to feel a need for the prayers of holy men. New monastic foundations as well as gifts to established family monasteries proliferated during the troubled years. Towards the end of the century William of Newburgh was to note that an exceptionally large number of monasteries had been founded during the period when Stephen 'held the title of king'.[27] The foundations were spread among houses of all kinds. This was, however, a period of considerable expansion everywhere for the Cistercians, the congregation of Savigny, the Augustinian canons and the houses of religious women, and England was no exception to the general trend.[28] New work on some of the sources for the history of individual houses, such as the new edition of *The Foundation History of the Abbeys of Byland and Jervaulx*, which has shown how the congregation of Savigny profited from the prevailing conditions, has emphasised the monastic expansion.[29] All orders attracted patronage from the supporters of both Stephen and Matilda.

In attempting to determine how far the reign should be regarded as a period of anarchy two aspects need to be considered: regional variations in disorder and the degree to which central government broke down. There were some grounds for the complaints of chroniclers. Even though Stephen continued to control some of the wealthiest regions in England he did not succeed in raising all the revenues to which he was entitled. Neither his resources nor Matilda's were sufficient to support the armed garrisons necessary to hold castles that were under constant threat and to maintain an effective presence on both sides of the Channel. The most difficult period in the administration of justice came after the king's capture in February 1141. Before that time there is evidence of some effective action by the courts. In the long run the growing profits of royal justice were to become the most important item in the royal revenues, but this did not take place until Henry II had been on the throne for a number of years.[30]

The cases for which evidence survives illustrate the problems exacerbated by uncertainties in rights of inheritance. Two decades of violence led to confusion in the descent of property and this stimulated speculation about law. Some early

---

[26] For example the nuns of Holy Trinity Caen. See C. Letouzey, 'L'organisation seigneuriale dans les possessions anglaises et normandes de La Trinité de Caen au xii siècle', *Annales de Normandie*, 55 (2005), 213–45, 291–332.

[27] *Newburgh*, i, 53.

[28] See J. Burton, 'English Monasteries and the Continent in the Reign of King Stephen', below, 98–114.

[29] J. Burton, *The Foundation History of the Abbeys of Byland and Jervaulx*, Borthwick Texts and Studies (York, 2006).

[30] See White, 'Royal Income and Regional Trends', below, 27–43.

attempts to record perceptions of law date from this reign. Bruce O'Brien has made a good case for dating the *Leges Edwardi Confessoris* and the *Leis Willelmi* after 1136 and before 1154 and for their modification during this time.[31] In spite of periods of civil war and of acute local disorder, they are 'a testament to the resilience of the Old English state' and to the adaptability of its institutions. Whatever the sufferings in some parts of the country during the nineteen years of Stephen's reign it was not a time of anarchy. War weariness and the brutalities of continuing civil war gradually worked together to produce a greater readiness for compromise than had existed during Matilda's brief period of apparent triumph in 1141, when for a short while she had been at her most headstrong.

In the later years of the reign major events affecting the whole of Europe continued to play their part. In particular the second crusade in 1148–9 had an important impact, for Louis VII led a large contingent of crusaders including Waleran of Meulan and William of Warenne in a costly and unsuccessful venture. Even if the immunity from attack that should have protected the property of crusaders was never wholly respected there was some diminution in the active fighting. Moreover one consequence of major importance was the final breakdown in the marriage of King Louis and Eleanor of Aquitaine. While the battered French contingent rested at Antioch as the guests of the queen's kinsman Raymond prince of Antioch, rumours began to spread about Eleanor's enjoyment of Raymond's company. She herself is said to have questioned the legality of her marriage to Louis because of consanguinity. On the way home after a total failure to conquer Jerusalem a temporary reconciliation between the king and queen was brought about by Pope Eugenius,[32] but the outcome was only the birth of a second daughter to Eleanor. Marital relations remained extremely fragile, and Louis was unwilling to wait indefinitely in the hope that Eleanor might yet bear the son he so urgently needed. He sought and obtained annulment of the marriage. This left Eleanor as something of a loose cannon until young Henry of Anjou took the decisive step of marrying her without the consent of King Louis. She brought her immense but troubled inheritance to swell his resources and increase his problems.[33] These, however, remained to be tackled later; Henry's immediate task was to secure the English throne.

In 1149 he had been knighted by his uncle King David of Scotland and so could assume active leadership of the Angevins and help his mother to recover from the loss of her ablest supporter, Robert of Gloucester, who had died in 1147. Meanwhile the hold on Normandy that had been won by Count Geoffrey remained firm, in spite of serious temporary threats. Stephen struggled in vain for papal recognition of the right of his son Eustace to succeed to the throne, and when Eugenius died in 1153 Stephen reluctantly consented to accept Henry as his heir. The magnates in England showed extreme unwillingness to engage in

---

31 See B. O'Brien, 'Legal Treatises as Perceptions of Law in Stephen's Reign', below, 185–95.
32 *Historia Pontificalis*, 52–3, 61–2.
33 W. L. Warren, *Henry II* (London, 1973), 42–4.

another pitched battle and Henry gradually became ready to compromise.[34] He accepted that the hostilities could be ended only if he were prepared to agree to compensation for Stephen's kinsmen. By the time Stephen died on 25 October 1154, although Henry was in France there was no need for him to hurry back to England. Even after reaching Barfleur he was able to wait for a favourable wind, and finally on 19 December he and Eleanor were crowned at Westminster by Archbishop Theobald.[35] His next tasks were to resume the crown lands, demolish recently built castles, expel the Flemish mercenaries and set about restoring the royal revenues. These things were not done in a moment, but the king had the will and means to undertake them. When his second son, Henry, was born on 28 February 1155 the succession at least was secure,[36] and the Anglo-Norman realm was still intact. Nevertheless some ground had been lost in 1151, when for the first time a duke of Normandy had done homage in Paris to the king of France, and the growing wealth and prestige of the French monarchy threatened in time to outweigh any advantage that might have accrued from the acquisition of Queen Eleanor's huge duchy of Aquitaine.

[34] C. W. Hollister, 'The Aristocracy', in King, *Anarchy*, 37–66, at 65–6.
[35] E. King, 'Introduction', in King, *Anarchy*, 1–36, at 35–6.
[36] *Torigni*, 181–2.

1

Henry I and the Origins of the Civil War

JUDITH A. GREEN

WHEN CONTEMPORARIES wrote of the conflict that broke out in England and Normandy after the death of Henry I, they described it as a struggle centred around the succession, about the actions of individuals, about castles and inheritances.[1] On the whole subsequent historians have followed suit: ethnic conflicts, religious differences, or economic issues were not fundamental causes, to compare with the central contest for power in which lesser folk were caught up. Where there have been different views, these have centred on motivation and timing: how deep-rooted were the origins of the war? What were the motives of the leading protagonists? How far-reaching were its effects? This article is concerned with the first of these questions, the origins of the war, and specifically with the role of Henry I, whose actions in his later years are judged to have had a direct bearing on the events that followed his death.

The assessments made of Henry's contribution to the civil war have varied considerably.[2] On the one hand, some historians have played it down: it has been argued, for instance, that Henry had planned ahead as best he could, but that his intentions were wrecked by his daughter and her husband's intransigence on the issue of castles.[3] The outbreak of conflict was therefore due to the actions of others. Another view which has seen the causes of war as attributable less to individuals than to structural weaknesses in the Anglo-Norman realms is that of Keith Stringer, who has argued that the very effectiveness of Henry's rule masked growing challenges to the 'Anglo-Norman empire', as neighbouring powers grew

---

[1] This paper has benefited from the helpful comments of members of the conference at Liverpool Hope University and on a later occasion by staff and students in the Department of Medieval History, University of St Andrews. A special note of thanks is due to Professor Edmund King for his comments and suggestions.

[2] King, *Anarchy* is an important collection of conference papers delivered in 1992 which review scholarship to that point. The first four chapters of Matthew, *King Stephen* are also particularly useful from an historiographical viewpoint.

[3] C. W. Hollister, *Henry I*, edited and completed by A. Clark Frost (New Haven and London, 2001), 477.

stronger.[4] On the other hand, many historians have argued that Henry either deliberately or by the law of unintended consequences bore a good deal of responsibility for what was to happen. It has been suggested, for example, that he did not do enough to smooth his daughter's path when the dynastic and political considerations which had led to the advancement of his daughter's claim and her marriage became less pressing, after William Clito's death.[5] Another view is that Henry's centralizing rule was of a kind to provoke a baronial reaction from those wishing for greater freedom: his strong rule had kept them in check.[6] The motivation of the barons has inevitably come in for a great deal of scrutiny, but whether they were 'selfish',[7] or searching for security in a politically uncertain world,[8] Henry's patronage had inevitably favoured some at the expense of others.

The charge against Henry, reduced to its crudest, is that he made a major contribution to the outbreak of war by promoting the claim of his daughter to succeed him, thus fatally dividing his court. It is alleged, too, that he compounded this error first by arranging her marriage to an outsider, an Angevin, and then by failing to do enough to ease her accession after his death, especially by his obduracy over the role of her husband, Geoffrey of Anjou. If in 1126–7 the marriage seemed vital both for the succession and also to protect Henry's regime in Normandy, then subsequent events, most obviously the death of William Clito, may have diminished its importance, and Henry may even have begun to veer towards nominating one of the sons of his sister, Adela of Blois. If he was still keen to advance Matilda, why choose Henry of Blois for the bishopric of Winchester in 1129, given that the bishop would be very well placed to assist either Theobald or Stephen to make a bid for their uncle's legacy?[9]

Yet there is perhaps more to be said at various points about the options Henry faced and the decisions he took in the last years of his life. First, factors outside the narrow issue of the succession to England and Normandy had a major part to play: the fate of the crown of Jerusalem, the outcome of the Papal Schism of 1130, and the competing ambitions of the houses of Anjou and Blois. Secondly, there is a case for saying that whilst presenting his daughter as the representative of his line, Henry wanted to keep his options open over the succession. Consonant with

---

4 K. J. Stringer, *The Reign of Stephen: Kingship, Warfare and Government in Twelfth-Century England* (London, 1993), 13.
5 Matthew, *King Stephen*, 52–7.
6 F. Stenton, *The First Century of English Feudalism 1066–1166* (2nd edn, Oxford, 1961), ch. 7.
7 As, for instance, J. H. Round argued in *Geoffrey de Mandeville: A Study of the Anarchy* (London, 1892), v. Round was following up the comments of W. Stubbs, *The Constitutional History of England*, 3 vols. (6th edn, Oxford, 1897), 353: 'the barons were in earnest only for their own interests'. For comment see E. King, 'King Stephen and the Anglo-Norman Aristocracy', *History*, 59 (1974), 180–94.
8 For the argument that the central issue was inheritance, see R. H. C. Davis, 'What Happened in Stephen's Reign', *History*, 49 (1964), 1–12. For the magnates' perspective see, most recently, Crouch, *Reign of Stephen*, ch. 9.
9 As pointed out by Matthew, *King Stephen*, 56–7.

this approach, he did take steps which, it may be argued, he saw as sufficient to secure a smooth transfer of power in the kingdom after his death.

After the wreck of the White Ship and Henry's speedy remarriage, the general expectation must have been that Henry's second marriage would produce children. Stephen's fortunes meanwhile continued to rise with his marriage to a great heiress. His bride was Matilda, only daughter of Eustace III count of Boulogne, a descendant through her mother of the pre-Conquest kings of England. Like Henry himself, therefore, Stephen was to marry someone whose lineage helped to bind the new world to the old.

The timing of Stephen's marriage has never been precisely established: all that is known is that by 1125 the bride's father had retired from the world to a Cluniac priory. In fact the marriage and the preceding negotiations must have been concluded before 1125.[10] The alliance has usually been interpreted in terms of the politics of northern France and England. The small county of Boulogne, north of the duchy of Normandy, included the port of Wissant, and the count held great estates in England, concentrated in Essex.[11] From Henry's point of view, whilst the marriage was not, strictly speaking, in his gift, it was important that the county and its port should pass into a 'safe' pair of hands.[12]

However, we should also consider its wider ramifications. Eustace came from a crusading family. In 1118 he may have taken seriously his claim to succeed his brother, Baldwin I, as king of Jerusalem: according to the chronicler William of Tyre, Eustace, a widower at this point, may have reached Apulia before abandoning this plan.[13] Baldwin was instead followed by Baldwin II, but between 1123 and 1124 the latter was imprisoned.[14] The future of the kingdom of Jerusalem was thus in some jeopardy, as Baldwin II had no sons to succeed him. Stephen of Blois was the son of another, not wholly successful, leading figure of the first crusade, and he too may have felt drawn to the crusade, for his own sake and to redeem his father's reputation for having deserted the siege of Antioch.[15] A marriage between Stephen and Eustace's daughter was thus attractive to both families.

Yet, as the months wore on and Henry's young queen did not produce a child, his anxieties can only have increased. By 1123, as Orderic pointed out, the cause

---

[10] *Cal. Docs France*, 507.

[11] J. H. Round, 'The Counts of Boulogne as English Lords', in his *Studies in Peerage and Family History* (London, 1901), 147–80.

[12] For a discussion of the options facing the count, see H. Tanner, *Families, Friends and Allies: Boulogne and Politics in Northern France and England c. 879–1160* (Leiden and Boston, 2004), 178–80.

[13] William of Tyre, *Chronicon*, ed. R. B. C. Huygens, Corpus Christianorum, Continuatio Mediaevalis, 63 (Turnhout, 1986) (12, iii), 550; A. V. Murray, *The Crusader Kingdom of Jerusalem. A Dynastic History 1099–1125*, Occasional Publication of the Linacre Unit for Prosopographical Research, no. 4 (Oxford, 2000), 122–3.

[14] Ibid., 135–50.

[15] Davis, *King Stephen*, 2–4.

of Henry's nephew, William Clito, began to reanimate.[16] Between 1123 and 1124 Henry was occupied in dealing with a major revolt in Normandy, which drew in the dangerous alliance of Count Fulk V of Anjou, the latter's uncle, Amaury de Montfort, and King Louis VI of France. On the other side of the Channel, the death of Henry's daughter, Sibyl, queen of Scots, without children meant that King Alexander was a widower. David, Henry's brother-in-law, was last in line of the sons of Malcolm III, but his position in the succession was by no means guaranteed. It has recently been suggested that Henry may have needed to exert some pressure to ensure that David's position in the succession was recognized,[17] and this in turn may help to explain David's continuing loyalty to Henry.

In 1125 news came from Germany of the death of the Emperor Henry V, leaving Henry I's only legitimate daughter, Matilda, a widow, and at this point if not before – as Karl Leyser suggested – the king began to think of recognizing her as the heir to his lands and rights.[18] She returned to Normandy and in 1126 father and daughter went to England where intensive negotiations between the king and leading lay and ecclesiastical magnates took place, preceding the council at Windsor. It seems likely that a number of deals were struck in the lead up to the oath-swearing. The ones we know about were, first, the transfer of Duke Robert from the custody of Bishop Roger of Salisbury to that of Earl Robert of Gloucester and, secondly, the grant of Rochester castle to Archbishop William of Canterbury, who would be of central importance to a smooth transition of power.[19] It seems likely, too, that the archbishop was assured of permission to hold the legatine council which followed in 1127.[20] King David of Scots, Henry's brother-in-law and, through his wife, earl of Huntingdon, was placated over the vexed issue of the consecration of a bishop for St Andrews without a profession of obedience to York, on which Archbishop Thurstan had been insisting.[21] Queen Adeliza, whose position was not only Henry's wife but still the potential mother of a son, received a munificent grant of land.[22] Behind the scenes, too, there may have been other deals with interested parties which have left no traces in the record.

When it comes to the oath-swearing itself, although we are well informed about who was present and took the oath, headed by King David of Scots, Stephen of Blois and Robert of Gloucester, it is hard to be sure exactly what they were signing up to. William of Malmesbury, who provides the most detailed account, was writing after the event, not earlier than 1140 or 1141.[23] King Henry, he wrote, told the assembled company of the tragic death of his only son William, who

---

[16] *Orderic*, vi, 328.
[17] R. Oram, *David I: The King Who Made Scotland* (Stroud, 2004), 71–2.
[18] K. Leyser, 'The Anglo-Norman Succession 1120–25', *ANS*, 13 (1990), 225–41.
[19] *ASC* 1126; *Regesta*, ii, no. 1475.
[20] *Councils & Synods*, ii, 743–9.
[21] *John of Worcester*, iii, 174–5.
[22] *Historia Novella*, 6.
[23] Ibid., xxx–xxxi.

would have claimed the kingdom as of right. As it was, his daughter remained, *cui soli legitima debeatur successio*. Her paternal and maternal lineage was outlined: since the days of King Ecgberht of Wessex the line of English kings had not failed until the time of King Edward the Confessor, who had arranged the marriage of his great-niece Margaret to Malcolm king of Scots, the grandparents of the empress. The chronicler thus omitted from the presentation King David of Scots, and obviously no comment was made about the freedom to marry of the empress's mother, who had spent some time before 1100 wearing the veil.

There are several noteworthy points about the way the oath-swearing was reported. The first is William of Malmesbury's choice of words: the oath was of loyalty to the empress's right of succession, not to her as her father's heir.[24] Women could be *haeredes*, or heirs, as Henry's Charter of Liberties explicitly recognized, but the word *successio* might suggest that the empress was to be seen as the channel through which Henry's blood was to be transmitted (to a grandson). If the empress was indeed to be heir, *haeres*, then to what?

The issue of succession to the English throne involved several elements, of which designation was only one. Henry had been present at his father's bedside when the Conqueror is said to have entrusted his throne to God, whilst sending Rufus to England with a letter for Archbishop Lanfranc, as a result of which the archbishop performed the coronation. Could the empress undergo an inaugural coronation, as opposed to simply assuming power, as Queen Urraca seems to have done in Castile after her father's death?[25]

Then there is the question of the succession to Normandy. By 1127 Henry was using the title 'duke of the Normans' as well as 'king of the English', but in the eyes of many Normans the legitimate duke was his brother Robert, still in prison after twenty years, or Robert's son William Clito. The last thing Henry would have wanted was to goad King Louis into recognizing William Clito as duke. The French king was keeping a close watch on events at Henry's court. He had about ten years earlier made a commitment to William Clito which he had subsequently

---

24 The Worcester chronicler stated explicitly that the king lacked an heir, *John of Worcester*, iii, 166–7, 176–83. The Anglo-Saxon Chronicle makes no reference to her status, saying merely that the great men swore 'to give England and Normandy after his death into the hand of his daughter', *ASC* 1127. Henry of Huntingdon referred to the oath later, when writing of Stephen's accession, as an oath of fealty 'concerning the kingdom of the English', *Huntingdon*, 700–1. Robert of Torigny, in his interpolations to the *Gesta Normannorum Ducum*, also referred to an oath of fealty by the great men 'to ensure that after her father's death the empress would obtain the monarchy of the greater Britain now called England', *Jumièges*, 240–1, cf. 264–5 for the statement that Henry had, long before his death, appointed Matilda as his heir. John of Salisbury also referred to the oath in his *Historia Pontificalis*: that Stephen had sworn fealty and had undertaken 'to help her secure England and hold Normandy against all men after her father's death', John of Salisbury, *Historia Pontificalis*, ed. M. Chibnall (Oxford, 1986), 83–4.

25 B. F. Reilly, *The Kingdom of León-Castilla under Queen Urraca 1109–26* (Princeton, 1982), 55. Her son Alfonso Raimúndez was crowned in 1111, ibid., p. 73. For a recent review of the queen's artistic patronage, see T. Martin, 'The Art of a Reigning Queen as Dynastic Propaganda in Twelfth-Century Spain', *Speculum*, 80 (2005), 1134–71.

gone back on, and – apparently as soon as he had wind of the oath to the empress – he had created William Clito count, but of the Vexin, not of the Normans. He had also permitted him to marry Jeanne de Montferrat, sister of the queen.[26] Whatever else, Louis was standing by his man. If English chroniclers were perhaps not concerned to specify that Normandy was included in the oath, then such unconcern would not have been true of those who swore it, many of whom had considerable estates and interests across the Channel.

It is surely most likely even at this stage that Henry hoped to live long enough to see Matilda remarried and the mother of a son to whom her right of succession would descend. There were several examples of queens and countesses who ruled on behalf of absent husbands or minor sons. Henry's mother Matilda had been left as regent in Normandy when William invaded England, and presumably had he been killed, she would have taken charge on behalf of her young sons.[27] Urraca of Castile was a widow with a baby son at the time of the death of her father, King Alfonso VI of Castile, in 1109. Henry's sister Adela of Blois had ruled her husband's dominions during his absence on crusade, and then after his death.[28] Clemence of Flanders[29] and Adelaisia of Sicily[30] provide other examples.

We have no inkling that a marriage for Matilda to anyone other than Count Fulk or his son was ever proposed, either to a member of the Capetian dynasty or to one of the great families of the empire. Any such marriage to a ruling prince would remove Matilda and her children physically from England and Normandy and place her within her husband's family. In such circumstances, was it likely that any of her sons could secure enough support to make good their claim? An alliance within the kingdom or the duchy was possible, and there were possible candidates amongst the leading baronial families, such as Ranulf II, earl of Chester, but the trouble was that by allying with one family others would be alienated.

The likelihood that Henry would marry Matilda off to the son of Count Fulk of Anjou must have been glaringly obvious. The considerations which had led Henry to work for the marriage of his son William and Matilda of Anjou, to detach Count Fulk from allying with King Louis and Norman rebels, remained pressing, as events in Normandy in 1123 and 1124 had demonstrated, reinforced

---

[26] *Orderic*, vi, 368–70. The 'Hyde Chronicler' supplies the detail that Louis had agreed to accept a large sum of money to grant Normandy to Henry's son William, only to be dissuaded by the count of Nevers, who pointed out Louis's prior commitment to William Clito. No date is supplied by the author, but the incident must have occurred before the arrest of the count of Nevers in November 1115, *Liber Monasterii de Hyda*, ed. E. Edwards (RS, 1866), 309.

[27] *Orderic*, ii, 208, 210.

[28] K. Lo Prete, 'Adela of Blois: Familial Alliances and Female Lordship,' in *Aristocratic Women in Medieval France*, ed. T. Evergates (Philadelphia, 1999), 7–44, and especially 25–39.

[29] K. S. Nicholas, 'Countesses as Rulers in Flanders', in *Aristocratic Women in Medieval France*, 117–20.

[30] *Orderic*, vi, 428–32.

by King Louis's backing of William Clito first as count of the Vexin, and then as count of Flanders, following the murder of the childless Count Charles of Flanders.

There was never any chance at this stage that Henry would have recognized any claim of William Clito to be his successor. Quite apart from personal considerations, it would have removed any possibility of a son of his own succeeding. Those who supported William in the duchy would not have waited for Henry's death to challenge his power, and enough of them had lands in England to cause a major headache. Not only would Henry lose the possibility that a son or grandson of his would follow him, but he would run the risk of a major challenge to his own power. Nor was there any indication that Henry ever thought of his eldest illegitimate son Robert as his successor.

Whilst he continued to hope for a son by Adeliza, the question of Matilda's marriage could not be postponed, and that brought up the future position of his son-in-law, Geoffrey of Anjou. Contemporary opinion recognized the right of a husband to rule his wife's lands. If young at the time of his marriage, Geoffrey of Anjou could not be sidelined for long. He would expect to control his wife's dowry in Normandy, including the castles, and would expect assurances about his role after his father-in-law's death. Should Matilda predecease her father, and she came dangerously close to death in 1134, then Geoffrey would expect to rule Normandy and England on behalf of his infant sons. Henry might try to ensure that the levers of power would rest with his daughter and her advisers, but this would not be easy. Meanwhile, Henry had to balance the need to leave the succession open for a son of his own (who would almost certainly inherit as a minor and need a regency council) with securing the Angevin marriage. He may well have been dilatory, even evasive, over Matilda's dowry and Geoffrey's future role.

In May 1127, Matilda was dispatched to Rouen for her betrothal in the company of her half-brother Robert earl of Gloucester, and Brian fitz Count lord of Wallingford, but the formal wedding did not take place for a year.[31] This was because it was only one of three being negotiated in the same period within the house of Anjou, and which were all interdependent: Count Fulk proposed to marry Melisende, the heiress to the kingdom of Jerusalem, and to leave France for the Holy Land, so that Anjou would pass to his eldest son Geoffrey, whilst his younger son Helias was to marry the heiress to the county of Perche, a grand-daughter of Henry I. From Henry's point of view, all three marriages had to work to make the political costs of the marriage of Matilda and Geoffrey worthwhile.

Once again the succession to Jerusalem had a bearing on the future of the Anglo-Norman realms. King Baldwin II of Jerusalem, lacking a son, had decided that his daughter Melisende was to succeed him.[32] Accordingly he sent to France to find her a husband. Fulk of Anjou was deemed to be acceptable: he was a

---

[31] J. Chartrou, *L'Anjou de 1109 à 1151* (Paris, 1928), 21–2.
[32] William of Tyre, *Chronicon* (13, xxiv), 618–19.

widower who had previously been to the Holy Land on pilgrimage. The terms of the marriage, and Fulk's role during his father-in-law's lifetime and after his death, needed to be worked out carefully and may indeed have paralleled those for Geoffrey and Matilda. The sources in fact are not unequivocal about Fulk's role in Baldwin's lifetime, and after his death he seems to have shared power with his wife.[33] Fulk's younger son Helias might have been expected, from his name, to inherit his mother's county of Maine, but it looks as though Maine, a county over which Henry had asserted a claim to Norman overlordship, was to pass to Geoffrey and Matilda. Hence provision for Helias had to be made elsewhere. The widowed Count Rotrou of Perche, Henry's son-in-law, did not remarry and his daughter was married to Helias, with the prospect of the latter's succession to the county.[34]

What remains most obscure about the marriage negotiations is what assurances were given to the Angevin party about the English throne. Henry could argue that he had done what he could: he had 'designated' Matilda as his successor, and had had the great men swear oaths of allegiance. He had established at least one Angevin, Payn of Clairvaux, in the Sussex estate of Harting, possibly to provide a base and revenue for the Angevins in the south of England.[35] Matilda had evidently been concerned about her uncle, the imprisoned Duke Robert, who was transferred from the custody of Roger bishop of Salisbury to that of her half-brother, Robert earl of Gloucester.[36] The bishop controlled several castles, and his nephew Alexander was bishop of Lincoln. There was no overt indication that Bishop Roger did not support the king's plans at this stage, and he orchestrated the oath-swearing, but Matilda was clearly wary of him. Another important figure was Archbishop William of Canterbury, and there was no reason to suggest that he would not be loyal to the king's wishes. Robert earl of Gloucester was important to the success of his father's plans, and at some stage he gained custody of the castle of Dover.[37] Robert II d'Oilly, married to one of Henry's illegitimate daughters, became sheriff of Oxfordshire in 1129, and probably held the constableship of Oxford castle which his father had held.[38] Brian fitz

---

[33] Orderic believed that Fulk had been offered the crown during Baldwin's lifetime, but that he had refused, *Orderic*, vi, 390. William of Tyre, however, believed Fulk had been offered the succession, *Chronicon* (13, xxiv), 618–19. For discussion, see H. E. Mayer, 'Studies in the History of Queen Melisende of Jerusalem', *Dumbarton Oaks Papers*, 26 (1972), 95–182; B. Hamilton, 'Women in the Crusader States: The Queens of Jerusalem 1100–90', in *Medieval Women*, ed. D. Baker, Studies in Church History, Subsidia, 1 (Oxford, 1978), 148–9; P. Edbury and J. G. Rowe, *William of Tyre: Historian of the Latin East* (Cambridge, 1983), 80–3; L. L. Huneycutt, 'Female Succession and the Language of Power in the Writings of Twelfth-Century Churchmen', in *Medieval Queenship*, ed. J. C. Parsons (Stroud, 1993), 194–6, 198–200.

[34] K. Thompson, 'Dowry and Inheritance Patterns: Some Examples from the Descendants of King Henry I of England', *Medieval Prosopography*, 17 (1996), 55–6.

[35] *PR 31 Henry I*, 42.

[36] *ASC* 1128.

[37] *Orderic*, vi, 518.

[38] For the marriage, see *Complete Peerage*, xi, Appendix D, 108–9; for the shrievalty *PR 31*

Count was lord of Wallingford,[39] and the influence of Baldwin de Redvers, who was one of the very few not to do homage to Stephen in 1136, was growing stronger: his man Geoffrey de Furneaux became sheriff of Devon in 1129.[40]

Yet if the principal players were persuaded to back the king's plans in public, they must have been gloomy at the likely prospect of the violence which would spread after the old king's death, and of the possibility that the duchy and the kingdom would fall into different hands, thus imperilling their own interests. Such plans must also have been unwelcome to the house of Blois, and the three sons of Adela whose fortunes were most closely connected to those of King Henry, Count Theobald, Stephen, and Henry, the latter a monk of Cluny who had been elected abbot of Glastonbury. Matilda's accession was unlikely to benefit them. Finally, there was the position of David of Scots. He had a claim to the English throne himself, but he had publicly committed himself to Matilda. He had more immediate claims on territory in what was currently northern England, and might be able (as we know he later did) to extend his sway there after his uncle's death.

Meanwhile the war in Flanders continued. King Louis as overlord recognized William Clito as count and the latter fought valiantly to establish his authority over the other contenders.[41] If he succeeded, he would become a much more serious threat to Henry, for he would have the resources and allies to challenge Henry's power in both the duchy and the kingdom. Henry therefore distributed subsidies to William's rivals via his nephew Stephen (the only clue we have as to Stephen's activities during this period).[42]

Matilda's marriage was finally solemnized in June 1128, after her father-in-law Fulk had taken the cross at Le Mans and following Henry's solemn knighting of Geoffrey and thirty of his companions.[43] The description by John of Marmoutier of the solemn ceremonies, often cited by historians in the context of the history of chivalry, represented the young man's formal coming of age.[44] Within weeks of the wedding the political context had changed yet again, because William Clito died of a wound received in Flanders. His death at last brought to an end the most serious threat to Henry's position.[45] And whilst there was no going

---

Henry I, 1–6. Although the start of the sheriff's account is missing, there is little doubt that the Robert named on pages 1–2 was Robert d'Oilly. Robert I's responsibility for Oxford castle is reported in the annals of Oseney, see *Annales Monastici*, ed. H. R. Luard, 5 vols. (RS, 1864–9), iv, 9.

[39] For Brian fitz Count's tenure of Wallingford, see K. S. B. Keats-Rohan, 'The Devolution of the Honour of Wallingford, 1066–1148', *Oxoniensia*, 54 (1989), 311–18.

[40] *Charters of the Redvers Family and the Earldom of Devon 1090–1217*, ed. R. Bearman, Devon and Cornwall Record Society, ns, 37 (1994), 38.

[41] Walter of Thérouanne, *Vita Karoli*, PL, clxvi, col. 937.

[42] Ibid.

[43] Chartrou, *L'Anjou*, 21–2.

[44] John of Marmoutier, *Historia Gaufredi Ducis Normannorum et Comitis Andegavorum*, *Chroniques des Comtes d'Anjou*, ed. L. Halphen and R. Poupardin (Paris, 1913), 177–81.

[45] S. Burton Hicks, 'The Impact of William Clito upon the Continental Policies of Henry I of England', *Viator*, 10 (1979), 1–21.

back on the Angevin marriage, there was less urgency for Henry to take the next obvious step, that of presenting his daughter and her husband at great courts, where oaths of allegiance would be sworn to the couple. From Henry's point of view, the best tactic was to delay, until he had a son of his own, or until Matilda's own ability to have sons had been proved. Yet no such ceremonies are reported to have occurred on either side of the Channel.

The way was now eased for the release from custody of two of the leading rebels of 1124, Waleran count of Meulan and Hugh fitz Gervase, lord of Châteauneuf-en-Thymerais.[46] Henry could not have afforded the risk of freeing them earlier, but now there was every reason to restore them to their lands, if not their castles. They might rebel again, but William Clito's death had removed a figurehead round whom they could rally. Henry must have hoped, too, that Waleran, the son of his old friend, would have learned from his experiences and would henceforth remain loyal. Moreover, Waleran and his twin brother controlled an important tract of territory in central Normandy, and Hugh a castle close to the frontier of the duchy.

Once again events were moving quickly, because almost as soon as Henry had arrived in England in 1129, he received news that his daughter's marriage had broken down. She was on her way back to Normandy, and it was said that her husband had repudiated her.[47] Matilda herself may not have welcomed the marriage to the son of a count, but she had done her father's bidding. The break-down may have been rooted in personal factors, but Geoffrey's resentment at the way he was being treated is a more likely explanation. Matilda must have judged the breakdown to be fundamental, because she had returned to Normandy.

Thinking of the options facing Henry at this point, we can see that he had little choice but to work to salvage the marriage. Empress Matilda and Geoffrey were related within the prohibited degrees – to the same degree which had been used as the basis for a papal annulment of the marriage of William Clito and his wife Matilda. Geoffrey might seek to free himself from the marriage, and this would mean a delay in Matilda being able to produce a grandson for Henry. Henry had to ensure that any annulment did not happen. Meanwhile, in England in the autumn of 1129, his nephew Henry of Blois was consecrated as bishop of Winchester.[48] Was this a sign that the king had begun to change his mind about the future? Perhaps, but this appointment was only one element in a great outpouring of favour to the Cluniacs at this time, and the important see might well have been intended for the king's nephew for some time.[49] In February 1130 there was an added complication to any plans to repair the marriage in the form of a disputed papal election. Support for Peter Pierleoni, which included two men well known in England and Normandy, John of Crema and Matthew of Albano, was strong

---

[46] *ASC* 1129.
[47] *Symeonis Monachi Opera Omnia*, ed. T. Arnold, 2 vols. (RS, 1882–5), ii, 283.
[48] *ASC* 1129.
[49] Hollister, *Henry I*, 413–33.

outside Italy and especially in France. He was elected by one party and took the name Innocent II, whilst Gregory, cardinal deacon of St Angelo in Pescheria, who was supported by Roger II of Sicily and many in western France, took the name Anacletus.[50]

Henry would have to recognize one pope or the other: remaining at a remove from the problem as his father had done after 1080 was no longer an option. If he opted for Innocent, then Geoffrey might go to Anacletus for an annulment. By the end of 1130, Henry had chosen to support Innocent, persuaded, it was said, by Abbot Peter the Venerable of Cluny and St Bernard of Clairvaux.[51] In January 1131 Henry prostrated himself before Innocent II at Chartres, and five months later solemnly received him at Rouen.[52]

Henry's spectacular gifts to the church between 1129 and 1131, especially to Fontevraud and Cluny, cannot be detached from his concerns about the succession.[53] Some were set in train before the collapse of the marriage. Henry made very generous gifts to Fontevraud in 1129, not long after his daughter-in-law Matilda of Anjou, entered the community and Count Fulk visited her, prior to his departure for Jerusalem.[54] However, it seems that before the grants could be made effective, the empress's marriage had broken down, and so in 1131 there was a revised version, confirmed by the pope.[55] The king is said to have been one of the principal contributors to the rebuilding of the abbey church at Cluny, which was consecrated by Innocent II on 24/5 October 1130.[56] Henry at once demonstrated his piety and generosity, and his loyalty to Pope Innocent, should Geoffrey of Anjou seek a dissolution of his marriage.

Henry may also have been especially concerned about the loyalty of the major cities at this time.[57] Disorder in the towns and cities of England and Normandy might well imperil the prospects of a peaceful succession. London was a particular concern. The farm had been set at a high figure and in 1129–30 citizen sheriffs had tried and failed to collect much revenue.[58] The Tower is thought to

---

[50] *Historia Novella*, 14–18; *Councils & Synods*, ii, 754–7; I. S. Robinson, *The Papacy 1073–1198* (Cambridge, 1990), 69–78.

[51] *Vita Petri Venerabilis, PL*, clxxxix, col. 20; *Orderic*, vi, 418–21.

[52] Ibid., 420.

[53] J. A. Green, 'The Piety and Patronage of Henry I', *HSJ*, 10 (2001), 8–12.

[54] *Grand cartulaire de Fontvraud par Jean-Marc Bienvenu avec la collaboration de Robert Favreau et Georges Pon*, Société des Antiquaires de France, 2 vols. (Poitiers, 2000, 2005), ii, no. 874. For Juliana's presence at Fontevraud, see *Grand cartulaire*, i, nos. 223, 287, 453, 473; ii, no. 635. Matilda entered the community after her return from England, *Orderic*, vi, 330.

[55] *Regesta*, ii, no. 1688.

[56] *Orderic*, vi, 418–20.

[57] A point made by C. N. L. Brooke, G. Keir and S. Reynolds, 'Henry I's Charter for the City of London', *Journal of the Society of Archivists*, 4 (1972), 568.

[58] *PR 31 Henry I*, 143–4. For the view that the sheriffs of 1129–30 were the first chosen under the new arrangement, Round, *Geoffrey de Mandeville*, 362–4, cf. S. Reynolds, 'The Rulers of London in the Twelfth Century', *History*, 57 (1972), 341.

have been in the custody of one of Henry's west Normans, Hasculf de Tany,[59] and Baynard's Castle had possibly passed with the lands formerly held by Ralph Baynard to Robert fitz Richard.[60] Meanwhile, Geoffrey de Mandeville, a figure who was to be valuable in delivering London to the Empress in 1141, had succeeded to the bulk of his great landed inheritance, but not to his father's offices.[61] Thus there was a balancing act between the interests of the townsmen, military security, and the king's financial interests. Similar concerns may have been involved in the balance of power at Lincoln. Here the royal castle was in the custody of Robert de la Haye, a royal steward, and Bishop Alexander was granted custody of the Eastgate.[62] In 1129 Ranulf II succeeded his father as earl of Chester, and he and his half-brother, William de Roumare, were very rich in lands in Lincolnshire. The king may thus have been alive to the desirability of some counterpoise to their power.

In 1130 Henry's dealings with the archbishop of Canterbury may also have been conditioned in part by the need to ensure the latter's continuing loyalty over the succession. Henry was present at the dedication of the great new church at Canterbury, and, a few days later, was at Rochester for the dedication of the cathedral there.[63] On the former occasion he granted the collegiate church of St Martin to Archbishop William, a grant made at the council of Northampton in September 1131.[64]

During the later months of 1130 and the first of 1131, negotiations with Geoffrey were proceeding, and by the time Henry returned to England in 1131 these had been successful. On this occasion Henry had a vivid reminder that matters were pressing, as he was said to have narrowly escaped shipwreck.[65] On 8 September 1131 a great council met at Northampton, and it was decided that the empress should return to her husband 'who was asking for her', and those present made or renewed their oaths of allegiance.[66] Bishop Roger of Salisbury continued to be indispensable, and in 1131 he received a royal charter confirming his tenure of the abbey of Malmesbury.[67]

At Christmas 1132 the king fell ill, the first and only time before his final illness that a bout of ill-health is reported.[68] Stephen was with him, and it has been pointed out that it was from around this time that he began to associate himself

---

[59] C. W. Hollister, 'The Misfortunes of the Mandevilles', in his *Monarchy, Magnates and Institutions in the Anglo-Norman World* (London, 1986), 124 note.

[60] Brooke, Keir and Reynolds, 'Henry I's Charter for the City of London', 565 note.

[61] Hollister, 'The Misfortunes of the Mandevilles', 124.

[62] For Robert's tenure of the royal castle, see *Ancient Charters*, ed. J. H. Round, Pipe Roll Society, 10 (1888), 58; J. W. F. Hill, *Medieval Lincoln* (Cambridge, 1949), 87–91; for the grant of the Eastgate, see *Regesta*, ii, no. 1784.

[63] *ASC* 1130.

[64] *Regesta*, ii, no. 1736.

[65] *Huntingdon*, 486; *ASC* 1131.

[66] *Huntingdon*, 486–8.

[67] *Regesta*, ii, no. 1715.

[68] *Huntingdon*, 488.

more closely with his uncle's court.[69] By the end of 1132, however, Matilda was pregnant, and on 25 March 1133 she gave birth to a healthy son, named Henry after his grandfather.[70] The impasse over the succession had been broken, but if Henry now could hope to be succeeded, if not by a son, then by a grandson, then Geoffrey (and Matilda) might now expect a clearer commitment from Henry.

It is possible that after the births of Henry and Geoffrey their grandfather was at last prepared to arrange a public ceremony by which their mother was presented to the Norman magnates, perhaps wearing one of her crowns.[71] Duke Robert I had presented his young son William to the Norman magnates on the eve of his departure on crusade a century earlier.[72] The death of Robert Curthose in 1134 might also have removed any practical objection to such a ceremony.[73] However, an issue was raised which was to cause a deep rift between Henry and his daughter and son-in-law who were now, significantly, acting in accord, and this was over the custody of castles. Henry was very tenacious over the custody of castles, especially in Normandy, and upheld the view, reflected in the inquest of 1091 into ducal customs, that they were at his disposal.[74] This view, it was alleged, did not accord with the views of those who held lands close to the frontiers.[75] The custody of certain castles was included in Matilda's dowry,[76] but Henry proved loath to hand them over.

A second dimension of the issue was the friction that developed in the last months of Henry's life with William Talvas, son of Robert de Bellême. Robert's lands, but not his castles, had passed to William in 1119, and when Robert died, some time after 1130, his son must have requested the right to succeed to his inheritance in full. Henry thrice summoned William to his court, and when William stayed away, Henry confiscated the castles of Almenêches and Alençon. William fled over the border into Maine, and launched attacks across the border from his castles of Mamers and Peray.[77]

However, Robert of Torigny suggests over and beyond personal friction

---

[69] E. King, 'Stephen of Blois, Count of Mortain and Boulogne', *EHR*, 115 (2000), 291.

[70] *Torigni*, 123.

[71] Howden, *Chronica*, i, 187. Chibnall suggested that Henry may have contemplated a crown-wearing in Normandy, on the basis of Henry's confirmation charter to Saint-Etienne in 1129, which refers to the crowns, but this text is problematic, *Regesta*, ii, no. 1575. I should like to thank members of the Anglo-Norman Acta project at the University of Oxford for discussion of this charter. We have no means of knowing which crowns Henry or his daughter may have worn in Normandy.

[72] *Jumièges*, ii, 80.

[73] *John of Worcester*, iii, 212.

[74] *Consuetudines et Iusticie* c. 4 in C. H. Haskins, *Norman Institutions* (Cambridge, Mass., 1918), 282. For discussion, see C. Coulson, *Castles in Medieval Society: Fortresses in England, France, and Ireland in the Central Middle Ages* (Oxford, 2003), 66–70 and part II section 3.

[75] *Jumièges*, ii, 252.

[76] Argentan was one of these, Chibnall, *Empress Matilda*, 66. In 1135 Wigan the marshal handed over Exmes and Domfront to the Angevins as well, *Orderic*, vi, 454.

[77] Ibid., 446.

between the king, his daughter, and her husband, that the latter demanded that Henry himself should swear an oath of allegiance about the castles of *all* his realms.[78] Is this to be taken at face value? The author was writing at a later date, and his view may have been coloured by the Angevins' determination in 1153–4 to secure assurances about castles.[79] Nevertheless, if such an oath was requested, it could have been on the lines of the oath said to have been sworn by Harold Godwinson to Duke William.[80] A smooth handover of castles would certainly be critical in the succession. In his account of the weeks following Henry's victory at Tinchebray, Orderic wrote that Duke Robert freed the castellans of Normandy from their oaths to him, and they then were prepared to swear allegiance to Henry.[81] No similar undertaking was made to Geoffrey, and it was only when Stephen was imprisoned in 1141 that many of the Norman castellans handed over their castles. It does seem highly unlikely that a reigning king would have taken such an oath, in that again there would have been the danger of his power ebbing away in his own lifetime, and this may be another instance where the past was being remembered selectively.

It does not look as if Henry had much inkling in 1135 that his life was drawing to an end. He was still active and preparing to go hunting in November when he fell ill. As he lay dying he might have made some kind of indication that Stephen should succeed him: we shall never know.[82] Stephen was not at Henry's bedside, nor therefore bound by the pledge enjoined on those present to escort the corpse to the coast,[83] and was free instead to take swift action. He landed at Dover, and here and at Canterbury was refused access. According to the *Gesta Stephani*, he proceeded thence to London, where he was warmly received by the Londoners.[84] Stephen's London property, and the importance of trading links for Londoners via the port of Wissant in the county of Boulogne, may have predisposed the Londoners in his favour, but money, mentioned by the *Liber Eliensis*, and luck, may also have played a part.[85] Both the bishopric of London and the abbacy of Westminster, the coronation church, were vacant, thus removing any possibility

---

78 *Torigni*, 128.
79 For the latter, see the provisions of the Treaty of Winchester, *Select Charters and Other Illustrations of English Constitutional History*, ed. W. Stubbs, 9th edn rev. H. W. C. Davis (Oxford, 1913), 141–2.
80 *Gesta Guillelmi*, 70.
81 *Orderic*, vi, 92.
82 This was to be claimed later by Stephen's supporters. Arnulf of Lisieux speaking in Stephen's defence at the papal court claimed that Henry had extorted the oath, which had been conditional in the event his wife did not have a son; that afterwards he changed his mind, and on his deathbed had designated Stephen, as Hugh Bigod and two knights subsequently testified, *Historia Pontificalis*, 84.
83 *Orderic*, vi, 448.
84 *Gesta Stephani*, 4–7.
85 *Liber Eliensis*, ed. E. O. Blake, Camden Society, 3rd ser., 92 (1962), 285.

of potential opposition from these quarters. The Londoners asserted their 'right' to choose the next king, and Stephen, for his part, confirmed their liberties.[86]

Stephen now needed the support of Archbishop William, and Bishop Roger of Salisbury, the archbishop because he was to perform the coronation, and Bishop Roger as the person who was effectively in charge of royal administration.[87] Bishop Henry of Winchester, Stephen's brother, was another central figure. Whilst the sources allow us to gain some sense of who said what to whom, it is not wholly easy to understand when and why the first two decided to back Stephen. Archbishop William is said to have been particularly exercised about the next ruler's governance of the church. Stephen accordingly made a promise about the 'restoration and maintenance of the church' of which Bishop Henry made himself guarantor. The terms were subsequently recorded in writing.[88] Even then, according to the *Gesta Stephani*, the archbishop argued for careful discussion, and reminded the king's supporters about the oath they had sworn. They responded by arguing that the oath had been exacted under pressure, for the application of which the old king himself had repented, that the Londoners had accepted Stephen, and that a king who could restore order was needed.[89] John of Salisbury and Gervase of Canterbury named Hugh Bigod as one who, present at Henry I's deathbed, could testify that the king had freed those who had taken the oath from keeping it.[90] The archbishop may also have been concerned that if *he* refused to crown Stephen, Archbishop Thurstan might.

Bishop Roger may never have relished the prospect of an Angevin succession: the fact that Duke Robert had been removed from his custody in 1126 is possibly revealing on this point.[91] If Stephen became king, the odds of a smooth transfer of power, better both for his own family and for the church, were improved. Bishop Roger may also have been swayed by Stephen's pledges over the church. According to William of Malmesbury, Stephen brought over to his side both Bishop Roger and William de Pont de l'Arche, who had the keys of the royal treasury.[92]

Meanwhile Theobald travelled to Normandy and took soundings from the Norman magnates, either at Neubourg or Lisieux.[93] Robert, lord of Neubourg, was a cousin of the Beaumont twins. He had been at odds with the young Count Waleran in 1118–19 and was to become a staunch supporter of the Angevins, but nothing is known of his views at this juncture. For many of the Normans, Theobald would have been a more agreeable prospect as duke than either Stephen

---

[86] *Gesta Stephani*, 6–7.
[87] *Newburgh*, i, 32.
[88] *Historia Novella*, 28–9.
[89] *Gesta Stephani*, 8–13.
[90] *Historia Pontificalis*, 84; *The Historical Works of Gervase of Canterbury*, ed. W. Stubbs, 2 vols. (RS, 1879–80), i, 94.
[91] *ASC* 1126.
[92] *Historia Novella*, 28–9; cf. *Huntingdon*, 700.
[93] *Orderic*, vi, 454 (Neufbourg); *Torigni*, 129 (Lisieux).

or Matilda, but the speed of Stephen's coronation persuaded them Theobald's claim would not succeed. Stephen granted him lands in England in compensa-tion.[94] The brothers may have been working independently, or they could have agreed beforehand to aim for different portions of Henry's realms, but if so, Theobald's chances were blighted by the speed of his brother's coronation. Earl Robert too was slow to cross to England, delayed by his duty to fulfil his dying father's commands to pay off his servants and by the time he did arrive, he had little option but to do homage to Stephen.[95] How far were these events foreseeable by Henry? Whenever he died, his daughter was likely to be in the 'wrong' place, and he would have to rely on the loyalty to his memory of his sons and daughters, and on the ties built up during many years of service by men like Bishop Roger and Bishop John. It would perhaps have been too much to hope that his nephews would not try to assert their right to the succession, but he may have believed that his other measures would allow the empress time to marshal her forces.

The interpretation placed here on well known events is necessarily specula-tive: there is an obvious danger both of trying to second guess Henry I's thinking from his actions, or of assuming a rationale where none existed. Perhaps the ageing monarch did lose his sureness of touch, or simply avoided confronting difficult realities. Yet we know that for most of his life Henry was a shrewd and calculating ruler, and it is hard to believe that he made up his mind about the succession as early as 1125–6, or that he stubbornly clung to a plan which would inevitably be wrecked after his death. It is much more likely that he was trying both to plan for the succession and to keep his options open, in case his wife bore a son, until signs of his own mortality in 1132, followed in short order by the birth of a healthy grandson in 1133, injected a new sense of urgency and pointed the way ahead. Then, one could argue, he should have done more to recognize Geoffrey's role, but he must have believed that the resolution of the problem could be postponed, only to be wrong-footed by the speed of his last illness and death.

---

94 *Torigni*, 132; this was later granted to Geoffrey de Mandeville, *Regesta*, iii, no. 274.
95 D. Crouch, 'Robert, Earl of Gloucester and the Daughter of Zelophehad', *Journal of Medi-eval History*, 11 (1985), 227–9; idem, *Reign of Stephen*, 34–5; Matthew, *King Stephen*, 70–2.

2

Royal Income and Regional Trends

GRAEME J. WHITE

ANY CONSIDERATION of royal income in twelfth-century England is bound to rely very heavily on the pipe rolls. The fact that none survive from Stephen's reign, though an obvious impediment, has not deterred scholars such as Judith Green and Kenji Yoshitake from making important contributions to our knowledge of the king's finances[1] but this paper takes a different approach from that which they adopted. The task in hand here is to compare figures from Henry I's extant pipe roll, that of 1130, with those of the first full roll of Henry II (1156) and to extend the analysis to selected pipe rolls from the rest of Henry II's reign. As a result, some conclusions can be offered about the state of the country and the fortunes of different regions in the period when Stephen was king.

The limitations of the pipe rolls as evidence scarcely need rehearsing here. As Richardson and Sayles put it, they 'are not concerned with the whole of the revenue and they record the expenditure of but a fraction of the king's resources'.[2] With occasional damage, several entries open to conflicting interpretation, and the risk of human error in transcription and addition (whether in the twelfth century or the twenty-first), it is pointless to press too hard for precision. But Judith Green's masterly study of the 1130 pipe roll showed what could be done, provided that one accepted these limitations and celebrated the lessons to be learned rather than worrying about the pipe rolls' reliability down to the last penny.[3] Those who have ventured into this territory more recently[4] owe a great deal to Judith Green's work and also to that of Sir James Ramsay, whose *History of the King's Revenues*, published in 1925, remains a useful work of reference.

---

[1] J. A. Green, 'Financing Stephen's War', *ANS*, 14 (1992), 91–114; K. Yoshitake, 'The Exchequer in the Reign of Stephen', *EHR*, 103 (1988), 950–9.
[2] H. G. Richardson and G. O. Sayles, *The Governance of Mediaeval England* (Edinburgh, 1963), 170–1, 216–17 (quotation at 216).
[3] J. A. Green, ' "Praeclarum et magnificum antiquitatis monumentum": the Earliest Surviving Pipe Roll', *Bulletin of the Institute of Historical Research*, 55 (1982), 1–17.
[4] For example E. Amt, *The Accession of Henry II in England: Royal Government Restored, 1149–1159* (Woodbridge, 1993); G. J. White, *Restoration and Reform, 1153–1165: Recovery from Civil War in England* (Cambridge, 2000).

This paper presents some calculations of the sums collected for the king from the different shires in a given year, as recorded in the relevant pipe roll. The sums include all payments into the treasury in that year, whether due for the current or for previous years, and also reimbursements to the sheriff (or other accountant at the exchequer) for advance expenditure, on the grounds that these represent moneys actually raised. Sums owing, pardoned or in other ways 'written off' (such as those for *terrae datae*, the lands granted out of the royal demesne), though forming part of the accounts rendered at the exchequer, have been excluded from the calculations on the grounds that the king did not benefit from them financially in the year in question. Payments recorded in the pipe rolls as 'blanch' have been converted to *numero* (the face value of coins) by the addition of one-nineteenth, following the convention adopted by Emilie Amt in *The Accession of Henry II*, and the same formula has been used to convert sums 'ad pensum' in the 1130 pipe roll;[5] even though, in practice, there would have been variability in the conversion-rate, this does allow a consistent approach to the presentation of all figures in the face value of current coin. And in the interests of making broad comparisons, payments have been placed in one of three catego-ries: 'farms' (covering the king's income from estates, including escheats and sees in hand), 'taxes' (such as danegeld, scutage and the *donum comitatus*) and 'fines' (the so-called 'profits of jurisdiction' from pleas, 'feudal incidents' and various offerings for the king's favour).[6] As for the assignment of payments to particular shires, this also poses problems when there are accounts for escheated or forfeited estates stretching over several counties. In this case, they have been calculated as part of the shire to which the pipe roll assigns them; where they are dealt with outside the accounts of a shire, they are presented here as 'not assigned'.

Much of this is open to challenge, especially the placing of certain indetermi-nate items in one category or another, but the quest is for broad conclusions, not precise numerical results where precision is not to be found. Accordingly, although several of the figures which follow have been calculated in pounds, shil-lings and pence, the presentation of the results is consistently to the nearest whole pound, even where the rounding up or down may have thrown out a total by one or two pounds: to have done otherwise would have been to imply an accuracy of detail which is unwarranted.

With due regard to the various imperfections in source material and method-ology, let us turn to the figures from the 1130 pipe roll. These were analysed in great detail by Judith Green, and the fresh calculations offered here fully bear out her conclusions. We do indeed see 'a vigorous and predatory government, trying to keep up land revenue though the stock of land had diminished since the Conqueror's day, maintaining the old system of taxation whilst applying newer

---

5   Amt, *Accession*, 189; cf. J. A. Green, *The Government of England under Henry I* (Cambridge, 1986), 220–2.

6   Ibid., 55–94.

forms, but above all exploiting justice and jurisdiction in a way that is the most striking characteristic of this roll'.[7] The figures given here – with land revenue represented by 'farms' and most 'profits of jurisdiction' by 'fines' – differ a little from those published by Green, but this is to be expected given minor changes in methodology: the overall message is the same.

The 1130 pipe roll – showing 'farms' producing over half the king's income and 'fines' over a quarter – may be taken as a benchmark, against which to compare the figures yielded by subsequent pipe rolls. If we move immediately to the first full roll of Henry II, that for 1155–6, the most striking conclusion is that by then total income had (in broad terms) halved, the total income from land ('farms') had also halved, 'fines' yielded a very small sum, but taxes had increased, not only in proportion to other sources of income but also in absolute terms. Whatever conclusions are drawn from this regarding the king's income during the intervening period under Stephen, it is clear that Henry II's financial advisors deemed the country to be capable of paying more in taxes in the immediate aftermath of civil war than it had paid in the years preceding it. Even danegeld yielded almost as much in 1156 as it had done in 1130, despite substantial write-offs as 'waste'.[8] To this we shall return.

The pipe roll of nine years later, that for 1164–5, serves to demonstrate the extent of Henry II's success in restoring the financial position of his grandfather's time, on the eve of the judicial reforms which heralded a new phase of the reign. By then both 'farms' and the total paid in had reached levels not far short of those of 1130, while taxes were higher than in 1130 and comparable with those of 1156 (though mainly reliant on scutage, not danegeld). 'Fines', however, remained a relatively minor contributor to the overall income.

1176–7 may be taken as a representative year from the middle-to-later part of the reign. Among all Henry II's pipe rolls, it was in fact second only to 1186–7 in terms of the recorded amount paid to the king[9] and the substantial increase in 'fines' is immediately apparent; this was the direct result of the expansion of the king's justice, through the introduction of new processes and the systematic despatch of itinerant royal judges, which had been a feature of the previous decade. Income from land and taxes was much as it had been in 1164–5, but fell as a proportion of the total because of the dramatic rise in the significance of the 'fines'.

Finally, the pipe roll of 1188–9 gives us the position at the end of Henry II's reign, although the absence of a tax levy or any new judicial eyre during the course of the year make it atypical in the emphasis on landed income as a result. Total income from land was very similar to what it had been – on the evidence of the 1130 pipe roll – at the close of Henry I's reign over half a century before.

Taken as a whole, this run of figures testifies to the enduring importance of the

7   Green, 'Earliest Surviving Pipe Roll', 13.
8   G. J. White, 'Were the Midlands "Wasted" during Stephen's Reign?', *Midland History*, 10 (1985), 26–46.
9   J. H. Ramsay, *History of the Revenues of the Kings of England, 1066–1399* (Oxford, 1925), 191.

Pipe Roll 31 Henry I (1129–30)

Paid in as farms: **£14444** (approximately 58% of total paid in)
Paid in as taxes: **£3356** (14%)
Paid in as fines: **£6988** (28%)

Total paid in: **£24788**

It is also instructive to set the different shires in rank order of their contributions, with the following results.

Rank Order	Shires	Farms	Taxes	Fines	Totals
1	Essex-Hertfordshire	£1637	£204	£512	£2353
2	Lincolnshire	£947	£251	£943	£2141
3	London-Middlesex	£448	£149	£1166	£1763
4	Norfolk-Suffolk	£906	£367	£452	£1725
5	Dorset-Wiltshire	£991	£270	£187	£1448
6	Durham	£1095	£211	£16	£1322
7	Yorkshire	£453	£159	£694	£1306
8	Surrey-Cambs.-Hunts.	£497	£238	£464	£1199
9	Berkshire	£1015	£112	£63	£1190
10	Kent	£693	£60	£411	£1164
11	Northants-Leicester	£492	£135	£477	£1104
12	Hampshire	£760	£32	£232	£1024
13	Buckingham-Bedford	£569	£199	£106	£874
14	Devon	£384	£91	£288	£763
15	Nottingham-Derby	£314	£93	£293	£700
16	Gloucestershire	£405	£115	£145	£665
17	Warwickshire	£348	£85	£109	£542
18	Oxfordshire	£152	£130	£123	£405
19	Staffordshire	£243	£37	£69	£349
20	Northumberland	£202	£86	£11	£299
21	Cumberland	£103	£162	£2	£267
22	Sussex	£52	£94	£67	£213
23	Cornwall	£72	£13	£53	£138
24	Pembroke	£59	£—	£42	£101
25	Westmorland	£33	£48	£6	£87
26	Rutland	£37	£4	£10	£51
27	Isle of Wight	£—	£11	£—	£11
	Not assigned	£1537	£—	£47	£1584

(There is occasional minor damage, for example to figures in Sussex and Lincolnshire, and parts of the roll are missing for Hampshire.)

Pipe Roll 2 Henry II (1155–6)

Paid in as farms: **£6887** (approximately 53% of total paid in)
Paid in as taxes: **£5099** (40%)
Paid in as fines: **£849** (7%)

Total paid in: **£12835**

The rank order of shires was as follows.

Rank Order	Shires	Farms	Taxes	Fines	Totals
1	Hampshire	£760	£298	£151	£1209
2	Lincolnshire	£595	£443	£10	£1048
3	Yorkshire	£374	£540	£55	£969
4	Northamptonshire	£543	£203	£—	£746
5	Essex	£480	£179	£—	£659
6	Kent	£242	£159	£242	£643
7	Buckingham-Bedford	£429	£165	£39	£633
8	Nottingham-Derby	£455	£99	£14	£568
9	Worcestershire	£278	£191	£89	£558
10	Somerset	£220	£278	£36	£534
11	London-Middlesex	£336	£152	£—	£488
12	Devon	£198	£226	£5	£429
13	Wiltshire	£75	£284	£38	£397
14	Gloucestershire	£174	£196	£—	£370
15	Berkshire	£186	£144	£—	£330
16	Sussex	£69	£202	£55	£326
17	Shropshire	£182	£117	£7	£306
18	Cambridgeshire	£161	£112	£2	£275
19	Dorset	£23	£240	£0	£263
20	Herefordshire	£127	£131	£1	£259
21	Surrey	£94	£137	£20	£251
22	Suffolk	£171	£57	£21	£249
23	Huntingdonshire	£147	£69	£3	£219
24	Norfolk	£56	£107	£52	£215
25	Oxfordshire	£96	£102	£8	£206
26	Hertfordshire	£101	£75	£1	£177
27	Staffordshire	£96	£74	£—	£170
28	Warwickshire	£104	£56	£—	£160
29	Leicestershire	£75	£57	£—	£132
30	Rutland	£40	£6	£—	£46

(There is minor damage to figures in Dorset.)

Pipe Roll 11 Henry II (1164–5)

Paid in as farms: **£12882** (approximately 61% of total paid in)
Paid in as taxes: **£4843** (23%)
Paid in as fines: **£3307** (16%)

Total paid in: **£21032**

The shires yielded payment in the following rank order. (For this and subsequent pipe rolls, categorisation into farms, taxes and fines is not shown at the level of individual shires.)

Rank Order	Shires	Total
1	Kent	£2750
2	Norfolk-Suffolk	£2274
3	Lincolnshire	£2200
4	Yorkshire	£1679
5	Hampshire	£1390
6	Buckingham-Bedford	£1124
7	London-Middlesex	£964
8	Essex-Hertfordshire	£942
9	Nottingham-Derby	£813
10	Northamptonshire	£654
11	Cambridge-Huntingdon	£635
12	Berkshire	£567
13	Gloucestershire	£537
14	Dorset-Somerset	£514
15	Warwick-Leicester	£483
16	Wiltshire	£452
17	Cumberland	£439
18	Oxfordshire	£388
19	Northumberland	£388
20	Sussex	£353
21	Shropshire	£346
22	Devon	£317
23	Worcestershire	£286
24	Surrey	£220
25	Herefordshire	£197
26	Staffordshire	£120

Pipe Roll 23 Henry II (1176–7)

Paid in as farms: **£12528** (approximately 42% of total paid in)
Paid in as taxes: **£4806** (16%)
Paid in as fines: **£12811** (42%)

Total paid in: **£30145**

The shires may be listed in the following rank order.

Rank Order	Shires	Total
1	Yorkshire	£2960
2	London-Middlesex	£2746
3	Hampshire	£1827
4	Norfolk-Suffolk	£1689
5	Northamptonshire	£1681
6	Lincolnshire	£1562
7	Buckingham-Bedford	£1559
8	Essex-Hertfordshire	£1543
9	Dorset-Somerset	£1511
10	Nottingham-Derby	£1082
11	Devon	£1044
12	Kent	£1022
13	Staffordshire	£946
14	Warwick-Leicester	£720
15	Wiltshire	£667
16	Oxfordshire	£612
17	Cambridge-Huntingdon	£587
18	Northumberland	£576
19	Gloucestershire	£570
20	Sussex	£569
21	Worcestershire	£545
22	Berkshire	£536
23	Cumberland	£528
24	Shropshire	£475
25	Cornwall	£426
26	Herefordshire	£338
27	Surrey	£323
28	Westmorland	£205
29	Rutland	£22
	Not assigned	£1276

Pipe Roll 1 Richard I (1188–9)

Paid in as farms: **£14637** (approximately 87% of total paid in)
Paid in as taxes: **£243** (2%)
Paid in as fines: **£1883** (11%)

Total paid in: **£16763**

With this heavy focus on the king's lands, the rank order of shires was as follows.

Rank Order	Shires	Total
1	Kent	£942
2	Lincolnshire	£928
3	Norfolk-Suffolk	£902
4	Hampshire	£879
5	Yorkshire	£793
6	Essex-Hertfordshire	£767
7	Sussex	£646
8	London-Middlesex	£560
9	Northamptonshire	£559
10	Cambs-Huntingdon	£523
11	Northumberland	£484
12	Buckingham-Bedford	£479
13	Berkshire	£476
14	Dorset-Somerset	£465
15	Devon	£428
16	Wiltshire	£414
17	Warwick-Leicester	£326
18	Cornwall	£299
19	Cumberland	£265
20	Oxfordshire	£239
21	Gloucestershire	£237
22	Worcestershire	£208
23	Surrey	£187
24	Herefordshire	£184
25	Staffordshire	£175
26	Nottingham-Derby	£127
27	Shropshire	£111
28	Rutland	£22
	Not assigned	£4138

(There is minor damage to figures in Norfolk-Suffolk, Lincolnshire, Northamptonshire, Warwickshire-Leicestershire and Rutland.)

king's landed income as a substantial and reasonably stable source of revenue. Taxes could be levied when there was sufficient incentive to make the effort to collect them, and were clearly identified by Henry II's advisors as the best means to meet some of the shortfall in landed income at the very beginning of the reign. The extent to which 'fines' were a significant contributor to the overall income depended directly on the activity of the king's justices, whose perambulations led not only to pleas but to offerings for the king's favour and who left their legacy in accounts in the pipe rolls for several years to come. Pleas heard by a dozen royal justices are apparent in the 1130 pipe roll – not all from the past twelve months – while no less than seven judicial eyres during 1176–7, plus a host of forest offences and a backlog of previous cases, lay behind the high totals for 'fines' in 1177.[10] By contrast, there was relatively little judicial work of this kind in the periods covered by the pipe rolls of 1156, 1165 and 1189.

Beyond overall totals, the rankings of the individual shires repay close attention. Notwithstanding the difficulties faced in making direct comparisons from one year to another – the fact that in 1130 several shires were accounted for together, and that the totals for particular shires could be skewed in any given year by the temporary inclusion of escheated estates – it is clear that the crown tended to look in the same direction for a substantial portion of its revenue from one decade to the next: including either side of Stephen's reign. The large and well-populated county of Lincolnshire, for example, was the second highest contributor to the king's recorded income both in 1130 and in 1156 and appears in the 'top six' in all the lists. Yorkshire, seventh in 1130 and third in 1156, was also in the leading group every time. Essex (usually accounted for with Hertfordshire) was never out of the 'top eight' while only major omissions within the coverage of Hampshire in the 1130 pipe roll prevented it figuring as prominently in the list for that year as it did in all the others. Kent and Northamptonshire also featured consistently in the upper reaches of the table. Conversely, Oxfordshire, Gloucestershire and Staffordshire were among those which regularly appeared towards the lower end, as did Herefordshire and Shropshire (albeit absent from the roll of 1130).

Henry II's exchequer was of course well aware of the potential of certain shires to yield more revenue for the crown than others and obviously targeted them as sources of additional income. Lincolnshire and Kent had increments of £140 and £165 13s 4d *numero*, respectively, added to their shire farms in 1156.[11] The *donum comitatus* was, in effect, a variable levy based on perceived ability to pay, and, as Table 1 demonstrates, the sums imposed in 1156 and 1158 were particularly high in Yorkshire, Lincolnshire, Essex, Kent and Northamptonshire, but particularly low in Staffordshire and some of the western shires.[12] And in Henry

---

10 Green, *Government under Henry I*, 108–9; Ramsay, *Revenues*, 127–31.
11 White, *Restoration*, 223; smaller increments were added to the farms of London and Nottinghamshire-Derbyshire in the same year.
12 The system used for the levy of the *donum comitatus* (or common assize) is described in *Dialogus de Scaccario*, ed. C. Johnson, F. E. L. Carter and D. E. Greenway (Oxford, 1983), 47–8. *Dona* were also imposed on London in 1159 and 1161 (totalling £1700), Norwich in

II's first eleven years, before the advent of regular judicial eyres, Yorkshire appears on pipe roll evidence to have been visited four times by royal justices, when most shires saw them only once.[13]

Table 1. Rankings for assessment to *donum comitatus*, 1156 and 1158

Rank Order	Shire	1156 + 1158 = total (silver marks)
1	Yorkshire	500 + 500 = 1000
2	Lincolnshire	270 + 300 = 570
3	Essex	200 + 200 = 400
4	Devon	180(?) + 150 = 330(?)
5	Kent	150(?) + 120 = 270(?)
6	Northamptonshire	120 + 140 = 260
7	Somerset	100 + 150 = 250
8	Gloucestershire	100(?) + 130 = 230(?)
9=	Buckingham-Bedford	100 + 120 = 220
9=	Nottingham-Derby	80 + 140 = 220
11	Norfolk	200 + NIL = 200
12	Hampshire	90(?) + 100 = 190(?)
13=	Wiltshire	100 + 80 = 180
13=	Sussex	100(?) + 80 = 180(?)
15=	Oxfordshire	70 + 100 = 170
15=	Warwickshire	50 + 120 = 170
17	Surrey	80 + 80 = 160
18	Leicestershire	50 + 80 = 130
19=	Berkshire	60(?) + 60 = 120(?)
19=	London-Middlesex	80 + 40 = 120
19=	Suffolk	120 + NIL = 120
22=	Shropshire	40 + 70 = 110
22=	Herefordshire	40 + 70 = 110
22=	Worcestershire	50 + 60 = 110
25	Dorset	100(?) + NIL = 100(?)
26	Staffordshire	40 + 50 = 90
27	Cambridgeshire	80 + NIL = 80
28	Hertfordshire	60 + NIL = 60
29	Huntingdonshire	50 + NIL = 50

(?) Entry in pipe roll leaves the sum assigned as *donum* unclear.
(Northumberland (120 marks) and Cumberland (50 marks) were also liable for the *donum comitatus* in 1158 but not in 1156.)

1158, 1159 and 1161 (totalling £800) and York in the same three years (totalling over 1000 marks): White, *Restoration*, 153.
[13] Ibid., 184, 193.

So what is the significance of all this for our understanding of Stephen's reign? First of all, there is the obvious point that, insofar as Stephen managed to retain a measure of control over certain parts of his kingdom for most of the 1140s and early 1150s – as evidenced by writs, charters, coins and occasional financial levies within a broad belt from Yorkshire in the north through Lincolnshire, Nottinghamshire, Huntingdonshire, Cambridgeshire, East Anglia and the south-east as far west as a 'frontier zone' of Hampshire, Berkshire, Oxfordshire and Buckinghamshire – that control did at least embrace the more lucrative shires. The Angevins were left with the poorer counties to the west.[14] That said, broad allegiance and isolated evidence of success in raising money does not prove that Stephen was receiving more than a fraction of what he might have thought himself entitled to, even from the eastern and south-eastern shires. He had to contend with divided loyalties, notwithstanding the fact that a particular shire was supposedly in the royalist camp: witness the resistance he encountered from Hugh Bigod in Norfolk, from Brian fitz Count and John Marshal in Berkshire and Oxfordshire and from Walchelin Maminot and others in Kent.[15] The alienation of royal manors, including those with hundredal jurisdiction, also curtailed the king's income (a phenomenon particularly prevalent in Norfolk, Suffolk, Essex, Kent, Berkshire and Oxfordshire)[16] as did reliance on autonomous figures as the local representative, such as William of Aumale in Yorkshire.[17] A rare glimpse of the difficulties faced by Stephen's administration in the face of competing allegiances and independent-minded magnates is to be found within the pipe roll accounts for Norfolk and Suffolk early in Henry II's reign. There was no political settlement here until the summer of 1157, when Hugh Bigod and Stephen's son William de Warenne were both required to surrender their castles and William also had to return the Norfolk lands given as part of the 1153 peace settlement.[18] Less than half the shire farm for Norfolk and Suffolk was accounted for until 1158, there was no full list of *terrae datae* in the pipe rolls until 1158, references to 'waste' appear in shire farm accounts until 1159 and there are such sketchy references to danegeld in 1156 that while some account was taken of small sums owing, there is no sign of anything being paid into the treasury. The result is that shires which (accounted for together) appear among the most lucrative sources of royal revenue in 1130 and for most of Henry II's reign are to be found near the bottom of the list in 1156.

This is a warning against over-reliance on the pipe rolls if what one is seeking is an indication of economic conditions: the story they tell may be more

[14] Ibid., 25–45; M. Blackburn, 'Coinage and Currency', in King, *Anarchy*, 145–205.

[15] White, *Restoration*, 34–5.

[16] E. J. King, 'The Anarchy of King Stephen's Reign', *TRHS*, 5th ser., 34 (1984), 133–53; Amt, *Accession*, 149–68.

[17] P. Dalton, 'William Earl of York and Royal Authority in Yorkshire in the Reign of Stephen', *HSJ*, 2 (1990), 155–65.

[18] *Torigni*, 192–3; W. L. Warren, *Henry II* (London, 1973), 67–8; White, *Restoration*, 6.

concerned with political and administrative circumstances than with anything else. Yet Norfolk and Suffolk are exceptional in dropping from near the top to near the bottom of revenue-yielding shires between 1130 and 1156. If one puts to one side income from 'fines' – largely a reflection of the activity of the king's officers – and concentrates on 'farms' and 'taxes', as in Table 2, overall there is broad similarity in the placings of shires within the two lists, though it is instructive to note those which saw the most serious falls in income to the crown, in excess of 60%. Apart from Norfolk and Suffolk, these were Berkshire – which also had a large number of alienated royal manors by the beginning of Henry II's reign – and Warwickshire, where the shortcomings of the sheriff, Robert fitz Hugh, have been blamed elsewhere for the high proportion of danegeld written off as 'waste' in 1156.[19] Elsewhere, again looking only at 'farms' and 'taxes', a relatively buoyant picture is apparent within a broad geographical zone embracing northern and east-midland England from Yorkshire through Lincolnshire, Nottinghamshire, Derbyshire, Northamptonshire, Leicestershire, Rutland, Huntingdonshire and Cambridgeshire, where the figures show increases or only minor decreases in revenue returned to the crown when 1156 is set against 1130: to these may be added the southern shires of Sussex, Surrey, Hampshire and Devon.

Several caveats must be entered against these figures, which may misrepresent some shires accounted for jointly with others and in the case of Hampshire are affected by sections missing from the 1130 pipe roll.[20] But they do suggest a certain resilience in the economy, particularly in parts of the north, the east midlands and the south, which should be seen in the context of healthy economic development overall during the first half of the twelfth century, as discussed by Edmund King.[21] King has reminded us, for example, of the competition for trading privileges which continued throughout Stephen's reign, and has also demonstrated the speed with which economic advantage would be pursued as soon as political circumstances allowed. There are a score of grants or confirmations of fairs by Stephen in *Regesta Regum Anglo-Normannorum* volume III, almost all in the eastern counties, and King's example of the bishop of Lincoln establishing a new fair at Banbury 'at the first Pentecost after the concord made between the king and the duke of Normandy' is echoed by Stephen's grant of two three-day fairs and a weekly market to Great Bricett Priory (Suffolk) and of a coalmine in Weardale to Hugh bishop of Durham, both in the closing months of his reign.[22] This strikes a note of optimism, and it is reinforced by the tax returns from the beginning of Henry II's reign. If, instead of concentrating on what was written off as 'waste' in 1156, we look at what was actually paid in the form of one tax or another, we find that nearly every shire contributed more in tax in that

19 White, 'Were the Midlands "Wasted"?', 38; Amt, *Accession*, 141–7.
20 *PR 31 Henry I*, 40, 43.
21 E. J. King, 'Economic Development in the Early Twelfth Century', in R. Britnell and J. Hatcher, eds., *Progress and Problems in Medieval England* (Cambridge, 1996), 1–22.
22 *Regesta*, iii, nos. 118, 258.

Table 2. Comparison of total income from farms and taxes combined, by shire, 1130 and 1156

Increase 1130–1156

Shire	1130 £	1156 £	£ increase	% increase
Sussex	146	271	+ 125	(86%)
Yorkshire	612	914	+ 302	(49%)
Northampton-Leicester	627	878	+ 251	(40%)
Nottingham-Derby	407	554	+ 147	(36%)
Hampshire	792	1058	+ 266	(34%)
Rutland	41	46	+ 5	(12%)

Decrease 1130–1156

Shire	1130 £	1156 £	£ decrease	% decrease
Surrey-Cambs.-Hunts.	735	720	– 15	(2%)
Devon	475	424	– 51	(11%)
Lincolnshire	1198	1038	– 160	(13%)
London-Middlesex	597	488	– 109	(18%)
Buckingham-Bedford	768	594	– 174	(23%)
Gloucestershire	520	370	– 150	(29%)
Oxfordshire	282	198	– 84	(30%)
Staffordshire	280	170	– 110	(39%)
Kent	753	401	– 352	(47%)
Dorset-Wiltshire	1261	622	– 639	(51%)
Essex-Hertfordshire	1841	835	– 1006	(55%)
Warwickshire	433	160	– 273	(63%)
Norfolk-Suffolk	1273	391	– 882	(69%)
Berkshire	1127	330	– 797	(71%)

year than it had in 1130 (Table 3). If we focus specifically on one tax, danegeld, some two-fifths of the shires for which accounts were rendered in both years paid more in 1156 than in 1130 – with no convincing correlation with the proportions written off as 'waste' (Table 4).[23] One must of course beware of equating high tax

[23] This is not the place to reopen discussion of the meaning of the 'waste' in the 1156 danegeld returns. In my most recent treatment of this topic (*Restoration*, 155), the point was made that what mattered most to the exchequer was 'not how much physical damage there had been … but how realistic the tax assessments were in current circumstances'. The present analysis supports the argument made there that shires such as Kent and Yorkshire remained in a good position to pay their dues to the crown (and hence had relatively low sums entered

payments with good economic performance – as anyone who has studied government extortion, such as that practised on the starving peasantry during the Great Famine of 1315–17 knows only too well[24] – but at least we can say that Henry II's exchequer had the confidence to call on these resources within two years of the peace settlement, evidently considering some write-off for 'waste' to be a small price to pay.

Table 3. Rankings of shires for total tax payments in 1156, with 1130 tax payments for comparison

Rank order	Shire	1156	1130
1	Yorkshire	£540	£159
2	Lincolnshire	£443	£251
3	Hampshire	£298	£32 but gaps
4	Wiltshire	£284	£161
5	Somerset	£278	—
6	Dorset	£240	£109
7	Devon	£226	£91
8	Northamptonshire	£203	£78
9	Sussex	£202	£94
10	Gloucestershire	£196	£115
11	Worcestershire	£191	—
12	Essex	£179	£135
13	Buckingham-Bedford *	£165	£199
14	Kent	£159	£60
15	London-Middlesex	£152	£149
16	Berkshire	£144	£112
17	Surrey	£137	£106
18	Herefordshire	£131	—
19	Shropshire	£117	—
20	Cambridgeshire	£112	£76
21	Norfolk *	£107	£231

as 'waste') while those such as Warwickshire and Oxfordshire (with high 'waste' figures) did not. This does not, however, explain the high sums for 'waste' entered for Nottinghamshire-Derbyshire and Northamptonshire, which paid more in total to the crown in 1156 than in 1130 if 'fines' are excluded, nor the relatively low 'waste' figures for Dorset and Staffordshire where there was a substantial fall in revenue to the crown. Administrative reasons for the write-offs for 'waste', in circumstances in which full and accurate collections of danegeld must have been very difficult, continue to be attractive explanations.

24 I. Kershaw, 'The Great Famine and Agrarian Crisis in England, 1315–22', *Past and Present* 59 (1973), 3–50.

Rank order	Shire	1156	1130
22	Oxfordshire *	£102	£130
23	Nottingham-Derby	£99	£93
24	Hertfordshire	£75	£68
25	Staffordshire	£74	£37
26	Huntingdonshire	£69	£56
27	Leicestershire *	£57	£57
28	Suffolk *	£57	£136
29	Warwickshire *	£56	£85
30	Rutland	£6	£4

* Those shires which paid less in 1156 than in 1130.

Table 4. Comparison of danegeld payments in 1130 and 1156, by shire (omits minor sums owing from previous year in 1130)

Shires which paid more danegeld in 1156 than in 1130

Shire	1130	1156	% increase	% waste (1156)
Kent	£51	£89	75%	under 1%
Dorset	£98	£170	73%	7%
Sussex	£94	£158	68%	4%
Rutland	£4	£6	50%	14%
Wiltshire	£146	£200	37%	37%
Surrey	£85	£105	24%	17%
Gloucestershire	£96	£108	13%	30%
Middlesex	£35	£39	11%	12%
Yorkshire	£114	£125	10%	7%

plus a total of £589 paid in 1156 from Somerset, Hampshire, Worcestershire, Shropshire and Herefordshire, for which there are no danegeld accounts in the 1130 pipe roll.

Shires which paid less danegeld in 1156 than in 1130

Shire	1130	1156	% decrease	% waste (1156)
Devon	£62	£61	2%	9%
Staffordshire	£30	£25	17%	19%
Huntingdonshire	£46	£35	24%	20%
Hertfordshire	£61	£46	25%	27%
Lincolnshire	£191	£141	26%	27%

Shire	1130	1156	% increase	% waste (1156)
Essex	£134	£98	27%	26%
Northamptonshire	£78	£55	29%	32%
Berkshire	£112	£77	31%	38%
Buckingham-Bedford	£191	£118	38%	34%
Cambridgeshire	£66	£38	42%	30%
Nottingham-Derby	£79	£38	52%	52%
Leicestershire	£57	£25	56%	51%
Warwickshire	£79	£32	59%	63%
Oxfordshire	£116	£44	62%	39%

plus a total of £337 paid in 1130 from Norfolk, Suffolk and Cornwall, for which there are no danegeld accounts in the 1156 pipe roll. Northumberland was also liable for danegeld in 1130, but the sum of £100 for that year was owing.

All this contributes to an impression that, whatever physical or economic damage was done in Stephen's reign, it was quickly repaired; in Edmund King's phrase, it was soon 'business as usual'.[25] This is apparent not only from the broadly similar rankings of shires in terms of their revenue yield to the crown in 1130 and in 1156 – aberrations in Norfolk and Suffolk notwithstanding – but also from the speed with which restocking of the royal demesne was accomplished: although no less than £1178 was spent on this in 1155–6 according to the relevant pipe roll (embracing 21 shire farms and eleven separately-farmed estates), by the following year the total spent was down to £71 (in Norfolk-Suffolk, Berkshire, Surrey and Northamptonshire), less than the £86 devoted to the same purpose in 1130.[26] And while it would be quite wrong to underplay the horrific experiences of suffering arising from famine or warfare described in the chronicles, passages such as that in the *Gesta Stephani* describing 'villages with famous names standing solitary and almost empty because the peasants ... were dead'[27] need to be set against other evidence. While the Medieval Settlement Research Group recognises several settlements whose desertion is attributable to Stephen's reign, these are mostly the result of monastic foundations and their associated granges: the destruction of the eastern end of Rampton (Cambridgeshire) and south-western end of Burwell to make way for castle-works at Burwell during Stephen's campaign against Geoffrey de Mandeville in 1143 is a rare example of depopulation directly attributable to the civil war. Although sometime between 1163 and 1176 Thornton Abbey was allowed to graze sheep in the fields of

---

25 King, 'Economic Development', 22.
26 Amt, *Accession*, 142–8; on 1130, see *PR 31 Henry I*, 7, 24, 122, 130, 137 (Nottinghamshire-Derbyshire, Yorkshire, Berkshire, Durham, land of Roger de Mowbray); on 1157, see *PR 3 Henry II*, 72, 76, 81, 94, 104.
27 *Gesta Stephani*, 152–3.

Ulceby (Lincolnshire) 'until the same vill was repopulated and restored', this is not a deserted settlement site.[28] Ulceby clearly recovered and – in this era of population expansion – it is fair to suggest that most similar communities, other than the victims of monastic initiatives, would have done likewise.

Stephen's reign has been depicted in the past as one which, despite political and military upheaval, helped to maintain a tradition of administrative continuity from Henry I's reign to Henry II's.[29] The argument here is for economic continuity as well, in the sense that there was no lasting impact on the capacity of the kingdom to supply the royal treasury, nor on the relative importance of the various shires as contributors. There was certainly a serious fall in the king's landed income between the end of Henry I's reign and the beginning of Henry II's, but its impact was short-lived. The position steadily recovered and the drop was at least partly offset by a higher yield from taxes. Among the many problems which Henry II faced in his earliest years as king, revenue-raising was one which could most readily be solved. For, in economic as well as administrative terms, the reign of Stephen was essentially an interlude.

[28] M. W. Beresford and J. G. Hurst, *Deserted Medieval Villages* (Guildford, 1971), 5–6.
[29] G. J. White, 'Continuity in Government', in King, *Anarchy*, 117–24, and *Restoration*, 12–76.

3

King Stephen and Northern France

DAVID CROUCH

WHAT SORT OF WORLD VIEW did a twelfth-century man possess? A lot hinges on the answer to that particular question. As we now know, medieval aristocrats travelled very widely and travelled constantly. They knew the roads of their world well, and there is no doubt that they compiled mental maps of it, maps by which they navigated also their political world. Both Gerald of Wales and Bertran de Born give us in their writings excellent examples of how they visualized the world in which they lived: Gerald in his topographical writings, and Bertran in his sketch of the components of the Francophone cultural world that he drew up in 1183.[1] So if we wish to talk in terms of Stephen of Blois's geopolitical vision of his world, then I do not think we are begging questions. Such a vision was possible. Born in the Loire valley, at home from the frontiers of the Empire to the borders of Brittany, well-known in Paris, Bruges and London, Stephen of Blois could very easily have acquired a mental map of the world in which he was, from his adolescence, a significant player.

Whether he had the capacity to generate any sort of policy out of that vision is a different matter entirely. We should beware what Martin Aurell calls the 'statist' suppositions of earlier generations of historian, the suppositions that generated for English schoolboys the rather eccentric idea of an 'ecclesiastical policy' of Henry II of England, or for that matter the 'centralising policy' of Henry I. Policy is not the sort of word you could use happily of a medieval king, resonant as it is of the age of Gladstone and Disraeli.[2] You could also be begging the question of the mental capacities of Stephen of Blois, a king whose most sympathetic biographer would not say was a man of great intellectual distinction.

So the title of this paper is not the 'French policy of Stephen of Blois', but the much more anodyne 'Stephen and Northern France'. The cultural and political heartland of the Francophone world between the Loire, the Meuse and the

---

1   For Bertran's world picture, dating to 1181 x 85, *Poésies Complètes de Bertran de Born*, ed. A. Thomas (Toulouse, 1888), 162–3. For Gerald of Wales as topographer, R. Bartlett, *Gerald of Wales, 1146–1223* (Oxford, 1982), 178–210.
2   M. Aurell, *L'Empire Plantagenêt* (Paris, 2003), 181ff.

Channel was very much a political fact that any post-Conquest king of England – however limited his intellectual capacities – would have to recognize and to deal with. Some dimensions of the English king's situation in France are already well-known to historiography. Firstly there was the fact that the king was also the duke of Normandy, and that the elite of his aristocracy was powerful in the duchy as much as in England. Another was the increase in ambition and prestige of the Capetian king of France at the time of Louis VI. Louis's was no longer a dynasty fighting its own subject castellans in the Ile-de-France, it was shifting into expansionism. Flanders too was a factor in the English king's world view. It was the most economically dynamic region of France, and its counts had interests in England, both economic and territorial. Lastly there was the expanding principality of Anjou in the Loire valley, whose ambitions were pressing alike on Maine, Blois and Brittany.

So it can only be significant that at the end of 1135, at this point when Stephen became king, his advisers and he resolved on soliciting testimonials from two major players in northern France to present to the pope in support of Stephen's succession to Henry I. We do not know what these testimonials said, but they were certainly secured and they were sent with Stephen's embassy to Rome. The pope's bull sanctioning Stephen's succession mentions that the *curia* had viewed them.[3] They can only have been picked up as Stephen's envoys passed through Paris and Chartres at some time early in January 1136. They signified a major political shift in Northern France. Henry I in 1127 had staked much of his political capital on a new alliance with the Anjou of Fulk V and Geoffrey the Fair. It was meant to create a powerful barrier to Louis VI's ambitions and counterbalanced Louis's triumph in Flanders, where he placed his ally William Clito as count. The alliance was built on the marriage of Geoffrey and Empress Matilda.[4] The fact that Stephen had frustrated the old king's plan for his daughter's succession can only have caused a certain subdued delight in Paris, and a willingness to co-operate with Stephen's envoys on their way to Rome. No longer was there a threat of England, Anjou and Normandy under the same ruler. What had been created instead was a Normandy and Blois under the rule of brothers, who were now an imposing obstacle to any Angevin pretensions to expand up the Loire into Berry. The fact that Theobald of Blois was also prepared to support his younger brother's claims at Rome is significant as well. It shows that the count did not harbour the resentment at Stephen's coup with which one Norman chronicler – Robert de Torigny – credited him.[5] It also hints that before 1135 the house of Blois may have entertained the idea of furthering the family's power by seizing the succession to Normandy and England.

It was an idea first broached by Jim Bradbury that Theobald and Stephen of

---

3 Richard of Hexham, *De Gestis Regis Stephani et de Bello Standardii*, in Howlett, *Chronicles*, iii, 147–8.
4 For the Angevin marriage and its significance, see C. W. Hollister, *Henry I*, edited and completed by A. Clark Frost (New Haven and London, 2001), 322–5.
5 *Torigni*, 128–9.

Blois might have entertained plans to take advantage of the death of Henry I by agreeing on an intervention in the succession.[6] After all, the political union of Normandy and Anjou, not to mention England under Matilda and Geoffrey, was in no way to the advantage of Blois-Chartres, the next power bloc up the Loire beyond the Touraine. So why not do something about it? The Norman chroniclers of course believed that Theobald, the elder brother, had expected the succession, and indeed received the support of the Normans as soon as the old king was dead. The fact that Stephen nonetheless beat him to the throne of England may not have been due to the younger man's ambitions against his brother so much as the political chaos following Henry's unexpected death. After all, Stephen was in no position to consult with his elder brother when news reached him in Boulogne that the old king was dead. And so to England, where his own younger brother, Bishop Henry of Winchester was in a perfect position to engineer Stephen's succession, and where, we are told by the *Gesta Stephani*, that there was a strong pro-Blois party already in existence amongst the aristocracy.[7]

So, whether or not Theobald was annoyed that Stephen had beaten him to the throne, he did not stay annoyed for long. He has to have been solicited for testimonials for Rome by January at the latest, and he had provided them. There may have been inducements to soothe Theobald's annoyance. Arnold of Bonneval tells us that Theobald came by a large part of Henry I's gorgeous collection of household plate. On top of that, he also came by lands in England perhaps at this time, perhaps later, but certainly by 1139. The identifiable manors held by Theobald, at Maldon in Essex, Burbage in Wiltshire and Hurstwick in Hampshire, were all associated with the former royal demesne, Maldon as late as 1130.[8]

The other provider of testimonials in 1136 had been Louis VI. His support for Stephen's succession was rooted in the same concern as that of Theobald. He wanted to frustrate any increase in Angevin power. The fact that Stephen of Blois had taken the English throne rather than Theobald was the best he could have expected in the circumstances. It meant that at least the Anglo-Norman realm was not extended south-eastwards to include Blois-Chartres, and in terms of the polity of northern France, Stephen's succession was a distinct improvement on what the case had been under Henry I, for Anjou and Normandy were now at war.

So until Louis's death in 1137, a firm alliance linked Normandy, Blois-Chartres and Paris. It was expressed in a number of ways other than the writing of character references to Rome. In 1136, when Normandy was in some disarray, Theobald offered support to Waleran of Meulan, his brother's lieutenant in the duchy. On the expiry of his truce with Geoffrey of Anjou in June 1136, Count Theobald led a large force of knights into the duchy in support of Waleran's onslaught on Geoffrey's ally, Roger de Tosny. Theobald occupied the south-east

---

6   J. Bradbury, 'The Early Years of the Reign of Stephen', in *England in the Twelfth Century*, ed. D. Williams (Woodbridge, 1990), 20–2.

7   *Gesta Stephani*, 8.

8   *Vita Sancti Bernardi: Liber Secundus*, in *PL*, clxxxv, cols. 301–2; *Regesta*, ii, nos. 274, 543, 790.

of the duchy, pacifying the Seine and Eure valleys, while Waleran subdued the march towards Maine. It was partly Theobald's support that enabled Waleran to repulse the Angevin invasion of the duchy in September 1136.[9] Waleran of Meulan's lieutenancy is itself evidence of further connections with the Capetian court. Waleran was a close cousin of Louis VI and nephew of Louis's ally and adviser, Count Ralph I of Vermandois, the most considerable magnate of Picardy. The county of Meulan was within the French Vexin, and included within its fees a large part of the city of Paris. The Capetian alliance was therefore very much in Waleran's own interest, as King Stephen ought to have known – and even if he had not his brother and chief adviser at this time, Bishop Henry, most certainly did.[10]

By the time King Stephen made his triumphant return to the continent in March 1137, there is a good deal of evidence that an axis had grown naturally between Westminster, Paris and Chartres. It would be nice to think that Stephen himself had been the architect of this strategic bloc directed against Angers, but it has to be doubted. Bishop Henry, his brother, would be a more likely candidate, especially as he was the person most likely to have mobilized Louis's and Theobald's support over the succession, and he had preceded the king to Normandy in 1137 – one assumes for the purposes of organizing diplomacy.[11] But it is just as likely that shared anxieties and mutual interest would have made the alliance inevitable. The selection of Waleran of Meulan as the king's lieu-tenant in the duchy at Easter 1136 would have just cemented the arrangement. The axis became formalized at Easter 1137 when Louis VI, Theobald and Stephen met at Evreux and at Grossoeuvre near the Norman border. It was at around this time that, after many long years of confrontation, Theobald emerged as one of the ailing French king's principal advisers, being honoured with the revived title of 'count palatine'. The alliance with Westminster and Chartres became even more important for Louis at this time, as he was in the process of planning the marriage of his son and heir to Eleanor, the heir of Aquitaine. When the marriage came about in July 1137, it is no surprise to find that the faction at the Capetian court which seconded Louis VI in furthering it were listed as 'the leading and celebrated noblemen: Count Theobald of Blois, Count Ralph of Vermandois, Count William of Nevers and Count Rotrou of Perche', as the Morigny chronicle puts it.[12] Three of them were the princes most threatened by a potential expansion of Angevin power up the Loire. The marriage made Poitiers a Capetian citadel and opened a new southern frontier against Anjou which could not have made Count Geoffrey at all happy.

In fact the Angevin position against Normandy and Paris was as weak in the

---

9 *Orderic*, vi, 464; *Torigni*, 131.
10 For Waleran's connections with Louis VI and the Capetian realm, D. Crouch, *The Beau-mont Twins: The Roots and Branches of Power in the Twelfth Century* (Cambridge, 1986), 10–12, 20–1.
11 For Bishop Henry's directing role in this period, Crouch, *Reign of Stephen*, 50–2.
12 *La Chronique de Morigny*, ed. L. Mirot (Paris, 1909), 66.

summer of 1137 as it was ever to be. King Stephen had crushed all serious opposi-tion in the duchy, and even Geoffrey's die-hard supporters had submitted to him; only a toe-hold was left to Count Geoffrey in the south of Normandy, represented by his wife's castles. Anjou itself was surrounded now on three sides by hostile powers. This needs to be borne in mind whenever assessments are made of Stephen's 1137 tour of the duchy. Traditional historiography of the reign makes it a failure, an assessment largely reliant on William of Malmesbury and his dubious account of the failure of the ducal muster in the summer, which was intended to complete the job and oust Geoffrey from his last salient in the duchy.[13] Traditional historiography tends to forget what else was going on in northern France, and quite how isolated were the Angevins. The defection over the summer of stalwart Angevin adherents like Roger de Tosny and Robert du Neubourg makes sense if the weakness of the Angevin position is borne in mind.

But of course the cracks leading to the collapse of this very promising French situation for Stephen were already opening, even as barons deserted Geoffrey and Matilda for him. The principal disaster was the death of Louis VI. Louis has not had a particularly easy ride out of historians, he is often seen as yet another Capetian struggling to contain the unruly barons of the Capetian demesne.[14] In fact he was in his way as impressive a king as Henry I of England, his great rival. He was the first Capetian in several generations to expand his activities beyond the Ile-de-France. It is too often forgotten that the baronial bugbears of his early reign, Thomas of Marle and Hugh de Puiset, were castellans situated outside the previous Capetian orbit. And for all his mixed success, he was politically active in Flanders, Burgundy and Aquitaine. In many ways his reaction to the succession of Stephen in England was one of his finest hours. His reactions were politically agile and deft. He did not oppose it; far from it, he abruptly shifted from confron-tation with Count Theobald to close alliance. He caught Geoffrey of Anjou quite off balance, and the Aquitainian marriage ought to have been the killer blow for Anjou's power in western France. Had Louis not died, it might well have been.

The other of Stephen's French problems was less immediately obvious in 1137, but it was emerging. The problem was his links with Flanders. Stephen had been intimately linked with Flanders since he had acquired the county of Boulogne by marriage in 1125. Flanders had been Stephen's first serious outing into the world of high politics. In 1127 he had been despatched by Henry I to help oppose the succession of William Clito to Flanders. He had been active in chan-nelling English treasure to sympathetic Flemish cities and nobles and he had successfully opposed an all out Flemish assault on Boulogne during the summer of 1127.[15] It was during this crisis that Stephen had made the acquaintance of William of Ypres, the unsuccessful first candidate of Henry I for the county, and

---

[13] As in Davis, *King Stephen*, 25–6.

[14] A view of his reign still to be found in R. Fawtier, *The Capetian Kings of France*, trans. L. Butler and R. Adam (London, 1960).

[15] For Stephen's part in the Flemish crisis of 1127–8, see Crouch, *Reign of Stephen*, 26–7; E. King, 'Stephen of Blois, Count of Mortain and Boulogne', *EHR*, 115 (2000), 283–4.

of Thierry of Alsace, who eventually won the succession contest after Clito's death. He must have been instrumental in managing the renegotiation of the homage of Count Thierry to Henry I of England, and the affirmation of the military alliance that came with the homage.

What made these close Flemish ties ultimately a problem for Stephen was the degree of alienation that Flemings inspired in both Normandy and England. It seems that the mass recruitment of Flemish mercenaries began during the 1137 Norman campaign.[16] William of Malmesbury and three other contemporary writers all give resentment at the influx of Flemish mercenaries as the principal reason why large elements of the Norman army quit King Stephen's muster in disgust. This seems more than a little odd in the light of Henry I's predilection for recruiting Breton and French mercenaries for his Norman campaigns, as he did widely in 1118 and 1123. But it might be more accountable if we bear in mind that Stephen could have been thought to be giving his old Flemish friends priority at court. It was a tendency towards unwise concentration of patronage that was to be one of the less attractive features of his kingship. Henry I had never committed the political sin of factional favouritism.

Louis VI's commitment to Stephen as king of England left a long legacy. The new young king, Louis VII, initially maintained Count Ralph and Count Theobald as his principal advisers, and along with them went the continuation of the established alliance between Paris and Westminster. We see plenty of evidence of active engagement between Rouen and Paris in 1138. Count Ralph of Vermandois provided troops to support Waleran of Meulan in Normandy in the spring of that year, and there is evidence to reconstruct what amounted to an intensification of Louis VI's schemes. In the *Beaumont Twins* I presented the evidence for an embassy to Paris led by Waleran of Meulan at Easter 1138. The count went with at least one other English earl, his young half-brother William of Warenne, and several barons.[17] They may have gone simply to ratify with the new king the agreement reached with Louis VI the previous year. My feeling is, however, that there was more serious business. It is in the summer of 1138 that we first hear of the scheme to marry Stephen's eleven or twelve year old son, Eustace, to Louis VII's sister, Constance. Had this previously been proposed by Louis VI? It is possible, but the fact that it was being pushed so hard by Stephen and his advisers in the summer and autumn of 1138 – the proceeds of the overthrow of Bishop Roger of Salisbury went to finance the huge dowry payment – tend to indicate that it was a new scheme, one that the Meulan embassy had negotiated. It was a marriage alliance very close to the heart of King Stephen, and the dynastic union was the centrepiece of English engagement in northern France for the rest of his reign.[18]

---

[16] See Crouch, *Reign of Stephen*, 66–7 note. There is a late account of the dissension in Stephen's army as between Normans and Boulonnais knights, *Histoire des ducs de Normandie et des rois d'Angleterre*, ed. F. Michel (Paris, 1840), 73–5.

[17] Crouch, *Beaumont Twins*, 37–8, 42–3.

[18] Henry of Huntingdon associates the betrothal with the events of June 1139, as the

The first three years of Stephen's reign had seen a heavy engagement with the northern French powers, and not merely the inevitable hostile engagement with Anjou. The new circumstances of Stephen's succession had triggered an unprecedented period of diplomacy and restructuring of alliances in the region. It also triggered a realignment in the Capetian court that was to have some long-term consequences. For the most part these were highly successful years for Stephen though he cannot be given the entire credit for the success. Its keystone was the Anglo-Capetian alliance, and after the death of Louis VI there was a continuing impetus that affected both courts, but the year 1139 saw it begin to come apart, as Louis VII began to demonstrate his political ineptitude, and – more importantly – as civil conflict began to preoccupy Stephen in England.

The other key factor that emerged in 1139 was the slow shift in the military balance in Normandy. Geoffrey of Anjou had been confounded by Louis VI's alliance with Stephen, so much is indicated by his acceptance of 2000 marks for a three year truce in Normandy beginning in midsummer 1137.[19] The tendency has been to think of this arrangement as a mere stratagem. But when he made the deal, it may be that Geoffrey was cutting his losses and seeking to pull out of Normandy with some prestige still intact. But with no effort from his part, circumstances began to swing his way the next year. Despite the truce he was able to keep the pressure on Stephen in the duchy by proxy, through the defection to the empress of Earl Robert of Gloucester in May 1138. However, it was not till Stephen's capture at Lincoln in February 1141 that Geoffrey took once more to the field. The king's capture by his wife's forces seems to have voided the truce several months early, as far as Geoffrey was concerned. He then began a three year episodic campaign to bring the duchy under his control, resisting all distractions from England.[20]

The success of Geoffrey of Anjou has something to do with the man's remarkable persistence, something to do with Louis VII's inability to frame any sort of constructive response to the situation in northern France, but most to do with Stephen's obsessive and (as far as Ralph Davis was concerned) misplaced concern with his position in England at the expense of Normandy.[21] So Stephen's position in Normandy was nibbled to death as, year by year, Angevin campaigns took modest bites out of the duchy. The central march had gone with Robert of Gloucester's defection, military conquest obtained the Lieuvin in 1141, Mortain and the Avranchin in 1142, the Cotentin and the Evrecin in 1143 and the capital and the Caux finally in 1144. Stephen did next to nothing about it, trusting too much in the truce, perhaps. His justiciars were assassinated in 1139, and Waleran of Meulan preferred to stay in England from 1139 to the end of 1141. The count's

---

confiscated wealth of Roger of Salisbury is said to have contributed to its cash settlement, *Huntingdon*, 720.

[19] *Orderic*, vi, 486.

[20] For the military campaigns of Geoffrey of Anjou in Normandy, see J. Bradbury, *Stephen and Matilda: The Civil War of 1139–53* (Stroud, 1996), 152–5.

[21] Davis, *King Stephen*, 26.

absence from the duchy where he had so much success from 1136 to 1138 is difficult to account for, unless he, like Stephen, had become fixated on the destruction of Robert of Gloucester and the empress in England as the key to victory. If so, the battle of Lincoln proved them both wrong. The slow and painful defection of Waleran of Meulan to the Angevins late in 1141 was the final act in the destruction of the northern French order devised by Louis VI to contain Anjou in 1136. It took out of Stephen's party the man who had the most clout and connection at Paris.[22] Theobald of Blois himself must have realized that the game was up when, in 1141, he refused the invitation from the Norman nobility to assume the ducal sword in opposition to Geoffrey.[23] So Anjou and Normandy were united under Geoffrey's rule, and a different sort of political order was established in northern France, the one that was eventually to be the bane of Louis VII's political life.

In the meantime, there is the question of Stephen and Flanders. Boulogne was not lost when Normandy was, and it gave Stephen a continuing foothold in north-eastern France. The numbers of charters issued by Stephen and Queen Matilda in the county of Boulogne is testimony to the couple's continuing interest in it, as also is the large number of men of Boulonnais origins in Stephen's royal household. We find the queen in residence at Boulogne itself in 1142 and 1147 and again at the comital town of Steenvorde on the border of Flanders at some time in 1149 or 1150.[24] There is unfortunately little evidence as to Stephen's intentions in this corner of France. But that he had some ambitions in the region is at least clear from the later evidence of Lambert of Ardres. The counts of Boulogne and the counts of Guines were neighbours both in the Pas de Calais and in Essex, and it would be an obvious ambition for the greater of the two counts to try to extend his influence into Guines. Stephen had his chance in 1137 when Count Manasses decided to marry his granddaughter and heir to a suitable candidate, and in alliance with the lord of Bourbourg offered her to an Englishman, the younger Aubrey de Vere, son of another Essex landowner, the elder Aubrey de Vere, Stephen's chamberlain and intimate friend. The intention of the marriage could be interpreted as bringing Guines into an alliance with Boulogne and the lordship of Bourbourg, to extend Stephen's power deeper into Artois, or at least to secure the safety of his county.[25]

Aubrey's tenure of Guines was brief and ended with his divorce from Countess Beatrice before her death in 1142. The reasons given for the divorce by the Guines family historian was her poor health and Aubrey's reluctance to leave the

---

22 Crouch, *Beaumont Twins*, 49–51.
23 *Orderic*, vi, 548. Orderic says that Theobald was offered both England and Normandy by the Norman aristocracy, but it would seem more likely that Normandy alone was on offer.
24 For the queen's movements in Flanders, see Crouch, *Reign of Stephen*, 202, 248 note; see also, H. Tanner, 'Reassessing King Stephen's Continental Strategies', *Medievalia et Humanistica*, 26 (1999), 108.
25 For the Guines-Vere marriage, Lambert of Ardres, *The History of the Counts of Guines and Lords of Ardres*, trans. L. Shopkow (Philadelphia, 2001), 86–7. The editor fails to identify *Albericus aper* as Aubrey de Vere however, for which see, J. H. Round, *Geoffrey de Mandeville: A Study of the Anarchy* (London, 1892), 188–90.

English royal court. But there must have been more to it, as he was compensated in 1141 with an award of an English earldom, Oxford. As far as the rest of the north-east of France is concerned, there seems to have been little direct contact between the court of Count Thierry of Flanders and that of King Stephen, which is surprising considering the numbers of Flemings serving in Stephen's army and the potential usefulness of Thierry in any campaign to maintain Stephen's position in Normandy. There are reasons for this. Thierry had in fact married Geoffrey of Anjou's sister, Sibyl. Furthermore Thierry himself had problems with the aggressions of the counts of Hainault and St-Pol, and had reason to suspect the link between Stephen and William of Ypres, his former rival for the succession.[26] By 1140, as I have already suggested, Stephen had in any case begun to be absorbed in his own English struggle with Robert of Gloucester and the empress. There had been a reconciliation of sorts by 1142, when Stephen and his wife made grants to Thierry's Cistercian abbey at Clairmarais.[27]

Some indication of how the battle of Lincoln changed Stephen's status in northern France is also associated with Aubrey de Vere. In the creation charter of the earldom of Oxford for him in July 1141 the empress named as a surety for her good intentions both her husband and no less a person than King Louis VII of France.[28] This is both unexpected and revealing. What it reveals is that the empress considered herself in the summer of 1141 to be in friendly communication with the Capetian court. But it also reveals that by 1141 Louis VII had begun to make his own decisions on what to do about England and Normandy. One reason that Theobald of Blois might have decided against taking on Normandy that summer was the new hostility from Paris. He had refused to join the king on his expedition against Toulouse in June 1141. In the next year he was at war with Louis, desperately defending Champagne from Louis's invading army.[29]

In the meantime there was a new order in northern France. An uneasy alliance now linked Angers and Paris. It is difficult at first sight to think what it was that Louis got out of it. The union of Normandy and Anjou was not to his obvious benefit. But it might be that Louis had seen Normandy as a lost cause in any case, once Stephen was in the empress's prison. Another possible conclusion is that Geoffrey had sweetened the deal by putting on the table the possession of the Norman Vexin, which the Capetians had been aiming at since the reign of Philip I. Holding that key province would press the Capetian frontier to the valley of the Andelle, putting Rouen in easy range of Louis's troops. Robert de Torigny implies that the cession of the Norman Vexin occurred quite early, saying that although their part of the Vexin belonged of right to the Normans Geoffrey relinquished it to Louis 'for a time', the same way that he had allowed his magnates to

---

[26] Tanner, 'Reassessing King Stephen's Continental Strategies', 106.

[27] *Regesta*, iii, no. 194; see Tanner, 'Reassessing King Stephen's Continental Strategies', 106, 108.

[28] *Regesta*, iii, no. 634.

[29] Y. Sassier, *Louis VII* (Paris, 1991), 109–12.

enjoy ducal demesne in return for their help in mastering the duchy in the period 1141–4. This would lead to the conclusion that Louis was allowed to control it by 1144 at the latest.[30] This is all the sign of a new order in France. After late 1141 Louis was taking the advice of other men than Theobald of Blois, who was now dispensable, and was dispensed with. It was a dangerous gamble on his part, whatever, not least because Theobald subsequently had to ally with Geoffrey of Anjou for his own self-preservation. It was Theobald who knighted Geoffrey's younger son in 1151, and with him Theobald brought his ally, Rotrou of Perche, who was fighting with the Angevin army in Normandy in 1144.[31]

The best part of the next decade saw Stephen confined to England, completely consumed by the effort of fighting a difficult civil war in his kingdom. He let Normandy go. He had little choice in 1141, when he was out of the game till the autumn, but even afterwards he did nothing much to recover his position in the duchy. The way things were on his release, he had very little choice. Once Matilda and Robert of Gloucester were in England, the focus of the succession struggle moved to the south-west. It would have been as foolish on Stephen's part to cross to the continent in 1142 and try to revive the resistance in Normandy, as it had been for him to leave Normandy in 1137 and let the empress bring the war home to him in England.

In fact not a huge amount happened on the continent in any case. Louis's rule of his part of France was at this stage governed by idealistic concerns. The ideology of crusading was one that he began vigorously promoting in 1145. For the most part his concern seems to have been to duplicate the legendary achievement of the previous generation of French princes. But there might have been an element of calculation in it too. The huge enthusiasm in northern France in the mid 1140s for crusade is unmistakable. Nothing illustrates it better than the tournament ban that the French aristocracy imposed on itself between 1146 and 1148, so that there should be no distraction from the struggle against the Turks of Damascus.[32] The spirit affected magnates in both England and France, and allowed Louis to pose at Paris in May 1146 as the leader of the entire western aristocracy. No doubt it warmed Abbot Suger's heart to see a Capetian once again at the head of an army which far outstripped the king's actual territorial lordship, as Louis VI had done in 1125, and even proudly directing a large contingent of English knights and barons. We can assume this was so, because

---

[30] *Torigni*, 169. For the Norman Vexin and Louis VII see the brief treatments in J. A. Green, 'Lords of the Norman Vexin', in *War and Government in the Middle Ages: Essays in Honour of J. O. Prestwich*, ed. J. Gillingham and J. C. Holt (Cambridge, 1984), 48 note; and D. Power, *The Norman Frontier in the Twelfth and Early Thirteenth Centuries* (Cambridge, 2004), 392 and note.

[31] For Geoffrey's knighting, *Torigni*, 160. For Rotrou's change of side and death in Geoffrey's service, K. Thompson, *Power and Border Lordship in Medieval France: The County of Perche, 1000–1226* (Woodbridge, 2002), 83–4.

[32] D. Crouch, *Tournament* (London, 2005), 20–1.

Louis ostentatiously appointed the Anglo-Norman earl of Warenne as captain of his guard on the campaign.[33]

The whole world came to Paris in 1147, or almost the whole world, because Geoffrey of Anjou and his son were notable by their absence. Geoffrey, despite being the son of a king of Jerusalem, had no intention of taking the cross. Reforming and pacifying Normandy was his first objective, and would remain his single-minded concern until his death in 1151. Stephen also showed no interest in crusade in 1145, again, hardly surprisingly. He had a kingdom to try to salvage. Ironically, one of his wife's solutions to the difficulty of his captivity in 1141 had been that they both be exiled to Jerusalem, which indicates – along with their powerful advocacy of the Templars – that they both cherished the ideal of crusade, but in 1145 that was not an option.[34]

The Second Crusade was of course – as a crusade – a total disaster. There are grounds for believing it also a dynastic disaster for the Capetians. The marriage between Louis and Eleanor of Aquitaine came apart at the seams in 1148, and despite some desperate marriage counselling by Eugenius III in Rome in 1149, the pair sought and eventually obtained an annulment of their marriage. In this way, the great concluding achievement of Louis VI's life was undone, and Paris and Poitiers went their own way. Louis lost his ability to threaten Anjou from his Aquitanian lordships and from Berry, and the situation was initiated that stifled Capetian expansion in northern France until 1202 because Eleanor of Aquitaine evaded Louis's half-hearted attempts to control her and married the young Henry Plantagenet in 1152.

However, well before this the brief and uneasy peace between Paris and Angers had crumbled. The bone of contention was the Norman Vexin, which was now about the only place that Louis VII had any chance of successfully confronting the Angevins. As the letters of Suger make clear, Louis was already nervous about Angevin designs on reclaiming it as early as 1145. Louis, or perhaps his advisers, went about their ambitions in the Seine valley with some patience, determination and a definite end game. Louis very carefully seduced Waleran, count of Meulan, by bestowing on him the substantial honour of Gournay-sur-Marne, to the east of Paris, a lordship Waleran had a claim on through his wife, Agnes, daughter of Amaury de Montfort, count of Evreux. The transfer seems to have happened as early as 1145. The possession of Gournay made Waleran a substantial baron of the Parisian region, and augmented his great urban estate of La Grève. It also made him suspect to the Angevins, who had little reason to love him anyway. Since Waleran remained the greatest and most influential magnate in Normandy, doubts about his allegiance could do nothing other than destabilize the Angevin hold on the duchy.[35]

---

[33] Odo of Deuil, *De Profectione Ludovici VII in Orientem*, ed. V. G. Berry (New York, 1948), 54, 122.

[34] *John of Worcester*, iii, 296.

[35] Crouch, *Beaumont Twins*, 64–5.

In 1149, relations between the Angevin realm and Paris hit rock bottom. The trigger for confrontation was Geoffrey's incursion into Capetian-held Poitou in 1149, in pursuit of a grudge against Louis's seneschal of Poitou, Giraud Bellay, setting siege to Giraud's castle of Montreuil in the king's absence. On his return, still duke of Aquitaine, Louis ordered Geoffrey to withdraw. Instead he maintained the siege with his usual dogged patience, until Montreuil surrendered and Giraud Bellay was captured and imprisoned.[36] War naturally followed in 1150, a war that reintroduced King Stephen of England into the affairs of northern France. Stephen had little choice other than to re-engage with French affairs by this time, but he also had the opportunity. The civil war in England had burned down to embers by 1149. The empress had withdrawn and peace had been re-established over most of the kingdom, with the Angevin earls looking to make treaties with their neighbours. Stephen at last had leisure to look abroad. But the succession question also drew his attention to France. Probably in 1149, the king had requested Archbishop Theobald of Canterbury to crown his son Eustace as associate king, and so seal his succession. Stephen had been refused, and the case had gone to Rome. It was becoming clear however that the pope was not going to co-operate with Stephen's plan. Eustace's only certain chance of becoming king after his father was to eliminate his rival. We see him attempting to do just this in the summer of 1149, as he hunted Henry Plantagenet through the lanes of the west midlands of England in hopes of assassinating him. It must have become clear to Stephen and his council that they must send Eustace to Normandy in pursuit of Henry, as the only way to continue the duel between the new generation of claimants to England.

So the idea of a Capetian alliance was reactivated and late in 1149 Stephen's envoys reached Louis's court with offers of assistance and alliance. Indications are that the embassy was led by Queen Matilda and the king's brother Bishop Henry of Winchester, en route for Rome. The correspondence of Arnulf of Lisieux and Abbot Suger allows us to glimpse the parties at Louis's court forming against the proposed alliance. Suger was decidedly against it. He argued strongly for maintaining peace, and was in correspondence with Geoffrey of Anjou at the beginning of 1150, arguing that he should come to terms with the king of France so as to deflect the threat of an alliance with the king of England. Stephen was well aware of Suger's attitude and attempted some subtle bribery through guarantees of restoration of the lands of the abbey of St-Denis in England and, eventually, if he were successful, in Normandy.[37]

War did not happen in 1150, in part perhaps because of the appalling famine and consequent disease that laid waste England and northern France. But in 1151, with Suger now departed this life to his expected reward, the alliance was concluded and Count Eustace, the king's son, arrived in Boulogne with English troops. The course of the subsequent campaign is not easy to reconstruct,

---

[36] J. Chartrou, *L'Anjou de 1109 à 1151* (Paris, 1928), 69–74.
[37] For an analysis of this, Crouch, *Reign of Stephen*, 245–9.

although there is little doubt that it could have been very dangerous for Angevin control of Normandy, and it is also clear that Stephen had deployed his connections in Flanders and Artois to make it so. He and Eustace enlisted the help of the count of Ponthieu and substantial numbers of Flemish troops. As Daniel Power has recently demonstrated, the border county of Aumale was also subverted and defected to Eustace.[38] Eustace certainly did his part. At some time in the early summer he and Louis marched into the Pays de Bray and threatened the formidable citadel of Arques. At the same time, Louis's brother Robert, count of Dreux and the Perche struck into southern Normandy and wasted the duchy as far as Séez, which was seized and burned. But at that time no battle was fought with the new Duke Henry. The campaign petered out as Louis withdrew to join his brother Robert in southern Normandy, as Robert de Torigny seems to imply.[39] A more serious strike against Normandy took place some time later, in August 1151. Louis crossed into the Vexin, and the fruits of his courtship of Count Waleran paid off when the fortified bridges of Mantes and Meulan were opened to him. So far so good, but as Louis moved to enter the Norman Vexin, he fell ill and the campaign was abruptly cancelled, with Louis returning to Paris and taking to his bed.

The next year, the campaign was renewed with an extended alliance. Things had changed in the spring, with the death of Theobald of Blois and Geoffrey of Anjou, and the divorce and remarriage of Eleanor of Aquitaine. Louis VII at midsummer 1152 marshalled in his support Eustace and Robert of Dreux once again, and added to them Stephen's nephew, Henry, the new count of Champagne, and Geoffrey, count of Nantes, the younger brother of Henry Plantagenet. Apart from Geoffrey, this grand army encamped in the Pays de Bray before the castle of Neufmarché. It eventually succeeded in securing the surrender of the castle, perhaps some time in July, but not before Henry was able to make a separate peace with his brother. This inconvenience might account for Louis's withdrawal back to the French Vexin. Henry encamped opposite him in the Norman Vexin, which was at the time Louis's, the price of his support for Geoffrey Plantagenet. Henry systematically laid waste to the province, burning down the castles loyal to the king, perhaps in order to tempt Louis to retaliate. Louis instead crossed the Seine at Meulan once again, and moved suddenly south to make an attempt on Pacy-sur-Eure. But he was once again countered by a swift march by Duke Henry, and withdrew rather than try battle. The duke raided into the county of Dreux, as the king retired to his town of Mantes, and the count of Dreux retaliated in kind on the Norman border towns, but that was the end of the campaign.[40]

Why the campaign petered out so inconclusively is difficult to say, although Louis's military caution seems to be the likeliest explanation. He seems to have been perennially anxious about being outmanoeuvred by his enemies, and lacked

[38] Power, *The Norman Frontier*, 395–6.
[39] *Torigni*, 161–2.
[40] Ibid., 165–6, 169–70.

decisiveness. So he was continually outflanked by Henry's swift marches and countermarches, and was driven remorselessly back across the frontier, losing his great asset of the Norman Vexin and all the allied castles there. What Count Eustace thought about it all is easy to imagine. The Norman campaign was his best chance to date of securing his kingdom in this world. But he was soon called away, as Henry Plantagenet made his decisive and daring crossing to England, and Eustace had no choice but to follow, to meet his death from typhoid fever soon after; and so ended the hopes of the house of Blois, not by a sword stroke but by a bacillus.

What conclusions do we make from this? The first thing is something that several authors have already said well enough. You could not divorce the fortunes of the king of England in the twelfth century from what happened on the continent. Henry I had known this, which was why he stationed himself in Normandy for most of his reign and developed means to govern England in his absence. Although he was count of Mortain and Boulogne, as well as lord of Eye and Lancaster, Stephen had not learned this lesson from his uncle. His failure to cross back to Normandy until spring 1137 was not fatal to his rule as king-duke, but his failure to stay there after 1137 certainly was. Had he stayed in Normandy, the empress could never have crossed to England, there would never have been a factional civil war, and Robert of Gloucester could never have been an effective rebel. Stephen would also have been able to interact much more effectively with his fellow French princes. It would be too much to expect that Stephen could have devised alliances and a diplomacy to subvert Geoffrey Plantagenet, but just by stationing himself in Rouen or Alençon, he would have checkmated Geoffrey's greater ambitions.

The second conclusion is that the best of twelfth-century French kings and princes had quite a sophisticated view of the geopolitics of their world. By these I mean Henry I of England, Theobald of Blois and Louis VI of France. Their activities reveal that they could comprehend a mental map of their political world, and use it to navigate a path towards their objectives. They could make what we would call policy. The less bright clearly could not, and by these I mean principally Stephen of England and Louis VII of France. Interestingly, the 1152 campaign in the Vexin reveals that Louis VII also had a blank incomprehension of the use of castles, which were the essential tools of medieval geopolitics. Whether or not Stephen and Louis VII were effective soldiers, they floundered when faced with the demands of international politics. There were of course other ways of being king, and both Stephen and Louis VII had their strengths, but their intellectual equipment was not up to policy. They could not be great kings.

4

A Week in Politics:
Oxford, late July 1141

EDMUND KING

A WEEK CAN BE a long time in politics. We owe the observation to Harold Wilson, Prime Minister of the United Kingdom from 1964 to 1970 and again from 1974 to 1976. His predecessor, Harold Macmillan, asked about the main difficulties that he faced in office, is reported to have responded very simply, 'events, dear boy, events'.[1] A political historian, writing of Britain in the 1960s and 1970s, when these men were in power, can hope to provide a detailed analysis which takes proper account of these maxims. There is every need for a similar political history of the reign of King Stephen. Yet the difficulties in writing one would appear to be insuperable. We do not lack for stirring 'events'. It is the 'weeks' that are the problem. The documents which should provide the spine for any political analysis, the royal charters, are not dated as a matter of routine. We look enviously at the contemporary charters of the kings of France, the counts of Flanders, and the popes in Rome.[2] With their *acta* there may be scope for scholarly discussion of such matters as regnal years but there is a real security in these texts nonetheless. In England, on the other hand, we cannot say with complete confidence where the king of England was on any specific day at any time

Quotations from *Regesta Regum Anglo-Normannorum*, iii, ed. H. A. Cronne and R. H. C. Davis (Oxford, 1968), xxix and nos. 68, 180, 271–2, 274–5, 391, 393, 582, 634–5 are used by permission of Oxford University Press.

[1] The two quotations, though familiar, have proved difficult to pin down. The 'week in politics' was 'probably first said at the time of the 1964 sterling crisis', but 'events' are simply an attribution, in *The Oxford Dictionary of Quotations*, ed. E. Knowles (5th edn, Oxford, 1999), s.v. 'Wilson, Harold' and 'Macmillan, Harold'.

[2] *Recueil des actes de Louis VI, roi de France (1108–1137)*, dir. R.-H. Bautier, ed. J. Dufour, 4 vols. (Paris, 1992–4); *De Oorkonden der Graven van Vlaanderen, ii/1: Regering van Diederik van de Elzas (Juli 1128 – Januari 1168)*, ed. T. de Hemptinne and A. Verhulst (Brussels, 1988); *Papsturkunden in England*, ed. W. Holtzmann, 3 vols. (Berlin and Göttingen, 1930–52).

between 7 June 1143 and 12 May 1146, a period of three years.[3] We know of some significant events which occurred within this period but the dates can only be approximate. This is an extreme case, as comparatively little business came to the courts of either king or empress during these years, while the two historians who had ambitions to write a political history of the day – Orderic Vitalis and William of Malmesbury – had recently died.

There is only the one year during Stephen's reign, the nineteen years during which men 'said openly that Christ and his saints were asleep',[4] in which we can hope to escape from these constraints. This was 1141. It was a year in which Stephen's reign appeared to have ended but, so it transpired, it had not. It had seemed to end on 2 February, when Stephen was captured at the battle of Lincoln. This is at the same time a fixed date in the biographies of many of the leading men. We know that the king in the course of the following week was brought to Bristol and presented to the empress. Then towards the end of the year, on 1 November, the king was released from captivity, in exchange for Robert, earl of Gloucester. We know of the detail of the exchanges, and of the discussions that preceded them, and that the king and the earl met. If these are the key dates there are several key weeks in between. There is the week beginning 7 April 1141. A legatine council met at Winchester and took steps to transfer power to the empress. In the summer there are up to two weeks when the empress was in London, about which in fact we know very little: there is the secure date of 24 June standing as a lonely sentry in a London annal. There is then the beginning of what would be a five week siege of Winchester, in or around 1 August. There is a fixed date for the end of the siege, and Earl Robert's capture, on 14 September. The empress was box office, the centre of attention, throughout the year 1141, and news of her actions, particularly of her dramatic escapes first from London and then from Winchester, travelled quickly.[5]

There is a strong narrative line in all of this. And it provides good material for political history not just because it is so vivid but because it is so solidly based. There are three main sources here, three writers, each of whom writes with authority, though we know the name of only one of them. The first writer is a monk of Gloucester, who interpolated and continued the chronicle of John of Worcester, a text which can now be used with confidence thanks to Patrick McGurk's fine new edition.[6] The author knew Miles of Gloucester, a magnate

---

3   *Regesta*, iii, p. xlii, for the king's itinerary. The earlier date is found ibid., no. 655, a charter for Peterborough Abbey; the latter in Roger of Wendover, *Chronica sive Flores Historiarum*, ed. H. O. Coxe, 5 vols., English Historical Society (London, 1841–4), ii, 236–7.

4   *ASC* 1137.

5   The main sources for 1141, discussed more fully below, are, *Gesta Stephani*, 110–37; *John of Worcester*, iii, 292–305; *Historia Novella*, 80–111, 114–21. There is valuable material also in, *Orderic*, vi, 538–51; *Huntingdon*, 724–41; John of Hexham, *Historia Regum*, in *Symeonis Monachi Opera Omnia*, ed. T. Arnold, 2 vols. (RS, 1882–5), ii, 306–11.

6   *John of Worcester*, iii, pp. xl–l.

who was never far from the centre of events during this year. The empress 'had had the counsel, and enjoyed the support, of this Miles to such an extent that (as he himself told us) she would not for even one day or one month have had provisions nor have had her table served without his munificence and stewardship'.[7] Not spoken of here, but very much in mind, was Robert of Gloucester, who pointedly is called earl not 'of Gloucester' but 'of Bristol' by the Gloucester monk.[8] It is a title that clearly reflects usage in the streets of Gloucester and in the hall of its castle, no less than reference in the *Gesta Stephani* to the empress as 'the countess of Anjou' reflects the usage on the streets of London and in the royal court.[9] William of Malmesbury, the second writer, was no longer, if he ever had been, 'far from the secrets of the court',[10] but had privileged access to it; he was an eye-witness of proceedings at the legatine council of April 1141, just as he had been at the earlier council – following 'the arrest of the bishops' – in August 1139. There is more than one dialogue being conducted within the pages of the *Historia Novella*. The first is with Robert of Gloucester, who had commissioned the work, and with the earl's courtiers. Thus when we read of the death of William Clito, in 1120, as being a 'misfortune' rather than a 'disaster', we may feel we can detect the earl's own hand in the margin.[11] The other dialogue is that of William with his wider readership, extending into the present day. 'My information may be at fault but not my judgement',[12] he asserts in one of his prefaces. He is looking to place his information in context; put another way, he is trying to write a political history. Stubbs commented that 'not a few of his more ambitious sections have a little of the look of leading articles'.[13] This is an aside, comparable to those of William of Malmesbury himself, that goes to the heart of the matter.

The *Gesta Stephani*, the third of the key authorities for 1141, is a more difficult source to use. Its author is a gifted reporter. He writes vividly of sieges and battles and is always concerned to give the precise terms on which castles were surrendered. He is interested in towns and is concerned to put them in rank order. London is first, in a league of its own, 'the capital, the queen of the whole kingdom'.[14] He writes with immediacy and some colloquialism of events in London during the summer of 1141. He describes the pressure placed on the Londoners,

---

7 Ibid., iii, 298–9: 'eiusdem Milonis precipue fruebatur consilio et fouebatur auxilio, utpote que eatenus nec unius diei uictum nec mense ipsius apparatum aliunde quam ex ipsius munificentia siue prouidentia acceperat, sicut ex ipsius Milonis ore audiuimus'.
8 Ibid., xlix, 252–3, 298–9, 300–1: 'comes Bricstowense'.
9 *Gesta Stephani*, 10–11 (which edits out her earlier marriage), 46–7, and thereafter.
10 *Gesta Regum*, i, 708–9, and for comment, *Historia Novella*, xxiii–xxiv.
11 *Historia Novella*, lxxxiv, 6–7.
12 *Gesta Regum*, i, 540–1, and for comment, *Historia Novella*, xxxiii–xxxiv.
13 William of Malmesbury, *De Gestis Regum Anglorum*, ed. W. Stubbs, 2 vols. (RS, 1887–9), ii, p. cxlii.
14 *Gesta Stephani*, 4–5: 'totius regionis reginam metropolim'. Winchester was certainly the second city and Exeter was reckoned the fourth: ibid., 8–9, 32–3. Lincoln may have been the third but the section where it would have been first mentioned is missing: ibid., 110–11.

after the empress had arrived in the city in June, by the queen mustering her forces at Southwark: 'their land was being stripped before their eyes and reduced by the enemy's ravages to a habitation for the hedgehog'.[15] He is clear about the geographical space between London and Westminster. It was a space that allowed the empress to escape after the Londoners had rung the bells of the city churches, 'and came out in a body, like thronging swarms from beehives'.[16] It is tempting to suggest that rather than being the bishop of Bath, the author was a monk or canon based in London or its suburbs.[17] In any event, we do feel that we see in the pages of the *Gesta Stephani* what could be said in favour of the king among those who continued to support him, among whom the Londoners were particularly tenacious over the years. We are given a clear insight into the position of those who would eventually carry the day.

This would not have seemed likely in the initial euphoria in the empress's camp in the immediate aftermath of the battle of Lincoln. There was no need to write a new script. The empress needed to acquire power and the route to power would take her through Winchester and on to London, the same route that Stephen had travelled in December 1135. The transfer of power took place at Winchester. The body transferring power was a legatine council of the English church. It sat from 7 to 10 April 1141. This meeting followed prior discussions with representatives of the church and the townspeople, which were led by Henry, bishop of Winchester. The empress herself tells us of this meeting, which took place, 'on the third Sunday of Lent, on which he came to me and spoke to me at Wherwell, this being the day before the Monday on which the said prelate and the citizens of Winchester received me honourably in the cathedral and the city of Winchester'.[18] You could not ask for a more precise date than that.[19] But what exactly was done at Winchester? There was no official communiqué, at least none survives. The fullest description comes from William of Malmesbury. He had been there, and his memory was very clear. In the context of Stephen's prior weakness, of his breaking of his concordat with the church, and now of his captivity, 'so that the kingdom may not totter without a ruler ... we choose as lady of England and Normandy the daughter of a king who was a peacemaker, a glorious king, a wealthy king, a good king, without peer in our time, and we promise her faith and support'.[20] I think we must take this as definitive. The

---

15 Ibid., 122–3, referring to Isaiah 14: 23.
16 Ibid., 124–5.
17 I have succumbed to this temptation: 'The *Gesta Stephani*', in *Writing Medieval Biography, 750–1250: Essays in Honour of Professor Frank Barlow*, ed. D. Bates, J. Crick and S. Hamilton (Woodbridge, 2006), 195–206.
18 *Regesta*, iii, no. 343: 'die dominica *tercia* quadragesime qua venit contra me et locutus est mecum apud Warewell que precessit diem lune qua idem prelates et cives Wintonienses honorifice in ecclesia et urbe Wintoniensi me receperunt' (reading 'dominica *tercia*' for 'dominica *intrantis*' and 'dominica *incarnacionis*' which are the readings of the cartulary copies).
19 It is confirmed by *Historia Novella*, 88–9.
20 Ibid., 92–3; 'in Angliae Normanniaeque dominam elegimus'.

empress was not crowned. She was not given the title of queen nor did she assume that title. She did have a new title, that of 'lady of England', *domina Anglorum*. In her charters she was now: 'Matilda the empress, the daughter of King Henry, lady of the English'.[21]

What did this mean? Was it enough? I do not think that we should be deflected from asking these questions by the assumption that this title is provisional, given to the presumptive ruler prior to coronation. There is every indication that this was it, that this would be the final formulation of the empress's title. The conferment of the title, *domina Anglorum*, meant two things. It was, firstly, sufficient of itself to allow the empress to assume regalian authority. She writes to the sheriffs of the counties and tells them to do as they are told. She writes to the barons of the exchequer, assuming that they will account to the last farthing.[22] She issues coins in her own name, including an attempt at a national coinage, the PERERIC coins (so identified by Mark Blackburn).[23] She speaks of the pleas pertaining *ad coronam meam*.[24] Nigel, bishop of Ely, significantly, stands at her side, ready to take over from his uncle, Roger, bishop of Salisbury, as every political commentator, prior to 1139, would have expected him to. It allowed, secondly, those who wished to do so to swear fealty to the empress. They had sworn fealty to the king. Now they could – indeed the church was presenting it to them as a moral duty that they should – swear fealty to the empress. These instructions were etched on the brain of Brian fitz Count. 'You yourself who are a prelate of holy church have ordered me to adhere to the daughter of King Henry your uncle, and to help her acquire that which is hers by right but which has been taken from her by force, and to retain what she already has.'[25] Some of the more scrupulous, headed by the archbishop Theobald, first went to the king under safe conduct and from him 'obtained courteous permission to change over as the times required'.[26]

The actual date of the legatine council was not seen as determinative in terms of the empress's authority; in the way, that is, that the king's coronation marked out to the day his regnal years. She had assumed authority on her arrival in England in September 1139. William of Malmesbury wrote of the whole district around Gloucester going over to the empress, 'partly under compulsion, partly

---

21 *Regesta*, iii, p. xxix; M. Chibnall, 'The Charters of the Empress Matilda', in *Law and Government in Medieval England and Normandy: Essays in Honour of Sir James Holt*, ed. G. Garnett and J. Hudson (Cambridge, 1994), 276–98.

22 *Regesta*, iii, no. 628. The empress informs the barons of the exchequer that she has granted the canons of Oseney 5s 5¾d yearly from the farm of Oxford.

23 M. Blackburn, 'Coinage and Currency', in King, *Anarchy*, 173–5: 'It is a large group, with more than seventy specimens known, struck at seven mints, namely Bristol, Canterbury, Ipswich, Lincoln, London, Stamford, and Winchester.'

24 *Regesta*, iii, no. 274 (the Westminster charter). Geoffrey is to be chief justice in Essex, 'de placitis et forisfactis que pertinuerint ad coronam meam'.

25 H. W. C. Davis, 'Henry of Blois and Brian Fitz-Count', *EHR*, 25 (1910), 301; E. King, 'The Memory of Brian fitz Count', *HSJ*, 13 (2004), 89.

26 *Historia Novella*, 88–91.

from goodwill'.[27] The Gloucester chronicler, writing from first-hand experience, is more direct: 'the ex-empress remained at Bristol for over two months, receiving homage from all and dispensing the laws of the English kingdom as she pleased'.[28] We know that she had received the homage of Miles of Gloucester, and thanks to Nicholas Vincent we can now answer Sir James Holt's question, 'homage for what?'[29] As well as St Briavel's castle and the forest of Dean,[30] the empress gave Miles significant crown demesne manors within Gloucestershire and she confirmed to him the custody of the castle and the sheriffdom of the county in inheritance.[31] What she had taken and what she had granted up to April 1141 and after April 1141 had alike to be treated as legitimate. The expectation was now, however, that the transfer of regalian authority should be complete, and that all should swear fealty to her. With just the odd pocket of resistance. 'The empress', said Henry of Huntingdon, 'was received as lady by all the English nation except for the men of Kent'.[32]

The Londoners received her only with great reluctance, but after negotiations at St Albans, 'concerning the surrender of the city', receive her they did. As in Winchester, and on the same authority, we know that the civic leaders and the churchmen put on a good show: 'she was received with magnificent procession at Westminster, where she remained some days deciding how to set the affairs of the kingdom in order'.[33] This was an important week, though we are not sure of its exact dates.[34] The discussions at Westminster were widely reported. The reports were highly critical of the empress and calculated to undermine her authority. As it was reported from London:

---

27 Ibid., 64–5: 'tota itaque regio circa Gloecestram usque profundas Walas, partim ui, partim beneuolentia … se dominae imperatrici applicuit'.
28 *John of Worcester*, iii, 270–1: 'consedit itaque ibi domina illa plus duobus mensibus, sumens ab omnibus hominia, et pro libito suo disponens Anglorum regni iura'.
29 J. C. Holt, '1086', in his *Colonial England, 1066–1215* (London, 1997), 33.
30 This much was known from *Regesta*, iii, no. 391.
31 A much fuller version of the above charter is found in BL Sloane MS 1301, fo. 422r–v. I am very much indebted to Nicholas Vincent for sharing this exciting discovery with me and for allowing me to cite it in advance of publication. The sheriffdom and the castellanship had been granted by the king in January 1136: *Regesta*, iii, nos. 386–7.
32 *Huntingdon*, 738–9; thence, M. Brett, 'The Annals of Bermondsey, Southwark and Merton', in *Church and City*, ed. D. Abulafia et al. (Cambridge, 1992), 299–300, and *Torigni*, 141; cf. *Newburgh*, 41.
33 *John of Worcester*, iii, 294–5, 296–7.
34 All the timings relate to the major feast, that of the Nativity of St John the Baptist, on 24 June (a Tuesday in 1141). Thus the empress arrived 'a little before' the feast: *Historia Novella*, 96–7 ('uix paucis ante'); she stayed in the city for 'a few days': *John of Worcester*, iii, 296–7 ('aliquantis diebus'); and during the feast she was driven out: Brett, 'Annals of Bermondsey, Southwark and Merton', 300; Symeon of Durham, *Libellus de Exordio atque Procursu istius hoc est Dunhelmensis Ecclesie*, ed. D. Rollason (Oxford, 2000), 286–7 ('cum omnibus suis discederet ipsa die a Lundonia imperatrix'). The townsmen may have gained cover from the midsummer revels; for the later connection between popular rising and church festivals, see S. Walker, *Political Culture in Later Medieval England*, ed. M. J. Braddick (Manchester, 2006), 166 and note 69.

Then she, on being raised with such splendour and distinction to this pre-eminent position, began to be arbitrary or rather headstrong in all that she did. Some former adherents of the king, who had agreed to submit themselves and what was theirs to her, she received ungraciously and at times with unconcealed annoyance, others she drove from her presence in fury after insulting and threatening them. By reckless innovations she lessened or took away the possessions and lands of some, held on a grant from the king, while the fees and honours of the very few who still adhered to the king she confiscated altogether and granted to others; she arbitrarily annulled any grant fixed by the king's royal decree, she hastily snatched away and conferred on her own followers anything he had given in unshakeable perpetuity to churches or to his comrades in arms. What was a sign of extreme haughtiness and insolence, when the king of Scotland and the bishop of Winchester and her brother the earl of Gloucester, the chief men of the whole kingdom, whom she was then taking around with her as a permanent retinue, came before her with bended knee to make some request, she did not rise respectfully, as she should have, when they bowed before her, or agree to what they asked, but repeatedly sent them away with contumely, rebuffing them by an arrogant answer and refusing to hearken to their words; and by this time she no longer relied on their advice, as she should have, and had promised them, but arranged everything as she herself thought fit and according to her own arbitrary will.[35]

These reports were no sooner carried out of the city, by traders and tourists, than the empress herself followed after them, with no ceremonial and in complete disarray. This too was widely reported. If we want to put this event into a precise context, the best evidence we have is that the empress was about to be crowned, for those driven out included 'bishops and belted knights' who had come to London 'for the enthronement of their lady'.[36]

The empress went from London to Gloucester, via Oxford, where she had discussions with Miles of Gloucester, and then returned to Oxford.[37] Now in the chronicles these few days at Oxford, at the very end of the month of July 1141, the focus of this paper, form a brief interlude. Yet the charter material makes it clear that for the empress and her followers this was a busy time, one of anxious calculation and hard bargaining. There are six charters of particular value, each issued by the empress in favour of one of her lay supporters: (i) for Geoffrey de

---

[35] *Gesta Stephani*, 120–1.

[36] Ibid., 124–5: 'ad dominam inthronizandam pompose ... et arroganter conuenerant'. The statement of the Durham chronicler that the empress planned to invest William Cumin with ring and staff on 24 June, whether or not it is to be taken literally, is further evidence that a ceremony of some kind had been organised for this day: *Libellus de Exordio*, 286–7, 312–13; Chibnall, *Empress Matilda*, 138–9.

[37] *John of Worcester*, iii, 298–9. *Gesta Stephani*, 126–7, says that after leaving London she 'came at full speed to the city of Oxford'.

Mandeville, at Westminster;[38] (ii) for Miles of Gloucester, at Gloucester;[39] (iii) for Geoffrey de Mandeville, at Oxford;[40] (iv) for Aubrey de Vere, at Oxford;[41] (v) for William de Beauchamp, at Oxford;[42] (vi) for Miles of Gloucester, at Oxford.[43] Of this list, no. (i) gives an insight into personalities and politics at Westminster in June 1141, before the empress was driven out by the Londoners, no. (ii) gives us a similar insight for Gloucester in early July 1141, whilst nos. (iii) – (vi) come from this week in Oxford. It is the Oxford charter for Miles of Gloucester, in which he was created earl of Hereford, which gives us the date, 25 July 1141, and where we feel that we can hear the empress once again speaking *viva voce*:

> I now have in my custody at Bristol King Stephen, who by the grace of God and with the assistance of Robert, earl of Gloucester, my brother, and with the assistance of the said Miles and other of my barons, was captured in battle before Lincoln on the day of the Purification of St Mary preceding the said day of St James the apostle.[44]

The other three of the Oxford charters are undated but they can be assigned to this week with some confidence. If we are prepared to commit to them, they can tell us a lot. We may even hope to produce an analysis of which our colleagues who write on Harold Wilson or Harold Macmillan might approve.

If we are prepared to commit to them. The problem is that the two longest and most circumstantial of the charters, nos. (iii) and (iv) in favour of Geoffrey de Mandeville and his brother-in law, Aubrey de Vere, lie under a shadow of suspicion. It is not in doubt that they are a pair. The grants to the two men are many, varied, and different; but the security they are offered is identical. Because the charters are a pair, any hypothesis as to the date of one of them must take account of the provisions of the other. It is the Oxford charter in favour of Geoffrey de Mandeville that has monopolised the discussion. Round, whose commitment to these charters was not in doubt, said that it was 'absolutely certain' that this charter was issued subsequent to Christmas 1141; this was the date of King Stephen's second charter for Geoffrey. It was no less 'certain' that it could be dated prior to June 1142, when Robert of Gloucester crossed to Normandy to

---

38 *Regesta*, iii, no. 274.
39 BL Sloane MS 1301, fo. 422r–v; *Regesta*, iii, no. 391.
40 *Regesta*, iii, no. 275.
41 Ibid., no. 634.
42 Ibid., no. 68.
43 Ibid., no. 393.
44 Ibid.: 'Hanc autem donationem feci ei apud Oxineford die Sancti Jacobi apostoli, videlicet octava die ante festum Sancti Petri ad vincula, pro servitio suo quod mihi feceret; et ita quod tunc habebam in captione mea apud Bristol regem Stephanum qui, dei misericordia et auxilio Roberti comitis Gloucestrie fratris mei, et auxilio ipsius Milonis et aliorum baronum meorum captus fuit in bello apud Lincoln die Purificationis Sancte Marie proximo ante predictum diem Sancti Jacobi apostoli.'

assist in the campaigning of Geoffrey, count of Anjou.[45] Round's certainty came from his belief that Geoffrey was selling his support to the highest bidder, the final bid being this charter from the empress. Ralph Davis argued against Round's hypothesis and his dating, suggesting the date of July 1141.[46] This had seemed to be a problem resolved until Davis was challenged in his turn by John Prestwich, who sought to reinstate Round's date, specifically 'the late spring or early summer of 1142'. Davis took up the challenge, and reinstated his position; and there was then a further exchange of views.[47] The readers of the *English Histori-cal Review* had not seen anything quite like this since the great days of John Horace Round.

We need a political context for these charters and there can be no doubt that the context is found, where Davis found it, in Oxford, in the week of 25 July 1141.[48] They fit with other charters for laymen, which are all of them the result of discussions, *conventiones*.[49] This is stated in the empress's first charter for Geoffrey de Mandeville, issued at Westminster. He is to hold, as this charter confirms, 'lands and tenements, fees and farms, castles and liberties, and in respect of all the agreements that have been made between us'.[50] In her second charter for Geoffrey, issued at Oxford, the empress refers back to her first charter and the language of the *convencio* becomes more insistent. 'I make this agreement with the said Geoffrey earl of Essex that neither my lord the count of Anjou nor myself nor our sons will make any peace or concord with the burgesses of London, unless it be with the permission and agreement of the said Earl Geoffrey, for they are his mortal enemies.'[51] There is a similar statement in respect of Stortford castle, which the bishop of London held and which Geoffrey wanted. The empress said that she would facilitate an exchange; if not, 'then I make this agreement with him

---

[45] J. H. Round, *Geoffrey de Mandeville: A Study of the Anarchy* (London, 1892), 163.

[46] R. H. C. Davis, 'Geoffrey de Mandeville Reconsidered', *EHR*, 79 (1964), 299–307; revised repr. in his *From Alfred the Great to Stephen* (London, 1991), 203–11.

[47] J. O. Prestwich, 'The Treason of Geoffrey de Mandeville', *EHR*, 102 (1988), 283–312, followed by a 'Comment' by R. H. C. Davis, ibid., 313–17; Prestwich, 'Geoffrey de Mandeville: A Further Comment', ibid., 960–6; Davis, 'Geoffrey de Mandeville: A Final Comment', ibid., 967–8.

[48] In addition to Davis's 'Comment' and 'Final Comment', ibid., 313–17, 967–8, and his restatement of his argument in *King Stephen*, 157–60, see Chibnall, *Empress Matilda*, 105–12, and her, 'The Charters of the Empress Matilda', 281–3.

[49] On *conventiones* during this period see, M. Chibnall, 'Anglo-French Relations in the Work of Orderic Vitalis', in *Documenting the Past: Essays in Medieval History Presented to G. P. Cuttino*, ed. J. S. Hamilton and P. J. Bradley (Woodbridge, 1989), 5–19; D. Crouch, 'A Norman *Convencio* and Bonds of Lordship in the Middle Ages', in *Law and Government*, 299–324; E. King, 'Dispute Settlement in Anglo-Norman England', *ANS*, 14 (1992), 115–30.

[50] *Regesta*, iii, no. 274: 'et in omnibus conventionibus inter nos factis'.

[51] Ibid., no. 275: 'et conventiono eidem Gaufredo comiti Essex quod dominus meus comes Andegavie vel ego vel filii nostri nullam pacem aut concordiam cum burgensibus Lundonie faciemus, nisi concessu et assensu predicti comitis Gaufredi, quia inimici eius sunt mortales'.

that I will cause it to be levelled and destroyed utterly'.[52] The whole lengthy charter is seen as a *convencio* and the empress gives Geoffrey her hand in respect of both it and the parallel agreement with Aubrey de Vere, and offers him security. 'I make this agreement with the said Earl Geoffrey so far as I am able that Count Geoffrey my lord will give him security with his own hand to hold to this and so also will Henry my son.'[53] We may take it that similar specific provisions in charters of the empress in favour of other of her lay supporters reflect discussions in their regard also. In the case of Miles of Gloucester she had made such an arrangement before she came to England, as the price of his support. Miles in 1139 had been offered security in very much the same terms as Geoffrey de Mandeville in 1141: 'you should know that all this is the subject of an agreement which I have made with the said Miles, by the counsel and at the command of the lord Geoffrey, count of Anjou, who swore to him that he would do this and hold to this and I similarly swore to him before I came to England after the death of my father'.[54] This agreement with Miles of Gloucester helps place the agreement with Geoffrey de Mandeville in context.[55]

The charters are the result of discussions. It follows that if we are looking at a charter of the empress in favour of a magnate, whether it be issued at Westminster in June or at Oxford in July 1141, we should be listening for his voice as well as hers. It is Geoffrey de Mandeville who speaks of the Londoners as his 'mortal enemies', and they were besieging the Tower of London as he spoke.[56] It is he who is asking the empress for security and that he should hold as any earl in England best holds of her. It was seen as a problem that both in the Westminster charter and in the Oxford charter there are references to Stephen as king and Matilda as queen of England. It will be helpful here to set out the relevant extract in full and in context:

> I also concede to him that he should have those hundred librates of land which I gave him, and the service of those 20 knights as I gave them him and as I confirmed them in my other charter. Also those two hundred librates of land which King Stephen and Queen Matilda gave him. Also those hundred librates of escheated land which the said king and queen

---

52 Ibid.: 'tunc ei conventiono quod faciam illud prosternere et ex toto cadere'.
53 Ibid.: 'et conventionavi eidem comiti Gaufrido pro posse mea quod comes Andegavie dominus meus assecurabit ei manu sua propria illud idem tenendum et Henricus filius meus similiter'.
54 BL Sloane MS 1301, fo. 422r–v: 'et sciatis quod hec omnia ei conuentionaui predicto Miloni consilio et precepto domini Galfridi comitis Andegauie qui affidauit ei quod hoc ei facerem et tenerem et ego similiter idem antequam in Anglia venerim post mortem patris mei'.
55 It was not known to John Prestwich and it helps resolve the problems which he perceived in the involvement of Geoffrey of Anjou at this date: Prestwich, 'The Treason of Geoffrey de Mandeville', 290–1.
56 Brett, 'Annals of Bermondsey, Southwark and Merton', 300.

gave him, and the service of the knights which they gave him, in respect of which he has their charters.[57]

It is in this last phrase that we catch the echo of Geoffrey speaking, and once we hear him the problem disappears. 'From Geoffrey's point of view Stephen and his wife were still the king and queen whose charters he held.'[58] Exactly. And Geoffrey's views were shared by his peers. The empress, so it was reported, had snatched away what the king had granted to his comrades in arms. She was not going to snatch away the grants that the king and queen had made to Geoffrey. He had their charters.

If, as has been argued, we are able to hear the voices of the magnates in discussion with the empress, and if we can commit to a point of time, then we may hope to learn their view of the political situation at that time. In the Westminster charter for Geoffrey – whose date is not in question – the empress is depicted as putting together for him a package of escheated and crown demesne lands. These included Maldon, 'with everything that pertained to it on land and sea on the day that King Henry died'. She added a rider. 'If anything is lacking in making up this hundred librates of land, then I will make it up in an appropriate place ... with this proviso that if I shall give back to Count Theobald all the land which he held in England, then I will give Earl Geoffrey an exchange of the same value ... before he shall be disseised of the aforesaid lands.'[59] The place is Maldon in Essex, with its royal hall and its 180 burgess households.[60] The person is Theobald, count of Blois, who has been given the borough by his brother, possibly in lieu of the annual pension promised him in 1137, and who has installed in the royal hall a top manager trained in one of the Champagne fairs.[61] Round commented that, 'the empress, on obtaining the mastery, forfeited his lands at once'.[62] This is true, but the more interesting point in this context is not that the empress had forfeited Count Theobald's land but that she now acknowledges that she may have to give it back. And if she may have to do this for Count Theobald, Stephen's brother, most assuredly she will have to restore to Eustace, Stephen's son, the *comitatus*, the lands which Stephen had held before he acquired the kingdom of England. We know from the chroniclers that this was a major point of discussion in summer

---

[57] *Regesta*, iii, no. 275: '... et illas cc libratas terre quas rex Stephanus et Matildis regina ei dederunt, et illas c libratas terre de terris eschaetis quas idem rex et regina ei dederunt, et servicium militum quod ei dederunt, sicut habet inde cartas illorum'.

[58] Prestwich, 'The Treason of Geoffrey de Mandeville', 293.

[59] *Regesta*, iii, no. 274: 'tali tenore quod si reddidero comiti Theobaldo totam terram quam tenebat in Anglia, dabo Gaufrido comiti Essexe escambium suum ad valentiam ... antequam de predictis terris dissaisiatur'.

[60] *Domesday Book*, fos. 5v–6; ed. A. Williams and G. H. Martin (Harmondsworth, 2002), 973.

[61] The archive here is *Regesta*, iii, nos. 274, 276, 543 (naming Walter of Provins), 790 (giving details of other grants to Theobald); *EEA VIII: Winchester 1070–1204*, ed. M. J. Franklin (Oxford, 1993), nos. 68–9. On the promised pension, *Torigni*, 132.

[62] Round, *Geoffrey de Mandeville*, 102.

1141 and that the empress was intransigent.[63] We know that this was a significant issue for Stephen's other brother, Henry, bishop of Winchester, and that this was a major factor in Henry's withdrawing his support from the empress, claiming that she had broken the agreements that she had made with him.[64] The provisions relating to Maldon show Geoffrey de Mandeville's take on these wider discussions. A wise man would seek to factor in to any agreement that he made with the empress a future peace agreement, in which provision for members of Stephen's family would play a key part.

This was not the only way that the political situation might change, potentially to a magnate's disadvantage. The power that the empress sought would be gained when the earls and barons of England personally accepted her lordship. She would offer to protect their title from the date of that acceptance. Geoffrey de Mandeville would have his lands confirmed, 'from the day on which he became my man'.[65] For all the talk of the empress being accepted by all except the men of Kent, she knew that many of the greater magnates had not made this personal submission to her. Not yet. In her Oxford charter for Geoffrey she offers him as guarantors, 'other barons of mine whom he may wish to have and whom I am able to have'.[66] One great magnate whose support she hoped to have was Waleran, count of Meulan, whom Stephen had appointed earl of Worcester. The prospect was viewed with some misgiving by William de Beauchamp, the sheriff and castellan of Worcester, who did support the empress and who was at Oxford. In the charter which she issued for him there, the empress confirmed him in his lands and offices and granted him the forests of the county also:

> In respect of these he [William] has become my liege man against all men and specifically against Waleran, count of Meulan, in such a way that neither Count Waleran nor anyone else shall make fine with me concerning these things but he shall always hold of me in chief, unless of his own goodwill and with his own free agreement he shall wish to hold of the said count.[67]

Seldom does the dialogue that lies behind these charters come quite so clearly, and so rawly, out into the open.[68] In each of the two extracts we have considered –

---

[63] *John of Worcester*, iii, 296–7; *Gesta Stephani*, 122–3; *Historia Novella*, 98–101; *Orderic*, vi, 548–9.

[64] *Historia Novella*, 98–101.

[65] *Regesta*, iii, no. 274: 'sicut tenuerunt die qua ipse homo meus effectus est'. Similarly, as we have seen, with Henry of Winchester (in his capacity as administrator of Glastonbury Abbey): ibid., no. 343.

[66] Ibid., no. 275: 'alii barones mei quos habere voluerit et ego habere potero'.

[67] Ibid., no. 68: 'de hoc devenit ipse Willelmus meus ligius homo contra omnes mortales et nominatim contra Gualerannum comitem de Mellent et ita quod nec ipse comes Gualerannus nec aliquis alius de his predictis mecum finem faciet, quominus semper ipse Willelmus de me in capite teneat nisi ipse bona voluntate et gratuita concessione de predicto comite tenere voluerit'.

[68] Chibnall, *Empress Matilda*, 107. As to one of his main concerns here, William should not

what was said about Maldon to Geoffrey de Mandeville and what was said about Waleran of Meulan to William de Beauchamp – the empress has been forced to acknowledge that her grants were provisional. Her magnates knew only too well that a week could be a long time in politics.

It is possible to extend this point a little further. In their dialogues with the empress, we learn the views of the magnates as to what was proper when lands came to her by forfeiture or escheat. The most direct statement here is contained in a further extract from her charter for William de Beauchamp. 'I also give and concede to him the lands and inheritances of his close relations who have been against me in my war unless there be other of his closer relatives who have served me in my war.'[69] 'The fees and honours' – this, as we have seen, was the charge – 'of the very few who still adhered to the king she confiscated altogether and granted to others.'[70] In fact, she was not able to do so. One of her own followers is here telling her as much. It was argued against her also that she was not prepared to take counsel. In the charter for Aubrey de Vere counsellors were named for her. They were to advise on which earldom he should choose, in the event that his preferred choice was claimed by the king of Scots. The relevant extract is worth setting out in full.

> Besides this I give and concede to him that he shall be earl of Cambridge-shire and thence have the third penny as an earl ought to have, thus I say if the king of Scots does not have this county. And if the king shall have it, I will do everything that I can to acquire it from him by means of an exchange. If I cannot do this, then I give and concede to him that he shall be earl of one of the following four counties, namely Oxfordshire, Berkshire, Wiltshire, and Dorsetshire, [it to be chosen] by the counsel and agreement of the earl of Gloucester my brother and Earl Geoffrey and Earl Gilbert.[71]

The uncertainty here is not over what might happen in the future but rather over what had happened in the past. There was no ledger to hand to show the empress the assets which she had.

have had to ask. As a significant tenant-in-chief his service should have been reserved to the crown in any grant of the *comitatus*. *Regesta*, iii, no. 437, the king's grant of the *comitatus* of Herefordshire to Robert, earl of Leicester, is quite exact on this, and so also would be Duke Henry's charter for Ranulf, earl of Chester, ibid., no. 180.

69 *Regesta*, iii, no. 68: 'item dedi ei et concessi terras et hereditates suorum proximorum parentum qui contra me fuerint in werra mea et mecum finem facere non poterunt, nisi de sua parentela propinquiore michi in ipse werra servierit'.

70 *Gesta Stephani*, 120–1.

71 *Regesta*, iii, no. 634: 'Et preter hoc do ei et concedo quod sit comes de Cantebruggescira et habeat inde tertium denarium sicut comes debet habere, ita dico si rex Scotie non habet illum comitatum. Et si rex habuerit, perquirem illum ei ad posse meum per escambium. Et si non potero tunc do ei et concedo quod sit comes de quolibet quatuor comitatuum subscriptorum, videlicet Oxenefordescira, Berkscira, Wiltescira, et Dorsetescira per consilium et considerationem comitis Gloucestrie fratris mei et comitis Gaufridi et comitis Gisleberti.'

The advice which the empress received at Oxford may have unsettled her. She went unannounced to Winchester and there are no more charters for us. We rely on the chronicles for the outline of what followed.[72] Henry of Winchester, seeing himself as a target, escaped in haste and there was fighting and arson in the heart of the city. Gradually, however, the forces against the empress mounted up, with the Londoners active in supplying resources for the queen and her party, which included several of the earls who had fled from the battle of Lincoln and who had never attended the empress's court. The empress found herself under siege in the castle and she was forced to flee from Winchester, just as she had from London. An orderly retreat turned to panic when Robert of Gloucester, her brother and talisman, was captured by royal forces at Stockbridge ford. Peace discussions were reopened but failed; the Gloucester chronicle appears to conclude before any political settlement could be agreed. The settlement when it came involved the king's release, on 1 November, in exchange for Robert of Gloucester, 'no other condition being involved except that each should guard his own region to the best of his ability, as before'.[73] At another legatine council, early in December, the magnates were instructed by Henry of Winchester to return to their allegiance to the king. 'I would not say that these words of the legate were gladly received by all the clergy.'[74] The king was recrowned at Canterbury, by the archbishop, at Christmas 1141.[75] Geoffrey de Mandeville was one of those present at what Round called the 'restoration court'.[76]

1141 had turned into an *annus horribilis* for the empress. Not just that. It had been an *annus horribilis* for the country as a whole. The political process had failed to resolve the civil war and all political commentators were united in their condemnation of the leaders on both sides. This had been a year, said William of Malmesbury, 'that was ill-omened and almost mortal for England, which, after thinking it might now draw a breath of freedom, fell back again into misery'. The *Gesta Stephani* described the king's joyful reception by the Londoners but bemoaned the fact that no political settlement had been reached and that hostilities were simply resumed: 'these indeed were harsh and ill-judged terms and bound to do harm to the entire country'. Orderic Vitalis, who may not have lived to the year's end, commented sadly: 'I see the princes of this world overwhelmed with misfortunes and disastrous setbacks'.[77] Outside the Anglo-Norman world,

---

[72] *Gesta Stephani*, 126–37; *John of Worcester*, iii, 298–305; *Historia Novella*, 100–11, 114–21.

[73] *Historia Novella*, 106–7: 'nullo pacto alio interueniente, nisi ut quisque partes suas pro posse, sicut et prius, tutaretur'.

[74] Ibid., 110–11: 'Haec eius uerba non dico quod omnes *clerici* gratis animis exceperint.' Ce has deleted *clerici* here, to make the passage read '... were gladly received by everyone'. I would view this as another of the minor but deliberate changes in the Ce text, on which see ibid., lxxxii–lxxxv.

[75] *The Historical Works of Gervase of Canterbury*, ed. W. Stubbs, 2 vols. (RS, 1879–80), i, 123–4.

[76] Round, *Geoffrey de Mandeville*, 158.

[77] *Historia Novella*, 110–11: 'fuit ergo hic annus, cuius tragedias compendio digessi, fatalis et

the state of the English polity was written of with pity, not without a touch of *Schadenfreude*. The country 'had sunk from earlier wealth to great poverty because of the devastation and expense of persistent dissention'. It was seen as shocking, both inside and outside England, that an anointed king had fallen into the hands of 'that woman' and had been put in chains.[78] Our witnesses, sitting at the corners of the stage, here get up and come together and speak with one voice, like the chorus in a Greek tragedy.

Now the men, and most certainly the women, whom we are dealing with were not fools. They knew all of this very well. They knew that they had failed. And – since they were only human – they blamed somebody else. The empress and her supporters were particularly shocked and resentful, and they can now be seen in a mood of retrospection and recrimination. There is a section in the *Historia Novella* in which Robert of Gloucester is shown as looking back and defending the consistency and the propriety of his actions.[79] He was not the only one doing so. We can see, with much more immediacy, the raw anger in Brian fitz Count's surviving letter to Henry, bishop of Winchester, over the same ground. 'Do not look back', he had been urged, 'remember the wife of Lot.' It was one of the bishop's texts for the times. Brian fitz Count would have none of it. It was essential to look back and when you did so it became clear that the clergy, and especially the papal legate, bore a large measure of responsibility for what had gone wrong. They had insisted on taking the lead in 1141; they had first instructed Brian to 'adhere to the daughter of King Henry' and had then countermanded the instruction. Responsibility for the misery of the country was not the responsibility of Brian and his peers but of Henry of Winchester, Theobald, 'the so-called archbishop of Canterbury', and their colleagues: 'I am sorry for the poor and their plight when the church provides scarcely any refuge for them.'[80]

pene pernitiosus Angliae; in quo cum aliquo modo sibi ad libertatem respirandum putasset, rursum in erumnam recidit'; *Gesta Stephani*, 136–7: 'facta fuit ... conuentio ut ... ad priorem dissensionis punctum ex integro redirent, dura quidem et indiscreta, omnique regioni offutura conditio'. *Orderic*, vi, 550–1: 'optimates huius seculi grauibus infortuniis sibique ualde contrariis comprimi uideo'; cf. *John of Worcester*, iii, 304–5: 'per totum annum deinceps omne regnum cum patria rapinis pauperum, cedibus hominum, uiolationibus ecclesiarum crudeliter ...' (where the text ends); *Huntingdon*, 740–1, noting that the king, 'the Lord's anointed', was put in irons; 'Annals of Mortemer', s.a. 1141, *Recueil des historiens des Gaules et de la France*, 24 vols. (Paris, 1738–1904), xii, 782: 'Anglia fame et gladio atteritur, principibus terrae inter se discordantibus.'

78 Otto of Freising, *The Two Cities: A Chronicle of Universal History to the Year 1146 A.D.*, ed. C. C. Mierow (New York, 1928; rev. edn 2002), 429–30; Suger, 'Histoire de Louis VII', in *Oeuvres*, i, ed. F. Gasparri (Paris, 1996), 158–9: 'imperium siquidem Romanorum, regnum eciam Anglorum in defectu successive prolis multa imcommoda fere usque ad status sui ruinam sustinuisse conspicantes'. England had sunk 'from earlier wealth to great poverty because of the devastation and expense of persistent dissention': Herman of Tournai, *The Restoration of the Monastery of Saint Martin of Tournai*, ed. L. H. Nelson (Washington, DC, 1996), 34.

79 *Historia Novella*, 112–15.

80 Davis, 'Henry of Blois and Brian Fitz-Count', 301–303; King, 'The Memory of Brian fitz Count', 89–91.

We are then following the grain of our sources if, having run through the events of 1141, we now go back to scrutinise in more detail some of its key episodes. In the eyes of Brian fitz Count, the reception of the empress by the clergy, headed by Henry of Winchester, was such an episode. We come back to the council of Winchester, in early April 1141. We have the report of William of Malmesbury, which is of value here not just because he was an eye-witness but because he was writing during the period of retrospection, in 1142.[81] He describes a council of the clergy. Such consultation as took place involved the bishops, the abbots, and the archdeacons, meeting in separate groups. 'The case was discussed in secret yesterday before the chief part of the clergy of England, whose special prerogative it is to choose and consecrate a prince.'[82] They chose, they elected, the empress as *domina Anglorum*, 'lady of England and Normandy'. Our reporter allows us to see behind the legate's rhetoric. Henry of Winchester had introduced the proceedings by speaking of the need for peace. But he did not provide it. The empress at Oxford, more than three months later, writes of those 'who have been with me in my war': there is every sign that she saw it as still going on. Any peace would be a peace agreement and the key to that would be a settlement with Stephen's family. Henry of Winchester would work towards such a settlement but he would do so only after the Winchester council. The election of the empress as 'lady of England' was not made conditional on the *pax*. A clerk of the queen's appeared at the council and asked for the king's release, but the legate stuck to his prepared text.[83] The Londoners appeared also. Now the Londoners, according to what I would now identify as a London chronicler, also had claims to elect. They were received 'as if they were magnates', not as representatives of a commune, but they were ignored,[84] while the other magnates were absent from the discussions. The council itself, though it made extensive claims for its authority, did not become a matter of public knowledge.[85] It was reported rather that the legate had received the empress.[86] The reception was seen as very much his responsibility,

---

[81] *Historia Novella*, xxxi–xxxii, 80–1 (on the date), 90–7 (on the council).

[82] Ibid., 92–3: 'Ventilata est hesterno die causa secreto coram maiori parte cleri Angliae, ad cuius *ius* potissimum spectat principem eligere.' The Ce text omits the *ius* and so queries the *right* that the legate claimed. I should have noted this also as a significant change: cf. ibid., lxxxii–lxxxv.

[83] Ibid., 94–7.

[84] Ibid., lviii–lix, 94–5; M. McKisack, 'London and the Succession to the Crown during the Middle Ages', in *Studies in Medieval History Presented to F. M. Powicke*, ed. R. W. Hunt et al. (Oxford, 1948), 76–89.

[85] Aside from the *Historia Novella*, the only other reference to a church council comes in the Plympton annals: F. Liebermann, *Ungedruckte Anglo-Normannische Geschichtsquellen* (Strasbourg, 1879), 28; *Councils & Synods*, ii, 788–92 (no. 142).

[86] *Huntingdon*, 738–9; *Gesta Stephani*, 118–19 (the editors comment, at note 3, that the text represents 'a very off-hand allusion to the Council of Winchester', but in fact the council is not mentioned at all). The Gloucester chronicle is the one text which seeks to show that the political community was behind the empress's reception at Winchester, saying that she was welcomed by 'presules pene totius Anglie, barones multi, principes plurimi, milites innumeri, abbates cum suis diuersi': *John of Worcester*, iii, 294–5.

and this was a man, we are told, who would never abandon a course of action once he had set himself to it.[87] Henry of Winchester's reputation would never quite recover from the events of 1141, though he would live for another thirty years.

The empress here in Oxford, in July 1141, is seen to be exposed in terms of her title as well as in terms of her support. She waits for magnates to 'make fine' with her but they were under no compulsion to do so. The charters show those who were present, the majority of whom had been her supporters since 1139, and those whom she felt that she could rely upon. How can she warrant her grants? Standing behind her, vouching support, there is not the common counsel of the land but 'the Christianity of England which is in my power'.[88] In her charter for Aubrey de Vere, who is not present at Oxford, she states at one point: 'and besides this I give to Robert de Vere a barony to the value of the honour of Geoffrey de Vere within a year from when I acquire power over the kingdom of England'.[89] These are statements made when the empress had not yet acquired, but still had hopes of acquiring, power over the whole kingdom of England. They could only have been made prior to Stephen's release on 1 November 1141, after it was agreed that the parties should resume the *status quo ante* the battle of Lincoln. Most assuredly they did not come from the period of retrospection and recrimination. The charter for Aubrey de Vere makes the point even more clearly than the charter for Geoffrey de Mandeville. One of the promises made to Aubrey was that he should have 'the motte and the castle of Colchester', just as soon as she was able to hand this over to him.[90] The empress was driven back from London and the south-east of England, and hence had lost the possibility of gaining power over the whole kingdom of England, in 1141, in large part because of the resources enjoyed by Stephen and his family, which the queen and later the legate could mobilise. Colchester lay at the heart of their family lands. This lesson had been learned by the empress and her followers and in 1142 they were concerned to protect what they had.[91]

It is the lack of confidence of Geoffrey de Mandeville, combined with the attention to detail of a very capable manager,[92] that allows us to see clearly what the empress's power amounted to, and what advice she was being given, at Oxford, late in July, in 1141. My title, however, suggests something more, that over quite a short period there can be significant change, and it is time to address this point more directly. A case can be made, although it cannot be proved. We can say that after this week, in our records, some things have changed, most

---

87 *Historia Novella*, 108–9, 110–11.
88 *Regesta*, iii, no. 275: 'et quod Christianitas Anglie que est in potestate mea capiet in manu istam supradictam conventionem tenandam eidem comiti Gaufredo'.
89 Ibid., no. 634: 'et preter hoc concedo Roberto de Veer unam baroniam ad valentiam honoris Gaufridi de Veer infra annum quo potestativa fuero regni Anglie'.
90 Ibid.: 'et turrim et castellum de Colecestria sine placito finaliter et sine escampa quam citius deliberare potero'.
91 *Historia Novella*, 122–3.
92 *Waltham*, 78–9: 'rei sue familiaris prouidus dispensator'.

specifically in terms of the empress's title. In the two charters for Geoffrey de Mandeville there appears to be a change: at Westminster, in June, the empress refers to his 'accession to my service'; at Oxford, in July, to his 'adhering to the service of the count of Anjou and myself'.[93] In the Oxford charter there is an insistence on the involvement of her men folk; they are necessary for security, and they will become necessary for practical support. The change here seems to be matched in William of Malmesbury's contemporary history, which hereafter always associates the empress's title with that of her husband and her sons.[94] That title was being re-evaluated. I do not think that there is any doubt that the empress thought of herself as her father's heir. We have her own words, in her charter for Miles of Gloucester: 'he received me as lady and as she who was the rightful heir of the kingdom of England'.[95] I do not think that there is any doubt also that in the eyes of her supporters, at least after she had suffered the reverses of 1141, she was not. She was not *heres* but *successor*; she transmits title; it is her son, not herself, who is the heir. This is the formulation of William of Malmesbury, writing of the oaths sworn to the empress on 1 January 1127,[96] but it must be doubtful that this precise distinction was made as early as that. Was it floated at Oxford? We cannot say. The *Historia Novella* is sharp, and its author is well informed, but this visit to Oxford is only a staging-point in his narrative. We do, however, have our charters, if we will but trust them. They show us a gathering of the empress's supporters which, if it is not 'the common counsel of the land', is at least fuller counsel and it is speaking more frankly.

'Remember the wife of Lot.' Nowhere was that advice more disregarded, nowhere were the events of 1141 reviewed more closely, and more clear-headedly, than in the court of Henry, the empress's son, who would now describe himself as 'the rightful heir of England and Normandy'.[97] This is a paper on 1141 but it will help focus the issues raised in that year, and specifically here at Oxford, if we jump ahead to 1153. We can proceed, just as William of Malmesbury did, by way of recapitulation. We have seen, first of all, how in April 1141, the churchmen, led by Henry of Winchester, elected the empress as lady of the English, without involving the wider political community and without considering how the wider political community would be affected by this act. Most immediately affected was Stephen's family. No settlement could subsequently be made, to protect their interests, either in the spring or in the autumn of 1141, and

---

93 *Regesta*, iii, nos. 274 ('sicut tenuerunt die qua ipse homo meus effectus est', 'usque ad diem quo homo meus devenit'), 275 ('usque ad diem qua servicio domini mei comitis Andegavie ac meo adhesit').

94 *Historia Novella*, lxvii, 122–3, 124–5.

95 *Regesta*, iii, no. 391: 'Milo de Gloucestria quam citius potuit venit ad me apud Bristolliam et recepit me ut dominam et sicut illam quam iustam heredem regni Anglie recognovit.'

96 *Historia Novella*, 6–7: 'cui iure regnum competeret' (of William), 'cui soli legitima debeatur successio' (of Matilda).

97 *Regesta*, iii, no. 635, confirming the empress's grant to Aubrey de Vere; cf. Chibnall, *Empress Matilda*, 111–12.

in consequence no peace was made. When the peace was made in 1153 the provision for Stephen's family was an integral part of it. This can be seen at Winchester, in November 1153, where Bishop Henry presided just as he had done at the councils in 1141.[98] There is every indication that the peace discussions had started with this problem and that the heads of an agreement had been accepted by the time that Henry, duke of Normandy, and Stephen, king of England, met at Wallingford in August 1153. Eustace, king Stephen's heir, had died shortly after this. At Winchester the surviving son, William, was given the *comitatus* of his father, just as they had been requested for Eustace in 1141. And a great deal more. He was given 'whatever came to him with the daughter of the Earl Warenne, both in England and in Normandy', along with the *comitatus* of Norfolk and the honour of Pevensey, the latter grant being made 'to strengthen my goodwill and affection for him', as the king put it. The generosity of Duke Henry is most easily explained by suggesting that he was here confirming to Stephen's surviving son a landed settlement that was intended to provide for two sons, Eustace and William. When Eustace died the provision for William became sumptuous but Henry stayed with it, 'so as not to break an arrangement that had been made'.[99] When king and duke met again at Winchester this was a done deal and the detail did not need to be rehearsed there. William did homage to Duke Henry for his lands and this homage was his title to them.[100]

The magnates of England were no disinterested observers of these arrangements. The treatment of William earl of Warenne, now confirmed as one of the greatest magnates in the Anglo-Norman world, had implications for the other magnates also. We have seen how in 1141 it could be claimed that the empress had arbitrarily deprived individuals of their property. There was some substance to the charge. There are several references in her charters of 1141 to the grant of estates *sine placito*, 'without judgement'.[101] It was certainly expected that she would confiscate the estates of political opponents, even if it was thought that those estates should then be granted to close relations among her supporters. After Duke Henry had landed in England in January 1153 the same issues would recur. He initially expected that his opponents should be disseised. His earlier charters suggest as much.[102] The same charters, however, insist that he will hold court and give judgement there on disputed inheritances that his supporters claimed. His

98 *Gervase of Canterbury*, i, 156.
99 *Torigni*, 174: 'ne fidem illorum irritam faceret, predictum pactum concessit' (referring to the truce negotiated at Wallingford by his representatives).
100 *Regesta*, iii, no. 272. On the issues raised by this document, see J. C. Holt, '1153: The Treaty of Winchester', in King, *Anarchy*, 291–316; E. King, 'The Accession of Henry II', in *Henry II: New Interpretations*, ed. C. Harper-Bill and N. Vincent (Woodbridge, 2007), 24–46.
101 Such references are found in her charters for William de Beauchamp, Geoffrey de Mandeville, and Aubrey de Vere: *Regesta*, iii, nos. 68, 274–5, 634.
102 Ibid., nos. 180 (for Ranulf of Chester, 'de his que mihi ex hostibus meis adquisita acciderint'), 582 (for William Mauduit, 'de terris mihi accidentibus de primis meis conquisitionibus').

chancery was concerned to issue documents in proper form and may well have had a small archive of charters to serve as a formulary.[103] To advertise the meetings of his court was to advertise that he would take counsel. And as he took further counsel, in particular after he was joined by Robert, earl of Leicester, the references to disseisin fade away. In the record of the peace it could be stated that 'the earls and barons of the king' had done homage to the duke, while conversely 'the earls and barons of the duke' would perform homage or swear fealty to the king, depending on whether they had earlier done him homage or not. This network of homage now formally held the kingdom together. The swearing of homage protected title. If an agreement with Stephen's family was one key element in the making of a peace, recognising the integrity of those who had fought on either side and protecting their title was another.

The magnates were not all present at Winchester in November 1153. The king and the duke presided at a series of meetings,[104] and the oaths were sworn over a period of time. And yet it was stated in the Westminster charter that the swearing of the homages was complete. Why? Asking this question brings us back to what was the underlying political issue in 1153, as it had been in 1141. In whose name were these arrangements being made? The Westminster charter was issued in the name of the king. At the end of the charter and, it may be, at the end of the proceedings at Winchester, the king reserved the rights of justice, 'both in the parts that pertain to myself and the parts that pertain to the duke'. The king here in 1153 acknowledges the continuing existence of two camps, just as the empress had done in 1141. We know that the peace settlement in 1153 was followed by a peace process. John of Hexham describes this in the following terms. 'An edict was immediately promulgated by them for the suppression of outrages, the prohibition of spoliation, the dismissal from the kingdom of mercenary soldiers and archers of foreign nations, and the destruction of the fortresses which, since the death of King Henry, everyone had built on his own property.'[105]

While 'they' here are the king and the duke, John is concerned to stress that they spoke for the whole political community.[106] This is the difference between

---

103 It is known that two of the Oxford charters were brought to Henry for confirmation in 1141 (*Regesta*, iii, nos. 275, 634–5); and they may have been retained. In the Westminster charter for Geoffrey de Mandeville, ibid., no. 274, the empress said that he was not to be impleaded 'quamdui se defendere potuerit de scelere sive traditione ad corpus meum pertinente'. In Henry's charter for Ranulf of Chester, ibid., no. 180, he granted him the fee of William Peverel, 'nisi poterit se dirationare in mea curia de scelere et traditione'. The clerk here is Henry's chief clerk, *scriptor* xxiii, on whom see the comments, ibid., iii, p. xxxv; iv, plates xl(a), xli.

104 Holt, '1153: The Treaty of Winchester', 307: 'there were at least six courts, which they both attended, between Winchester on 6 November and Henry's departure for Normandy in early March 1154'.

105 John of Hexham, *Historia*, 331: 'continuo exiit edictum ab eis per omnes prouincias violentias comprimi, direptiones interdici, milites conductitios et sagittarios exterarum nationum a regno ejici, munitionesque quas quisque in sua possessione post mortem Henrici Regis construxerat dirui'.

106 Ibid.: 'consenserunt in hoc omnes principes regni'.

1153 and 1141. In 1153 the emphasis on 'common counsel' as conferring legiti-macy, the need for all to swear to the provisions of the peace, *unanimiter*, is unmistakeable.[107] The magnates had claimed responsibility. If we then ask how the magnates of England could be seen to have sworn to the peace before very many of them had physically done so, the answer may be here. Sir James Holt speaks of an evidentiary not a historic past.[108] Just so. The magnates could be seen to have sworn *unanimiter* because those present at Winchester had spoken for them.

In the course of the nineteen years of Stephen's reign there had been some distinctly partial claims made for the rights to elect a ruler of England, who would be able to claim legitimacy on the basis of such an election. In 1135 we are told of the rights of the Londoners to elect, though only at that time in one source, which may well emanate from London.[109] In 1141 we know that Henry, bishop of Winchester, claimed that it was the right of the church 'to choose and consecrate a prince'.[110] These were particular interest groups, or 'stakeholders' in the modern jargon, but their different roles in the ceremony of coronation did not entitle them to speak for the common counsel of the land. It was claimed against Stephen in 1135 that his coronation was attended by 'three bishops (the archbishop, Winchester, Salisbury), no abbots, and just a handful of the great men'.[111] It was in answer to such a claim that Stephen's coronation charter appeared only after his Easter court of 1136, 'which was more splendid for its throng and size, for gold, silver, robes and every kind of sumptuousness, than any that had ever been held in England'.[112] This charter is very properly included in the *Regesta* as a charter for 'England'.[113] The Westminster charter of 1153 follows it in the same collection, as a further charter for 'England', no less properly.[114] They each acquire such authority not just because of the name of the king, or the address, but from the list of names at the end of the document. The names represent the 'common counsel' of England.[115] And the 1153 document is more particularly

---

107 *Huntingdon*, 770–1, speaks of a 'glittering procession of bishops and famous men, and applauded by a countless multitude of the people'. *Gervase of Canterbury*, i, 156, calls the Winchester meeting a 'publicum conventum'. Stubbs, it is clear, was onto the case: 'the national claims for good government were strongly insisted upon', W. Stubbs, *The Constitutional History of England*, 3 vols. (6th edn, Oxford, 1897), i, 359–60.
108 Holt, '1153: The Treaty of Winchester', 296.
109 *Gesta Stephani*, 6–7; and for comment, M. McKisack, 'London and the Succession to the Crown', 76–89.
110 *Historia Novella*, 92–3.
111 Ibid., 28–9: '… paucissimis optimatibus'.
112 *Huntingdon*, 706–7.
113 *Regesta*, iii, no. 271.
114 Ibid., no. 272.
115 On this, see J. C. Holt, 'The Prehistory of Parliament', in *The English Parliament in the Middle Ages*, ed. R. G. Davies and J. H. Denton (Manchester, 1981), 25–6; cf. also, J. Hudson, 'Henry I and Counsel', in *The Medieval State: Essays Presented to James Campbell*, ed. J. R. Maddicott and D. M. Palliser (London, 2000), 109–26.

their document because it was a record of what they had done. 'The duke also willingly and gladly agreed to all that the clergy and barons had wisely arranged.'[116] If this had been the approach in 1141, had the bishops and lay magnates acted together, and had the king and the empress listened to them, the civil war might have concluded sooner.

---

[116] *Gesta Stephani*, 240–1: 'dux quoque omnibus istis que a clero et a baronibus erant discrete prouisa, libenter et ex animo consentiens'; cf. *ASC* 1140: 'the archbishop and the wise men went between them and made an agreement that the king should be liege lord and king as long as he lived and after his day Henry should be king; they should be as father and son; and there should be peace and concord between them, and in all England. This, and *all the other conditions that they made*, the king and the count and the bishops and the earls and powerful men all swore to keep.' (My italics.)

5

Allegiance and Intelligence in King Stephen's Reign

PAUL DALTON

AFTER THE DEATH of Henry I, according to the author of the *Gesta Stephani*,

> England, formerly the seat of justice, the habitation of peace, the height of piety, the mirror of religion, became thereafter a home of perversity, a haunt of strife, a training-ground of disorder, and a teacher of every kind of rebellion. The sacred obligations of hallowed friendship were at once broken among the people; the closest bonds of relationship were loosened; and those who had been clothed in the cloak of an enduring peace were assailed by the noise of war and the fury of Mars.[1]

According to this image, intended perhaps to help justify King Stephen's accession, the troubles following Henry I's death were inextricably linked with the breaking of obligations of friendship and the loosening of bonds of relationship. In this society, as is well known, aristocrats and others were bound to each other by various obligations and relationships. These included, naming just some, those inherent in kinship, lordship, friendship, tenure, service and neighbourhood, all of which might involve expectations of allegiance. Such allegiances could be highly complex in nature and were of fundamental importance in aristocratic conduct and reputation. They could be conditional, multiple, conflicting, limited and shifting, and their complexity was always likely to increase during times of political conflict. But while allegiance is often mentioned by historians of Stephen's reign, it has been less frequently examined in depth and sometimes considerably oversimplified. R. H. C. Davis's neat tabulation of the periods when magnates were supporting King Stephen, supporting the empress or Duke Henry, or

---

Quotations from *Gesta Stephani*, ed. K. R. Potter and R. H. C. Davis (Oxford, 1976), 3, 7, 23, 25, 41, 43, 49, 50, 67, 85, 89, 97, 113, 115, 201, 203, and from William of Malmesbury, *Historia Novella*, ed. E. King, trans. K. R. Potter (Oxford, 1998), xlvi, 33, 39, 41, 43, 59, 83, 85, 89, 91, 93, 97, 109, 110, 111, 123, are used by permission of Oxford University Press.

[1] *Gesta Stephani*, 2–3.

described as 'doubtful', is a case in point.[2] The reality was far more complicated than this. But the nature and extent of the complexity has still fully to be appreciated. This chapter seeks to make a further contribution to such an appreciation.

The complexity of allegiance, and the fact that it was and is open to a variety of – sometimes conflicting – definitions and interpretations, means that a brief study cannot hope to be comprehensive.[3] Used here the term allegiance is something of a convenience, embracing loyalty and the obligations arising from homage, fealty, friendship, obedience and service; all of which might be interrelated. There were and are many different forms and shades of allegiance, and medieval terminology may well have been much more precise or categorical than that used in this study. Some of the twelfth-century ceremonies and relationships fundamental to some forms of allegiance, such as homage, fealty and friendship are worthy of greater individual attention than can be devoted to them here. As recent work on medieval friendship has shown, medieval conceptions and interpretations of human relationships and of the words used to describe them could differ considerably from our own.[4] A study of allegiance in Stephen's reign also needs, ideally, to range far more broadly, chronologically and geographically, than is done here. What follows is intended, therefore, only as a modest contribution to knowledge. Its arguments and conclusions are provisional and limited. If it does no more than point to interesting lines of enquiry and raise constructive questions and objections, it will have served its purpose.

The securing and guaranteeing of allegiance was a major challenge for both King Stephen and Empress Matilda. After Henry I's death many magnates disregarded the oaths they had sworn to the empress in 1127 and 1131. In 1138 Matilda is described as writing to her uncle King David of Scots, the first layman to swear the oath of 1127, to appeal for his armed assistance against Stephen, to whom David's son Henry had done homage in 1136.[5] Matilda was proposing to act, as Matthew Strickland terms opposition of this kind, against 'the *christus domini*, the Anointed of the Lord, the divinely sanctioned receptacle of legitimate authority', and this had to be carefully justified.[6] Matilda is said to have done so with several arguments: she had been denied her father's will (and her father was a king); she had been deprived of a kingdom promised to her on oath; the fealty of

---

2 Davis, *King Stephen*, 142–3.
3 For discussion of loyalty, its limits, and the debates it stimulated, see D. Crouch, *The Birth of Nobility: Constructing Aristocracy in England and France 900–1300* (Harlow, 2005), 56–62.
4 For references to this work by B. P. McGuire, G. Althoff, J. Haseldine and others, see P. Dalton, 'Churchmen and the Promotion of Peace in King Stephen's Reign', *Viator*, 31 (2000), 84 notes 22–4.
5 *Gesta Stephani*, 54–5; Richard of Hexham, *De Gestis Regis Stephani et de Bello Standardii*, in Howlett, *Chronicles*, iii, 146.
6 M. Strickland, 'Against the Lord's Anointed: Aspects of Warfare and Baronial Rebellion in England and Normandy, 1075–1265', in *Law and Government in Medieval England and Normandy: Essays in Honour of Sir James Holt*, ed. G. Garnett and J. Hudson (Cambridge, 1994), 56–79, at 57.

the barons and the compact to which they had sworn had been disregarded, indicating that the nature of that fealty was defined by the terms of the compact; and the laws had been made of no account and justice trampled underfoot – an assertion that Stephen had not fulfilled key duties of a Christian king. Matilda also appealed to David more personally, as a kinsman bound to her by oath; and also, possibly, as a king, since it was the responsibility of monarchs to uphold peace and justice in the world. Her letter, whether real or imagined, nicely encapsulates some of the complexities and limitations of allegiance.

Central to Matilda's case was the argument that the magnates, including Stephen, had broken their oaths. This breach of allegiance was also carefully justified by those who thought it right. Some of the arguments were set out by the author of the *Gesta Stephani*, who supported Stephen's cause.[7] They follow a sensational account of the breakdown of law and order after Henry I's death, a description of Stephen's arrival in England (in which his close kinship with Henry I and many virtues are noted), and the choosing of Stephen as king by the Londoners. The Londoners 'took prudent forethought for the state of the kingdom [*regni statu*]', considering that it was worthwhile 'to appoint as soon as possible a king who, with a view to re-establishing peace for the common benefit, would meet the insurgents of the kingdom in arms and would justly administer the enactments of the laws'. Stephen was, they argued, a suitable candidate because of 'his high birth and ... good character'.[8] When the archbishop of Canterbury objected that Stephen's supporters were presumptuous to disregard their oath to the empress, they declared that Henry I had repented for forcibly imposing the oath and that it was acknowledged that the breaking of such an oath could not constitute perjury. They also argued that Stephen should be accepted because London had received him, he was closely related to Henry I, and (as a man of resolution and soldierly qualities) he would lessen the troubles of the disturbed kingdom.[9] Elsewhere, they added claims that Henry I had nominated Stephen as his successor and that Matilda could not succeed as the lawful heir because she was born of an illegitimate marriage.[10]

A crucial idea in support of Stephen's succession was that he would enforce peace and justice, one of the cardinal duties of a Christian king. This is also reflected in some of Stephen's charters. As David Crouch noted, 'several of Stephen's early ecclesiastical benefactions were granted "for the peace and security of the realm" ('*pro statu et incolumitate regni*') in a way that links king, subjects and the prayer of the Church into a common purpose'.[11] The phrase predates Stephen's reign and also appears in charters issued by Stephen, Empress Matilda and Henry of Anjou after 1136.[12] They form an interesting little

---

7 *Gesta Stephani*, xx–xxi.
8 Ibid., 2–7, quotations at 7.
9 Ibid., 10–13.
10 Chibnall, *Empress Matilda*, 75–6.
11 Crouch, *Reign of Stephen*, 85.
12 E. Mason, '*Pro Statu et Incolumnitate Regni Mei*: Royal Monastic Patronage 1066–1154',

archive.[13] One of its most interesting features is that many of the charters were issued at times when the grantors were establishing their authority, seeking to guarantee their support or dealing with crises.[14] The peace of the kingdom is prominent again in Henry, bishop of Winchester's, memory of why he and others had supported Stephen's accession, articulated in a speech given to an ecclesiastical council in April 1141 and designed to justify his recognition of Empress Matilda as lady of England after Stephen's capture at the battle of Lincoln. 'In the time of King Henry', declared the bishop, 'England had been the peculiar habitation of peace' but after Henry's death because the empress delayed going to England 'provision was made for the peace of the country and my brother allowed to reign'.[15]

The giving or breaking of allegiance could clearly be justified in various ways. These show that allegiance was contractual; and all contracts, as Edmund King noted, were conditional.[16] In his speech in April 1141 the bishop of Winchester set out some of the conditions on which he had accepted his brother's accession:

> though I made myself guarantor between [King Stephen] and God that he would honour and exalt holy church, maintain good laws and repeal bad ones, I am vexed to remember and ashamed to tell what manner of man he showed himself as king: how no justice was enforced upon transgressors, and how peace was at once brought entirely to an end, almost in that very year; bishops were arrested and compelled to surrender their property; abbacies were sold and churches despoiled of their treasure; the advice of the wicked was hearkened to, that of the good either not put into effect or altogether disregarded.[17]

Henry's justification for offering his allegiance to Matilda in 1141 was that Stephen had failed to fulfil the conditions on which Henry's allegiance to him in 1135 had been dependent. Stephen had failed in his obligations to the church, set out in a charter issued at Oxford in 1136; in his duty to provide peace and justice; and in his responsibility to listen to and act upon good advice.[18] In doing so, moreover, he had caused Bishop Henry to feel shame.

Bishop Henry's speech evoked a mixed reaction.[19] It is debatable whether Stephen had failed to fulfil his obligations to the church, and Bishop Henry's

---

in *Religion and National Identity*, ed. S. Mews, Studies in Church History, 18 (Oxford, 1982), 99–117.

13 *Regesta*, iii, nos. 327–8, 335, 337, 341, 368, 399, 592, 594, 598, 627, 629, 644, 648, 666–7, 681, 690, 698, 702, 716, 787, 798, 818–19, 836, 839, 921.

14 I hope to analyse these charters and their contexts in detail elsewhere.

15 *Historia Novella*, 90–3.

16 Ibid., xliv–xlvi.

17 Ibid., 92–3.

18 For the Oxford charter, see *Regesta*, iii, no. 271. The expectation that rulers were supposed to respect and protect the church, and maintain peace and justice already had a long history by the twelfth century. See Crouch, *Birth of Nobility*, 71–4.

19 *Historia Novella*, 94–5.

motives in 1141 are suspect. He was immensely powerful and wealthy, and coveted the leadership of the English church.[20] His concern to defend the possessions and liberties of the church, reflected in his opposition to the arrest of the bishops in 1139, was inseparable from a desire to protect his own interests.[21] And the good advice that he considered Stephen was obliged to hearken was probably his own. The conditions on which he gave his allegiance to Stephen were doubtless similar to those on which he gave it to the empress in 1141: 'The empress swore and gave assurance to the bishop that all important business in England, especially gifts of bishoprics and abbacies, should be subject to his control, if he and holy church received her as lady, and he kept his faith to her unbroken.'[22] After abandoning the empress later that year Henry claimed, at the council of Westminster (December 1141), that she had 'persistently broken all her pledges relating to the freedom of the churches' and that 'he had been informed on reliable authority that she and her men had plotted not only against his position, but against his life'.[23] According to Henry, his allegiance to Matilda was conditional upon her maintenance of his administrative and ecclesiastical power, and her protection of the liberty of the church.

Bishop Henry added a further element to the equation. He claimed in December 1141 that 'he had received the empress not of his own will but under compulsion [*necessitate*]', because when Stephen had been captured and the earls had either been put to flight or were waiting to see how things would turn out, the empress had surrounded Winchester with an army.[24] The use of the concept of necessity to justify breaches or changes of allegiance can be found elsewhere. Theobald, archbishop of Canterbury, consulted with the imprisoned king in 1141 about offering his fealty to the empress and received permission 'to change over as the times required [*in necessitatem temporis transirent*]'.[25] Necessity was also used to justify the extent of what a king could expect from his men. At the council of Winchester in 1139 Hugh, archbishop of Rouen, defended Stephen's seizure of the arrested bishops' castles on the grounds that 'either it is unjust, according to canon law, for them to have castles, or, if this is permitted by the king as an act of grace, they ought to yield to the necessities of the time by delivering up the keys'.[26] The relationship between necessity and the rendability of castles is also a feature of the famous *conventio* made by the earls of Chester and Leicester (1148 x 1153), which also shows that both earls envisaged that they might be compelled by necessity to join their liege lords in attacking each other.[27]

---

20 *EEA VIII: Winchester 1070–1204*, ed. M. J. Franklin (Oxford, 1993), xxxv–xlvi.
21 For the arrest of the bishops, see E. J. Kealey, *Roger of Salisbury: Viceroy of England* (Berkeley, 1972), 173–89.
22 *Historia Novella*, 88–9.
23 Ibid., 109–11.
24 Ibid., 108–9.
25 Ibid., 90–1. See also note 45 below.
26 *Historia Novella*, 58–9.
27 F. Stenton, *The First Century of English Feudalism 1066–1166* (2nd edn, Oxford, 1961), 250–3, 286–8; C. Coulson, 'The Castles of the Anarchy', in King, *Anarchy*, 74. See also

A statement made by an envoy of the empress at the council of Westminster in December 1141 complicates matters even further. The envoy said that the bishop of Winchester had given the empress a pledge not to assist Stephen 'unless perchance he sent him twenty knights, but no more'.[28] As Edmund King observed, this resembles some of the terms of the treaty of Dover in 1101 and some of those in the Chester-Leicester *conventio*.[29] Bishop Henry, it appears, made a *conventio* with the empress in 1141; but one which acknowledged the continuance of a military obligation to the imprisoned king.

Viewed against this background, King Stephen's reported exasperation at what he considered to be the disloyalty of some of his own supporters is understandable. It emerges at different times and places, in different sources, sometimes in quoted speech, but has about it a certain consistency. One of the occasions was while Stephen was dealing with disturbances in England after returning from Normandy in 1137: 'The king, it was reported, was often quick to say of his opponents, "When they have chosen me king, why do they abandon me? By the birth of God, I will never be called a king without a throne!" '[30] Another occurred just after Stephen's capture at the battle of Lincoln in February 1141. The king allegedly complained that his opponents 'were not innocent of a monstrous crime in breaking their faith, condemning their oath, caring nothing for the homage they had pledged him, and rebelling so wickedly and abominably against the man they had chosen of their own will as their king and lord'.[31] Similar views were voiced by Stephen at the council of Westminster in December 1141: the king 'laid a complaint before that holy assembly, saying that *his men* had both captured him and had almost killed ... one who had never refused them justice'.[32] And the rebellion in 1147 of one of these men, Gilbert de Clare, earl of Pembroke, is reported to have provoked another comparable outburst. Stephen declared that it was wrong that Gilbert, to whom he had given considerable wealth and promoted to an earldom, had taken up arms against him and was assisting his enemies, and asked 'Where is his faith, his honour, where is the man who should have kept his faith to me unshaken and reckoned any swerving from his devotion to me a brand of infamy? He neither keeps faith to me, *his one and only lord*, nor, while doing this, does he in any wise avoid the shame of public disgrace.'[33] Similar views were expressed elsewhere. During the council of Winchester in April 1141 a letter from the queen was read out begging the attending clergymen, including Henry, bishop of Winchester, 'to restore to the throne that same lord, whom cruel men, *who are at the same time his own men*, have cast into chains'.[34]

Gesta Guillelmi, 28–9, discussed in Strickland, 'Against the Lord's Anointed', 64.

[28] *Historia Novella*, 110–11.

[29] Ibid., 110 note 261.

[30] Ibid., 38–41.

[31] *Gesta Stephani*, 112–15, quotation at 113, 115.

[32] *Historia Novella*, 108–9. My italics. For discussion, see Strickland, 'Against the Lord's Anointed', 59 and notes 15–17.

[33] *Gesta Stephani*, 202–3. My italics.

[34] *Historia Novella*, 94–7. My italics. For similar views, see *Gesta Stephani*, 68–9.

The king and his supporters kept on emphasizing that he was being opposed by his own men and that what these men had done was legally and morally wrongful: it was not just criminal but dishonourable and shameful – concepts central to aristocratic reputation and self-respect.[35] They emphasized the voluntary nature of the acceptance of, and oaths to, Stephen as king, deliberately contrasting this with the oaths to the empress which they claimed were compulsory.[36] They also underlined the wrongfulness of the king's opponents by claiming that Stephen had never refused them justice, one of the principal obligations of a king, or failed to give them the honours and possessions they had asked for, as a good lord should. The case also underlines the contractual nature of the relationship between the king and his men. And some of the terms of the contract suggest further complexities. How and by whom was justice to be defined? What if the granting of possessions to one man led to the dispossession or disinheritance of another? What did the king's reported assertion that he was Gilbert de Clare's one and only lord imply?

The complexities increase when we consider the position and arguments of some of the men about whose lack of allegiance Stephen complained. To begin with those who defeated and captured him at the battle of Lincoln in 1141; they were led by Robert, earl of Gloucester. He had done homage to Stephen in 1136. William of Malmesbury depicts it as conditional: 'namely for as long as the king maintained his rank unimpaired and kept the agreement [*pacta*]'.[37] As Edmund King observed, Robert secured all his demands and did homage ' "Sub conditione quadam": the homage created a contract, and all contracts were conditional. William here emphasized an element of the ceremony of submission that no contemporary would have found remarkable, and which the circumstances of Stephen's accession had served to highlight.'[38] Shortly after 22 May 1138 Robert formally defied Stephen and renounced his homage.[39] William of Malmesbury set out his reasons. The king had unlawfully claimed the kingdom, disregarded the faith he had sworn to Robert, and acted contrary to law in that, after taking the oath to the empress, he 'had not been ashamed to give his hands to another in her lifetime'. Robert had consulted many ecclesiastics who told him that he could not escape 'disgrace, or win blessedness in the life to come' if he broke the oath he had made to Empress Matilda. Robert had also taken note of a papal letter which had bidden him to obey that oath.[40] The break with the king was clearly no easy thing. We have here a list of justifications for it, both legal and moral. It includes unlawfulness, broken faith and oaths, honour, shame, salvation, ecclesiastical advice, papal authority, and obligations to kindred. The credibility of the case, like the credibility of William of Malmesbury's claim that Robert's initial

---

[35] For honour and shame, see Crouch, *Birth of Nobility*, 79–80.
[36] See *Gesta Stephani*, 12–13, 24–5.
[37] *Historia Novella*, 32–3.
[38] Ibid., xliv, xlvi.
[39] Ibid., 40–1.
[40] Ibid., 40–3, quotations at 43. For discussion, see Crouch, *Birth of Nobility*, 60–1.

allegiance to Stephen was a pretence, is questionable.[41] But the arguments were considered worth making, to a knowledgeable audience. They must have had about them a degree of plausibility. They also encapsulated another series of conditions on which allegiance might plausibly have been dependent.

It was one thing to renounce allegiance to the king, another to defeat and capture him in battle. This is what Earl Robert did in 1141. He or his supporters were careful again to justify his actions, despite his *diffidatio*. The arguments are set out by William of Malmesbury. He states that when Robert's son-in-law, Ranulf, earl of Chester, appealed for Robert's help to march against Stephen at Lincoln, Robert was persuaded because 'he could not bear the shame of the situation', 'his noble country, for the sake of two persons, was being tormented by the plunder and slaughter of civil war', and 'the king had wronged his son-in-law who was in no way at fault, was besieging his daughter, and had turned into a castle the church of the Blessed Mother of God at Lincoln'. Considering that it would be 'better to die and fall with glory, rather than bear so signal an affront', and 'for the sake of avenging God and his sister, and to free his relatives', Robert decided to take the risk.[42] Here again we see armed opposition to the king justified by an imperative to act honourably and avoid shame, and by obligations to God, the church, kin, and the peace of the kingdom. Henry of Huntingdon makes Robert articulate some of the same arguments in a speech to his army shortly before the battle of Lincoln. The king, declared Robert, 'has cruelly usurped the realm, contrary to the oaths which he swore to my sister, and by throwing everything into disorder he is the direct cause of the deaths of many thousands' – another indictment of Stephen's failure to maintain peace. Henry has Robert add something else: 'and by his [the king's] example in distributing lands to those who have no legal right, he has plundered those who are in rightful possession. ... he must be attacked first by those who have been wretchedly disinherited'.[43] The losers in this alleged illegal distribution are described as present on the battlefield. They were those whom Stephen had disinherited, and they formed the front line of Robert's army.[44] Disinheritance, whether real or invented, is here depicted as deeply wrongful, as something that justified armed opposition to the king.[45]

Ranulf of Chester appears to have had a more personal agenda than Robert for fighting Stephen at Lincoln.[46] Henry of Huntingdon has him complain that Stephen was a 'treacherous king, who has broken the peace after a truce had been allowed'.[47] It has been suggested that this peace was linked to Stephen's increase

---

41 See Crouch, *Reign of Stephen*, 121.
42 *Historia Novella*, 82–3.
43 *Huntingdon*, 726–9.
44 Ibid., 736–7.
45 Disinheritance could be seen as dishonouring the victim, and resistance to it as not only justified but forced by necessity. See *The Letters and Poems of Fulbert of Chartres*, ed. and trans. F. Behrends (Oxford, 1976), 152–5.
46 P. Dalton, '*In Neutro Latere*: The Armed Neutrality of Ranulf II Earl of Chester in King Stephen's Reign', *ANS*, 14 (1992), 43–5.
47 *Huntingdon*, 726–7.

of Ranulf's honours before the siege of Lincoln at Christmas 1140, and that it was part of a *conventio* involving the grant to Ranulf of rights within the castle and city of Lincoln.[48] The king's peace-breaking without proper notice or procedure is also suggested by William of Malmesbury who states that Stephen's siege of Lincoln castle 'seemed unfair to many because ... he had left them before the [Christmas] festival without any suspicion of ill-will, and had not, in the traditional way, renounced his friendship with them, which is termed defiance'.[49] There are other references to defiance in Stephen's reign, in William of Malmesbury's account of Robert of Gloucester's renunciation of homage to Stephen, and in the Chester-Leicester *conventio*: 'the earl of Leicester may not for any cause or chance lay snares for the person of the earl of Chester unless he has defied him fifteen days before'.[50] It is not inconceivable that Stephen's *conventio* with Ranulf in 1140 contained similar terms. By this time Stephen must have had a reputation for surprise attacks against his own men. He had seized bishops in his court in 1139 and deprived them of their castles, did the same to Eustace fitz John in 1138, and tried to ambush Robert of Gloucester in Normandy in 1137.[51] The upshot, in Robert's case, was a reconciliation resembling a *conventio*. The king swore an oath, formulated by Robert, 'that he would never again take part in so great a crime. And ... added weight to the oath by putting the hand of Hugh, archbishop of Rouen, into Robert's.'[52] Such an oath is not dissimilar from a pledge of peace and truce to Ranulf of Chester or an expectation to provide Ranulf with a fifteen-day warning of intended entrapment. It is also possible that Ranulf regarded Stephen's siege of Lincoln castle as attempted disinheritance. One of the castle towers had been established by Ranulf's mother, Countess Lucy, and the increase of honours he received from Stephen before Christmas 1140 may have included the constableship of the castle in hereditary right.[53]

Disinheritance in relation to castles provoked, or was cited as the justification for, the rebellion of another lord about whose loyalty Stephen complained: Gilbert de Clare, earl of Pembroke. The rebellion occurred in 1147 after Stephen seized Gilbert's nephew, Gilbert fitz Richard, earl of Hertford, and held him until he surrendered his castles. Fitz Richard had given the castles and himself as hostage to the king for the release and good behaviour of his uncle Ranulf of Chester, who had been imprisoned by Stephen in 1146. When Ranulf was released and rebelled, Stephen seized fitz Richard. After his own release fitz Richard joined Ranulf's rebellion. Fitz Richard's uncle, Gilbert, earl of

---

48 Dalton, *'In Neutro Latere'*, 45–7.
49 *Historia Novella*, 82–3.
50 Stenton, *First Century*, 251–2, 287.
51 *Historia Novella*, 38–9, 46–9; *Huntingdon*, 718–23; P. Dalton, 'Eustace fitz John and the Politics of Anglo-Norman England: The Rise and Survival of a Twelfth-Century Royal Servant', *Speculum*, 71 (1996), 368.
52 *Historia Novella*, 38–9.
53 Dalton, *'In Neutro Latere'*, 45–7.

Pembroke, who had been mainly loyal to Stephen, then demanded fitz Richard's castles from the king, 'maintaining that they were his by hereditary right', and, when Stephen refused, also joined Ranulf's rebellion.[54] Stephen condemned the earl of Pembroke as an ungrateful, faithless, and dishonourable man. But David Crouch is probably right to view the earl's actions as patriarchal politics, looking after the landed interests of his family, rather than cynical opportunism.[55] Gilbert had commitments to kin as well as the king. He made his allegiance to Stephen conditional upon the king respecting hereditary possession of castles.

A similar stance was taken by Miles de Beauchamp. Towards the end of 1137 Stephen commanded Miles to hand Bedford castle over to Hugh Poer, promising to compensate Miles for the loss. Miles took the advice of friends to resist the king,[56] and told Stephen that he would happily serve and obey him as long as Stephen did not attempt 'to remove him from a possession that was the patrimonial right of him and his', and that if Stephen was 'really determined to do him this wrong he would endure his anger with what patience he could, but the king would never get the castle until Miles was reduced to the last extremity'.[57] Stephen responded by besieging Bedford castle, against the advice of Henry, bishop of Winchester, whose opposition to the siege was clearly known to Miles. Miles and his men held out until Bishop Henry's arrival five weeks later and then 'submitted to him, and on his advice, which they judged favourable to their interests, and with his help they made peace with the king and surrendered the castle'.[58] Sir Frank Stenton considered that 'In theory the custody of a royal castle must always have been revokable at the king's pleasure', an observation which calls into question Miles's claim of disinheritance.[59] But what matters here is that the claim was made, after taking advice, and seen by some as justified grounds for resistance. And the resistance is interesting in another respect. Stenton went on to note, on the basis of a passage in the *Leges Henrici Primi*, that 'feudal custom expected great forbearance from a man towards his lord'.[60] Read in conjunction with the *Gesta Stephani*, the passage suggests that Miles dealt with the king's aggression according to accepted custom. It states that

> If a lord deprives his man of his land or his fee by virtue of which he is his man, or if he deserts him without cause in his hour of mortal need [*necessitate*], he may forfeit his lordship over him. A man must endure his lord, if he affronts him or does him an injury of that kind, for a period of thirty days in war, or a year and a day in peace; and meanwhile in accordance

---

[54] *Gesta Stephani*, 197–205, quotation at 201.

[55] Crouch, *Reign of Stephen*, 129–30.

[56] *Orderic*, vi, 510–11.

[57] *Gesta Stephani*, 46–9, quotations (the first of which is modified) at 49. See also *Orderic*, vi, 510–11.

[58] *Orderic*, vi, 510–11.

[59] Stenton, *First Century*, 238.

[60] Ibid. For forbearance, see also Crouch, *Birth of Nobility*, 63–6.

with the law he shall privately seek right from him through his peers, neighbours, members of his household, or outsiders.[61]

This closely resembles what happened in practice at Bedford. Miles regarded Stephen as wrongfully depriving him of his patrimony, told the king that he would endure his anger with what patience he could, sought the advice of friends and the mediation of Bishop Henry, and on Henry's advice surrendered Bedford castle and made peace with Stephen about thirty-five days after the conflict began. The advice involved reference to other customs, governing the terms on which castles could be surrendered, to which Miles also adhered. Miles and his men eventually left the castle 'Sub militari igitur conditione'.[62] The siege was lifted, but the conditions governing relations and allegiances between men were harder to escape.

Our sources teem with conditions, or alleged conditions, on which allegiance was promised or secured. The *Gesta Stephani* depicts the magnates devoting themselves to Stephen's service through voluntary oaths and homages after receiving gifts and lands.[63] In the case of certain special and 'very intimate friends of King Henry' the nature of their conditions can be determined in more detail. Henry I had bound these friends to him by affection, enriched them with grants, endowed them with extensive estates, made them his chief officials at court, and appointed them as advocates in every case pleaded there. Stephen duly promised them 'the same favour of friendship and the same lofty position'. But they initially refused to obey him because of their oaths to the empress, because certain noblemen 'grudged their distinction and their splendour', and because they were afraid of being 'overwhelmed before the king by the cries of the poor and the complaints of the widows whose lands they had appropriated'.[64] The conditions implicit here include the retention of power held in the past, and royal protection and legal immunity against threats to that power in the future. Some of these conditions are made explicit, as Edmund King noted, in charters issued by Stephen for one of the individuals concerned, Miles of Gloucester, almost certainly early in January 1136.[65] Grants and confirmations continued to be made by Stephen, the empress, and Henry of Anjou after 1136 and were sometimes very generous. The famous charters for the earls of Chester and Leicester, Geoffrey de Mandeville, Aubrey de Vere, and William de Beauchamp stand out.[66] They are sometimes rivalled by major concessions noted by the chroniclers.[67] And the magnates also demanded substantial conditions from each other.[68]

---

61 *Leges Henrici Primi*, ed. L. J. Downer (Oxford, 1972), 152–3 (translation modified).

62 *Gesta Stephani*, 50.

63 Ibid., 12–13.

64 Ibid., 22–5, quotations at 23, 25.

65 E. King, 'Dispute Settlement in Anglo-Norman England', *ANS*, 14 (1992), 120.

66 *Regesta*, iii, nos. 68, 178–80, 273–6, 437–9, 634–5.

67 See, for example, John of Hexham, *Historia Regum*, in *Symeonis Monachi Opera Omnia*, ed. T. Arnold, 2 vols. (RS, 1882–5), ii, 322–3.

68 See, for example, the grants made by Ranulf, earl of Chester, to Robert, earl of Leicester,

As is now well known, the magnates made conditional agreements (*conventiones*) that could define, qualify or limit their allegiances to each other and their lords.[69] Edmund King has noted that there 'is much discussion in the documents, particularly from those late in the reign, about the constraints upon individuals' freedom of action presented by homage, and it may be that we see a development of the idea of liege homage'. King also observed that *Glanvill*'s comments on homage are reminiscent of terms in the Chester-Leicester *conventio*:[70]

> if it shall be necessary for the earl of Leicester to go upon the earl of Chester with his liege lord, he may not bring with him more than twenty knights ... Neither the earl of Leicester's liege lord nor any other may attack the earl of Chester or his men from the earl of Leicester's castles or his land.[71]

These terms indicate the imposition of serious limitations on the support which the earls' liege lords, the lords to whom they owed most obedience, could expect from them in particular military circumstances.[72] They suggest the existence of other lords to whom the earls were obligated. They betray limited commitment to the leading combatants in the civil war.[73] And they bring us back to Stephen's complaints about the lack of allegiance displayed at the battle of Lincoln. 'In that battle', wrote Orderic Vitalis, 'treachery ran wild. Some of the magnates joined the king with only a handful of their men and sent the main body of their retainers to secure the victory for their adversaries.'[74] Another contemporary saw that battle as one between King Stephen and Earl Ranulf rather than one fought for the English crown.[75] It is against this background that Stephen's reported assertion that he was the one and only lord of his men needs to be understood.

The limitations of baronial commitment to the leading combatants in the civil war is evident again in another *conventio*, the 'alliance of love' agreed probably in 1142 between Robert, earl of Gloucester, and Miles, earl of Hereford, who both supported the empress. The alliance was probably made when Robert was about to visit Geoffrey of Anjou in Normandy and demanding hostages from leading members of the empress's following, whose ability to protect her and whose

---

and Eustace fitz John: *The Charters of the Anglo-Norman Earls of Chester, c. 1071–1237*, ed. G. Barraclough, The Record Society of Lancashire and Cheshire, 126 (1988), nos. 73, 82, 89; Dalton, 'Eustace fitz John', 372–4.

[69] For discussion, see King, 'Dispute Settlement'.

[70] Ibid., 124–5, quotation at 124.

[71] Stenton, *First Century*, 251.

[72] On liege lordship, see also *Leges Henrici Primi*, 152–3; *The Treatise on the Laws and Customs of the Realm of England Commonly Called Glanvill*, ed. G. D. G. Hall (Oxford, 1993), 104.

[73] See also on this: *Historia Novella*, 110–11, 110 note 261.

[74] *Orderic*, vi, 542–3.

[75] Stenton, *First Century*, 243; Crouch, *Reign of Stephen*, 140.

confidence in her cause he doubted.[76] Robert promised Miles 'in faith and on oath' that he would guard Miles 'to the extent of his power without guile, in his life and members and landed honour'. He would help him to maintain his castles, rights, inheritance and tenements, and to acquire the part of his inheritance he lacked. If anyone wished to do ill to Miles or diminish his rights, Robert would 'hold to [Miles] and aid him in faith and to the best of his ability, without guile' and 'not make peace or truces with those who sought to do ill to or diminish Miles without Miles's consent and guarantee'. 'And especially in the war which there now is between the empress and King Stephen [Robert] shall hold with the earl of Hereford and they shall work as one; similarly with all other wars.'[77] The treaty, as David Crouch noted, 'has very little to say about the ideological struggle between king and empress in which [the two earls] were engaged, other than that they intended to "be as one" ... in fighting it; a strikingly ambiguous endorsement'.[78] Robert and Miles spoke of the war in almost a detached way, as one between the empress and King Stephen. They made it clear that there were other wars in England, in which they were or might become involved, distinct from the one being fought for the crown. And they recognized Stephen's royal title. The alliance reflects a magnate neutralism, a lack of full commitment to the cause of either Stephen or the empress, and a prioritization of self-interest and local needs that Crouch argues is first traceable in 1140 and grew thereafter until 1148 'when the magnates ceased to listen to Devizes and Westminster, and began to manage their own relations with little reference to partisan objectives'.[79] It also shows, especially in its elaborate security clauses, that the two earls had little trust for one another, despite their shared allegiance to the empress and Miles's homage and fealty to Robert.[80]

There are reasons for questioning the allegiance of some of the magnates to Stephen and the empress earlier than 1140. Some of them are to be found in the accounts of the battle of the Standard in 1138. The northern barons who opposed the Scots were about to capitulate until Thurstan, archbishop of York, inspired them by his speech and counsel.[81] Forced to choose between his loyalty to Stephen and his loyalty to King David of Scots, one of these barons, Robert de Brus, lord of lands in northern England and Annandale in Galloway, renounced his homage to David.[82] But one of Robert's sons fought on the Scottish side at the battle of the Standard, and Robert's lordship of Annandale duly descended in the line of this

76 *Historia Novella*, 122–5.
77 R. H. C. Davis, 'The Treaty between William Earl of Gloucester and Roger Earl of Hereford', in *A Medieval Miscellany for Doris Mary Stenton*, ed. P. M. Barnes and C. F. Slade, Pipe Roll Society, ns, 36 (1960), 145–6; *Earldom of Gloucester Charters*, ed. R. B. Patterson (Oxford, 1973), no. 95.
78 Crouch, *Reign of Stephen*, 235.
79 Ibid., 118, 133, quotation at 233.
80 *Historia Novella*, 62–3 and note 144; *Regesta*, iii, no. 391.
81 Richard of Hexham, *De Gestis*, 160.
82 Ibid., 161–2; John of Hexham, *Historia*, 293; Ailred of Rievaulx, *Relatio de Standardo*, in Howlett, *Chronicles*, iii, 192–5.

son thereafter.[83] Divided allegiances of this kind emerge even earlier, at the siege of Exeter in 1136 which occurred after Baldwin de Redvers seized the castle. Members of the besieged garrison, dying of thirst, intended to seek advice from those who had inspired Baldwin to resist Stephen 'who were then serving in the king's army with treacherous designs, tell them privately of the troubles that afflicted them within' and surrender the castle 'under a safe conduct for the garrison'.[84] When Stephen refused the garrison's appeal to be allowed to surrender and leave the castle unharmed, some of Stephen's barons 'were bitterly aggrieved for their relations who were shut up within ... others, accomplices and helpers in Baldwin's rebellion, were highly indignant at so determined a siege of their sympathizers'.[85] The rift between besieged and besiegers was bridged by ties and obligations of blood and possibly by other bonds of allegiance. Those in Stephen's camp who favoured the garrison sought to diminish the rift further by complicated arguments. They claimed that the besieged 'had not sworn allegiance to the king's majesty, and had taken up arms only in fealty to their lord; indeed could not show they were dealing directly with the king except by handing over to him what was his by right.' They considered it 'wiser and more to the advantage of the kingdom' to end the siege.[86] Arguments about the advantage or state of the kingdom we have met before. But there are other ideas here which seek to excuse, if not to justify, armed resistance and to place limitations on the allegiance the king could expect from his subjects. At Exeter in 1136 they won the day; Stephen allowed the garrison to go free. Henry of Huntingdon was unimpressed. Stephen, he wrote, 'taking the very worst advice ... did not execute punishment on those who had betrayed him'.[87] It was to be a different story at the siege of Shrewsbury two years later. This time the resistant garrison was executed.[88]

The commitment of some of the magnates to the principal combatants appears even more doubtful when we consider the frequency with which sieges and campaigns were downgraded, curtailed, or aborted because of magnate advice or lack of resolve. The most famous examples, towards the end of the reign, were admirably discussed by R. H. C. Davis in his chapter 'The Magnates' Peace', and require no further comment here.[89] But the phenomenon can be traced throughout the reign, from the siege of Exeter onwards.[90] There were, of course, good reasons for magnates to avoid sieges or battles, and some of the advice they gave to Stephen and the empress to avoid or limit combat was undoubtedly informed by

---

83 G. W. S. Barrow, *The Anglo-Norman Era in Scottish History* (Oxford, 1980), 12, 18; A. A. M. Duncan, *Scotland: The Making of the Kingdom* (Edinburgh, 1992), 140, 370 and note 4.
84 *Gesta Stephani*, 30–41, quotations at 41; Crouch, *Reign of Stephen*, 45.
85 *Gesta Stephani*, 42–3. On divided allegiance more generally, see Strickland, 'Against the Lord's Anointed', 74–7.
86 Ibid.
87 *Huntingdon*, 708–9.
88 *Orderic*, vi, 520–3; *John of Worcester*, iii, 250–1.
89 Davis, *King Stephen*, 115, 117–18.
90 See, for example, *Gesta Stephani*, 64–9, 80–3, 88–9, 90–3, 96–7, 102–5, 172–5; Richard of Hexham, *De Gestis*, 160; *Orderic*, vi, 540–1.

genuine military or strategic considerations.[91] But some of it, as at Exeter, is condemned as treacherous. Those who advised Stephen not to besiege Bristol in 1138 are described as men 'who only pretended to serve the king and rather favoured the earl [Robert of Gloucester]'.[92] Stephen's decision to allow the empress to leave Arundel in 1139 is attributed by Henry of Huntingdon either to his trusting treacherous advice or to his thinking that the castle was impregnable.[93] The advice was given, according to the *Gesta Stephani*, by Henry, bishop of Winchester, after Henry, according to popular report, met and ratified 'a compact of peace and friendship' with the earl of Gloucester without Stephen's knowledge.[94] Stephen abandoned the siege of Trowbridge in 1139 'on the advice of his counsellors', as some of his barons 'were grievously irked by the wearisome delay, and the service of others was merely pretence and treachery', and all feared that Robert of Gloucester might attack them.[95]

The frequency with which military confrontations were avoided or limited and the suspect loyalty of some of the magnates raise questions about the extent to which intelligence flowed between the two warring camps. Stephen's reign features less prominently than that of his Anglo-Norman predecessors in John Prestwich's important article on military intelligence under the Norman and Angevin kings.[96] Prestwich's comments on Stephen's reign focus mainly on the failure, limitations or ignorance of military intelligence, including two examples of intelligence leaks: the betrayal of the military plans of William of Ypres and Waleran of Meulan to Geoffrey of Anjou by Robert de Courcy in Normandy in 1138, and (possibly) the last-minute warning given by one of the Londoners to the empress which enabled her to escape from London in 1141.[97] Prestwich also astutely observed that although

> It is possible to construct a long list of the leading participants in the civil war showing the dates at which they supported Stephen or the empress and her son, Henry of Anjou ... this ignores the force of William of Newburgh's observation that the kingdom merely seemed to be divided in two, since neither the king nor the empress was in full control of the respective factions, each becoming involved in the military enterprises of their followers.[98]

As we have seen, this division was bridged by a multitude of ties, springing in part from the complexities and limitations of allegiance, along which correspondence, information, and secrets could flow.

---

91 For example, see *Gesta Stephani*, 90–3, 102–5, 172–3.
92 Ibid., 64–7, quotation at 67.
93 *Huntingdon*, 722–3.
94 *Gesta Stephani*, 88–9.
95 Ibid., 96–7.
96 J. O. Prestwich, 'Military Intelligence under the Norman and Angevin Kings', in *Law and Government*, 1–30.
97 Ibid., 14–17, 27.
98 Ibid., 14.

And flow they did, despite the fact that endangering a lord by betraying his secrets could be seen as a breach of fealty.[99] Stephen's attempt to capture Robert of Gloucester in Normandy in 1137 was thwarted because the plan was secretly divulged to Robert.[100] When Stephen returned to England later that year, he was informed of a secret plot to kill the Normans and transfer the government of England to the Scots.[101] Robert of Gloucester's decision to renounce his homage to Stephen in 1138 possibly leaked from his camp, since rumours of his impending defiance were circulating in England before it happened.[102] In 1139 Stephen lifted the siege of Corfe castle 'because he had heard' that the empress and Robert of Gloucester were about to arrive in England.[103] In 1140 when Robert was marching to engage the king, who was returning from Cornwall, Stephen was secretly notified of this and had time to marshal his men for battle.[104] Robert's difficulties in concealing his military objectives are revealed again during his march from Gloucester to Lincoln in 1141: he kept 'the whole army in uncertainty, except for a very few, by taking an indirect route'. It was only when his army confronted that of Stephen at the River Trent that Robert disclosed his intentions to Ranulf, earl of Chester.[105] Later that year Henry, bishop of Winchester, informed the council of Westminster that 'he had been informed on reliable authority' that the empress and her supporters were plotting against him.[106] In 1142 the proceedings of a secret conference convened by the empress at Devizes were 'so far made public that it was known all her adherents approved sending for the count of Anjou'.[107] In the early 1150s Stephen was aware of the duplicitous dealings of Roger, earl of Hereford, and the intention of Henry of Anjou to return to England.[108] It is clear, moreover, that individual barons and townsmen had their own intelligence networks.[109]

As well as the passage of intelligence, other unauthorized communication occurred between the two camps. The bishop of Winchester's meeting with Robert of Gloucester near Arundel in 1139 has already been mentioned. It looks even more sinister in the light of the claims made by an envoy of the empress in 1141 that she had been brought to England by letters from Bishop Henry who was also chiefly responsible for Stephen's capture and imprisonment.[110] There is evidence that the lord and lady of Arundel, William d'Aubigny and his wife

---

99   See, for example, *Letters and Poems of Fulbert of Chartres*, 90–3.
100 *Historia Novella*, 38–9.
101 *Orderic*, vi, 494–5.
102 *Historia Novella*, 40–1.
103 *Gesta Stephani*, 84–5. See also *Historia Novella*, 44–5.
104 *Gesta Stephani*, 104–5.
105 *Historia Novella*, 84–5.
106 Ibid., 110–11.
107 Ibid., 122–3.
108 *Gesta Stephani*, 228–31.
109 *The Book of the Foundation of Walden Monastery*, ed. and trans. D. Greenway and L. Watkiss (Oxford, 1999), 16–17; *Gesta Stephani*, 62–5.
110 *Historia Novella*, 110–11.

Queen Adeliza, and Miles of Gloucester were also involved in the communica-tions.[111] As David Crouch noted, the choice of Arundel as a landing point was no accident and Adeliza may have hoped to act as a peace-broker.[112] The *Gesta Stephani* claims that Roger, bishop of Salisbury, secretly promised to maintain his faith to the empress and Robert of Gloucester and to give them his help and his castles on their arrival in England, and was in receipt of frequent messages from them.[113] The unauthorized passage of information might also explain the empress's successful escape from Oxford in 1142, which some chroniclers could hardly believe.[114]

In conclusion, it is understandable, in light of the discussion above, why King Stephen complained, possibly with some regularity, about the lack of allegiance of some of those he considered to be his own men. Allegiance could be compro-mised or qualified, or represented as such, in a complex variety of ways: by the conditions on which it was first agreed; by loyalties to other lords, kin, and family possessions (especially hereditary possessions), friends, neighbours, men with shared interests or regional power, and *conventio*-partners; by responsibilities to God, the peace and stability of the realm, the majesty of the crown, the liberty of the church, and the honour and reputation of one's person and family; by the dictates of necessity; and by self-interest and personal ambition. It is hardly surprising, in these circumstances, that allegiance was a matter of interpretation, debate, and dispute. The magnates often appear deeply concerned to justify their actions, legally and morally, and to be seen to be behaving honourably rather than shamefully.[115] In some cases appearances probably reflected reality;[116] in others they were undoubtedly deceptive. The problems arising from the complexities and limitations of allegiance probably increased as the reign progressed, but were also present early on. They can be seen at Exeter in 1136, and Stephen was already complaining about them soon afterwards. The situation was exacerbated by an atmosphere of uncertainty, fear and suspicion manifest in Stephen's seizures or attempted seizures of magnates, and in the anxieties about plots to overthrow the Norman regime which brought him back from Normandy to England in 1137.[117] We need to bear in mind in all this that Stephen's position as a focus of loyalty was, from the outset of the reign, far from secure. However much Stephen and his supporters tried to defend his actions, the accusation that he was a perjurer gave his opponents grounds to resist him. Against this background, the

111 Ibid., 60–1 and 60 note 139.
112 Crouch, *Reign of Stephen*, 107–10, at 107, 109.
113 *Gesta Stephani*, 72–3. The claim is questionable.
114 Ibid., 142–5; *Historia Novella*, 132–3.
115 For self-justification, see Crouch, *Reign of Stephen*, 124.
116 Brian fitz Count's response to the suggestion of the bishop of Winchester that he was unfaithful seethes with genuine indignation, and there is other evidence indicating that Brian was tenaciously loyal to the empress. See H. W. C. Davis, 'Henry of Blois and Brian Fitz-Count', *EHR*, 25 (1910), 300–3; E. King, 'The Memory of Brian fitz Count', *HSJ*, 13 (2004), 75–98.
117 *Orderic*, vi, 494–5.

complaints about the treachery of Stephen's own men to their one and only lord may appear naive or dishonest. But they are not dissimilar from those of some modern politicians who seek to deal with opposition within their own ranks by simplifying or polarising issues of loyalty. They are another reflection of the complexities, ambiguities, limitations, and other difficulties of allegiance confronting Stephen and many other lords during the nineteen years when Christ and His saints slept.

6

English Monasteries and the Continent in the Reign of King Stephen

JANET BURTON

For at that time when all the vitality of the king's power had waned, the powerful men of the kingdom were setting up fortifications as best each could to defend their followers or to invade the territory of others. So while evils sprouted and abounded in this way through the laxity of King Stephen, or rather through the malice of the devil who always nurtures disagreements, the wise and salutary provision of the great King over-flowed, and was splendidly in evidence. To overcome the king of pride, the King of peace is known to have built for himself at that time more intensively than usual fortifications befitting him. In short, many more monasteries of servants and handmaids of God are known to have been founded in England during the brief period when Stephen reigned – or rather, held the title of king – than in the hundred years previously.[1]

THIS PASSAGE was written by William of Newburgh in his *Historia Rerum Anglicarum*, compiled in the 1190s at the Augustinian priory of Newburgh in Yorkshire. William was not the only one to notice the outburst of monastic foun-dations in Stephen's reign and to link it to the chaos of the period. It is often the Cistercians, who arrived in Britain in the last years of the reign of Henry I, who attract attention, but this was indeed a notable period of expansion for other groups: the congregation of Savigny, the Augustinian canons, and, often unno-ticed in this context, houses of religious women. The purpose of this paper is to set a discussion of developments in the monastic order in the context of the political relationship between England and the wider world, and in particular the conflicts between Stephen and the empress and her allies, leading to the loss of Normandy in 1144. My purpose is therefore to investigate how political events and trends affected the monastic order in England, and, conversely, the influence of monastic houses and orders on political developments. Within these broad

---

[1] *Newburgh*, i, 53; translated in William of Newburgh, *The History of English Affairs*, trans. P. G. Walsh and M. J. Kennedy (Warminster, 1994), 79.

political concerns this paper develops two main themes: the order of Savigny in England and Wales and its patrons, and the evidence for the operation of the Cistercian order as an international institution and the significance of its contacts outside England.

Let us start with the figure of Stephen, and with an event that took place over ten years before he became king. In 1124 he brought monks from the reformed abbey of Savigny (Manche) in his county of Mortain on the borders of Brittany, Normandy and Maine to found a house at Tulketh in Lancashire; in 1127 the monks moved to Furness. This was the first Savigniac house in England, and by 1147 Savigny had twelve more abbeys in England and Wales and one on the Isle of Man. Most colonization was direct from the Norman abbey. Eight houses – Neath (1130), Basingwerk (1131), Quarr (1132), Combermere (1133), Stratford Langthorne (1135), Buildwas (1135), Buckfast (1136) and Coggeshall (1140) – were founded from Savigny. Two of these, Buckfast and Coggeshall, were royal foundations, the first by King Stephen and the second by Queen Matilda. Rushen on the Isle of Man (1134), Swineshead (1135), and Calder I (1135) and Calder II (1142–3) were colonized from Furness. Jervaulx, which was not yet in 1147 an official Savigniac abbey, was assigned in 1150 as a daughter house of Byland.[2]

By far the best documented of these abbeys are Byland and Jervaulx. Their late twelfth-century *Historia Fundationis* sheds valuable light on the relationship between the houses of the order in England and the mother house, as well as the merger between the Savigniacs and the Cistercians.[3] The *Historia* was composed at Byland in 1197 by its third abbot, Philip, formerly abbot of Lannoy, and he was following what was by then an established Cistercian tradition of recording the origins and early history of his house. It is narrative interspersed in a manner not unlike the Cistercian *Exordium Parvum* with charters and letters.[4] The reason Philip gives for compiling the text is a conventional one – again in the tradition of the *Exordium Parvum* – to record for future generations of monks how the foundation came about. However the dominant theme in both parts of the work, that relating to Byland and that relating to Jervaulx, is affiliation.

The chronology of the expansion of the English congregation of Savigny, so often overshadowed by the success of the White Monks, bears testimony to the rapid diffusion of ideas among monastic founders. In the case of the English and Welsh houses of Savigny these were drawn from a tight network among the baronial and knightly classes surrounding the earl of Chester and the bishop of

---

2   For the foundation dates of these houses see D. Knowles and R. N. Hadcock, *Medieval Religious Houses: England and Wales* (2nd edn, Cambridge, 1971).

3   The *Historia* survives only in a seventeenth-century manuscript, Oxford, Bodleian Library MS Dodsworth 63, and was printed in two sections in *Monasticon*, v, 349–54 and 568–74. It is newly edited and translated in J. Burton, *The Foundation History of the Abbeys of Byland and Jervaulx*, Borthwick Texts and Studies, 35 (York, 2006).

4   For the most recent edition of this key Cistercian text, see *Narrative and Legislative Texts from Early Cîteaux*, ed. C. Waddell, *Commentaria Cisterciensia*, Studia et Documenta, 9 (Turnhout, 1999), 199–259 and 416–40.

Coventry and Lichfield.[5] Yet it was a full ten years after its own foundation that Furness seized the opportunity refused by Cistercian Rievaulx to establish what was its first daughter house on the Isle of Man at Rushen. The following year, 1135, Furness sent out a second colony, to Calder in Cumbria. However in 1138 the monks of Calder were forced to abandon the house because of damage sustained during a Scottish raid. The monks attempted to return to Furness but were refused entry, and set off across the Pennines to seek the advice of Archbishop Thurstan of York. Here is our first problem. Why, in such extraordinary circumstances, were refugee monks refused entry at their mother house? Abbot Philip of Byland recorded two oral traditions. One is that the monks of Furness were not willing to share their resources with their former colleagues. The other was that it was not appropriate to have two convents with two abbots under one roof.[6] One suspects that there was rather more behind this, and I think we may find the explanation in the political and tenurial situation in Cumbria in the late 1130s. Calder I was founded by Ranulf Meschin, lord of Copeland, at around the time of the death of his father, William, possibly on his succession to his estates. Ranulf himself died some time between 1135 and 1140, and Paul Dalton has argued convincingly that his death probably occurred shortly after the devastation, in 1137–8, of his lands in Cumbria and Lancashire by William fitz Duncan, nephew of the Scottish king.[7] William fitz Duncan then consolidated his position in the area by marrying one of Ranulf's sisters and co-heiresses, Alice de Rumilly.[8] Thus, the political and tenurial realignment in the region meant that the monks of Calder I could not do what monasteries often did in such circumstances, and look to their lay patron for assistance. It was into this void that Archbishop Thurstan of York stepped. He secured for the monks of Calder I the patronage of

5 Richard de Granville, founder of Neath Abbey, was a knight of Robert of Gloucester, illegitimate son of Henry I. Ranulf de Gernons, earl of Chester, founder of Basingwerk, was one of the mightiest of Henry I's landowners, with estates in England and Normandy, *The Charters of the Anglo-Norman Earls of Chester, c. 1071–1237*, ed. G. Barraclough, The Record Society of Lancashire and Cheshire, 126 (1988), nos. 36–8. Hugh Malbank (d. 1135) founded Combermere with the assent of his lord, that same Ranulf, earl of Chester, and of Bishop Roger de Clinton of Coventry, *Monasticon*, v, 323–4. Both men were witnesses to Hugh's foundation charter and the bishop added his episcopal seal to the document. Bishop Roger himself founded Buildwas and King Stephen's charter of confirmation stated that the bishop had granted the site of Buildwas 'coram me', *Regesta*, iii, no. 132. It was from Combermere that Robert, butler of Earl Ranulf, drew a colony to staff Poulton Abbey (later removed to Dieulacres), founded 'pro salute et incolumnitate domini mei perfulgentissimi Cestrensis comitis Ranulfi', *Monasticon*, v, 628; 'The Chartulary of Dieulacres Abbey', ed. G. Wrottesley, in *Collections for a History of Staffordshire*, ns, 9 (1906), 293–365, at 329–30.
6 Burton, *History of Byland and Jervaulx*, 1–3.
7 P. Dalton, *Conquest, Anarchy and Lordship: Yorkshire, 1066–1154* (Cambridge, 1994), 207, 211–13, and, on the Scots in the north in general, 196–230.
8 Ibid., 212–13; P. Dalton, 'Northern England in King Stephen's Reign', in *Studies in Northern History*, ed. J. E. Hollinshead and F. Pogson (Liverpool, 1997), 1–35, at 15–16, 18.

Gundreda de Gournay and her son, Roger de Mowbray, who had just attained his majority. They were given the site of a hermitage at Hood, at that time occupied by Robert d'Alneto, a relative of Gundreda and a monk of Whitby. This was a stroke of good fortune. However, within a monastic order that had a sense of hierarchy, there remained a constitutional problem.[9] What was the status of Hood? Could Furness really still claim to be its mother house? This was clearly an issue that exercised Abbot Gerald of Hood. At the Savigniac general chapter of 1141 he formally asked that Hood be reckoned as a daughter house of Savigny, thereby tying it more closely to the continental mother house. His request was granted. Abbot Philip, author of the *Historia*, explained Gerald's actions in terms of his fear that the growing prosperity of Hood would lead to resumption by Furness of its rights as a mother house. What the reaction of the monks of Furness was at that time is not recorded. However, it may have been the tension generated by these events that prompted the abbot of Savigny to secure a charter of confirmation from King Stephen, reaffirming that Furness had been granted to Savigny and was subject to it.[10] This suggests a need on the part of Savigny to reassert its authority over Furness. Abbot Gerald's action shifted the abbey of Hood out of the orbit of Stephen's foundation, and Furness seems to have accepted that the move to Yorkshire was a permanent one, for after the monks had moved to their second site of Old Byland in 1142 a further colony was dispatched from Furness to reoccupy the site of Calder.[11]

R. H. C. Davis commented on Gerald's request that Hood be subject to Savigny rather than Furness but mistakenly assigned it to the chapter of 1147 rather than that of 1141. He linked it to Stephen's cooling towards the order of Savigny after the fall of western Normandy to Geoffrey of Anjou in 1142.[12] Indeed it may have been as early as 1144 that Duke Geoffrey issued charters for Savigny.[13] But even though he was mistaken about the date, I am sure that Davis was correct to say that there was a political impetus behind the successful attempt to disengage Hood from Furness. As told by the Byland *Historia* the initiative came from Abbot Gerald. However it may also have come from Hood's patron, Roger de Mowbray, young as he was. From the time he came of age in 1138 Roger suffered territorial losses, in the north of England to David of Scotland and in Normandy to Geoffrey of Anjou.[14] A major blow came in January 1141, when

9   The order had only very recently (in 1132, according to the *Vita* of Abbot Geoffrey of Savigny) introduced the system of visitation and general chapter that characterized the Cistercian order. Visitation implied a hierarchy of mother and daughter houses. See C. Holdsworth, 'The Affiliation of Savigny', in *Truth as Gift: Studies in Honour of John R. Sommerfeldt*, ed. M. Dutton, D. M. LaCorte and P. Lockey, Cistercian Studies Series, 204 (Kalamazoo, 2004), 43–88, at 55–6.

10 *Regesta*, iii, no. 803, where dated between August 1138 and 1143.

11 This abbey was known as Calder II.

12 Davis, *King Stephen*, 100.

13 *Regesta*, iii, nos. 807–8.

14 *Charters of the Honour of Mowbray 1107–1191*, ed. D. E. Greenway, Records of Social and Economic History, ns, 1 (London, 1972), xxvi–xxviii. See also J. Burton, '*Fundator noster*:

Roger was captured at the battle of Lincoln by Ranulf, earl of Chester. In 1142 or 1143 Roger married, and his bride was Alice de Gant, sister of Gilbert de Gant, an uneasy ally of the earl of Chester. So at about the time Abbot Gerald was setting in motion the process of distancing his community from King Stephen's abbey, and affiliating it direct to the mother house of the order, now in Angevin hands, Roger himself was being drawn more firmly into the Angevin camp, particularly the network around the earl of Chester. The two processes may be related. Roger de Mowbay and Abbot Gerald removed Byland from affiliation to an abbey in royal patronage to close association with one in the control of Duke Geoffrey of Anjou.

It is clear from the account in the Byland *Historia* that, although the Savigniac general chapter was a fairly recent innovation, its responsibilities included deciding matters of affiliation and settling or preventing disputes. We have other glimpses of its operation. Abbot Roger, who succeeded Gerald in 1142, is recorded as having attended the chapter of 1147. There he complained about the troubles caused for his abbey by certain of his neighbours, and pleaded for the chapter's support for the small community settled at Fors in Wensleydale.[15] However, that only the abbots of Quarr and Neath attended that chapter with Abbot Roger of Byland confirms other evidence that suggests that the control of the abbot of Savigny over the British houses was weak.[16] This is evident from the early history of Jervaulx, established in 1145. This is how the second section of Abbot Philip's *Historia* begins:

> In the time of King Stephen, who succeeded Henry I in the kingdom of England, there was a certain knight of noble family named Acaris son of Bardolf, a great landowner in the county of Yorkshire. Inspired by divine grace, this man gave to a monk serving God, Peter de Quinciaco, who was well experienced and very knowledgeable in the skills of medicine, and to other monks of Savigny, a certain portion of his land in Wensleydale … There the said Brother Peter and his companions began, as best they could, to establish a new abbey and to construct simple buildings.

The author adds:

> In this location the monks repeatedly suffered difficulties and hardships. It is uncertain how or for what reason Brother Peter and his other companions came from Savigny to England. Some believe that Peter was staying at the court of Alan, count of Brittany and Richmond, for the purpose of treating the sick and wounded or to collect alms in the hall and distribute them to the needy.[17]

Roger de Mowbray as a Founder and Patron of Monasteries', in *Religious and Laity in Western Europe, 1000–1400: Interaction, Negotiation and Power*, ed. E. Jamroziak and J. Burton (Turnhout, 2006), 23–39.

[15] Burton, *History of Byland and Jervaulx*, 21–2.

[16] Ibid., 41–2.

[17] Ibid., 36.

This glimpse of a handful of monks in the household of the count of Brittany and Richmond is an intriguing snapshot of monastic life on the fringes. What the *Historia* gives us is an account of the pre-history of a monastic foundation so often missing from the documentary record. Earl Alan visited Savigny shortly before his death and granted the new house to it. The abbot's reaction is instructive. We are told that Abbot Serlo received it 'unwillingly and grudgingly'. Moreover,

> Peter, a zealous supporter of that new foundation, waited very eagerly, day in day out, for an abbot with a convent to arrive from the monastery of Savigny. Very often he wrote to his abbot, requesting him to send an abbot and a convent to him, to live there throughout the generations. But the abbot of Savigny turned over in his mind the dangers, hardships and deprivations suffered by his monks, who had been sent from Savigny to various other places in England to begin and construct abbeys and who had very often begged him to bring them home again ... He swore very angrily by the virtue of the Holy Trinity, in whose honour the church of Savigny had been founded, that he never wanted to send a convent there. He said that he would be very pleased if he could be completely relieved of and freed from the grant of that place for good and all. He wrote back to Brother Peter, telling him that he had acted very foolishly in that he and his companions had founded an abbey without asking the advice of the house of Savigny.[18]

That was in 1145. Two years later, at the 1147 chapter that preceded the merger with Cîteaux, Serlo reconsidered the matter at the request of Abbot Roger. The decision of the chapter was that Jervaulx should become a daughter house of Byland because 'of the congregation in England Byland was the nearest abbey to Jervaulx', but before this could take place a formal inspection of the site of the abbey and its resources was to be made by the abbot of Quarr – a process very much reflecting Cistercian practice.[19]

This brings us to the merger with Cîteaux and the impact this had on the English congregations of both orders. In her controversial book, *The Cistercian Evolution*, Constance Berman suggested that the merger did not take place in 1147 as traditionally thought; indeed, she argues that the Cistercian order as we know it was a product of the second half of the twelfth century.[20] Berman dismisses the date of 1147 for the merger – the only evidence for which she believes to be the Book of St Gilbert written *c.* 1202 – as a 'retrospective choice ... that [has] more to do with politics in the Anglo-Norman realm than the

---

[18] Ibid., 40–1.

[19] Ibid., 41–2. For the stipulation that the site of a prospective abbey should be shown to the two closest abbots see Waddell, *Narrative and Legislative Texts*, 337, 468. This institute belongs to series B, which Waddell suggests might have been drawn up in the brief abbacy of Guy I (1133–4): ibid., 299.

[20] C. H. Berman, *The Cistercian Evolution: The Invention of a Religious Order in Twelfth-Century Europe* (Philadelphia, 2000), 143.

Cistercians'.[21] Her arguments as a whole have not received universal acceptance.[22] Equally unconvincing is her suggestion that Alexander of Cologne, who
was elected abbot of Savigny in 1158 from the position of abbot of Grandselve, a
daughter house of Clairvaux, masterminded the merger.[23] Berman evidently did
not consult the Byland *Historia*. Had she done so, she would have found several
references to the merger, some linking it to 1147. Abbot Philip wrote: 'In this year
[1148] at the Council of Reims under the presidency of Pope Eugenius III the
church of Savigny with its thirteen daughter abbeys subjected itself to the church
of Clairvaux and the order of Cîteaux'. These thirteen houses are specifically the
English and Welsh houses. Abbot Philip also stated that after 1147 Abbot Serlo

> sent letters with Lord Guy his prior to all his family throughout England.
> He ordered them, on apostolic authority, to take and maintain the consti-
> tutions and habit of the Cistercian order, as Pope Eugenius had, in his
> general council at Reims in the year of our lord 1148, ordered all the
> Savigniac houses to do.[24]

There seem to be no grounds for rejecting the traditional date of 1147 for the
merger between the two orders, which was ratified in 1148. Indeed to accept those
dates makes sense of what happened both before and after. Before 1147 we have a
picture of a group of houses in England and Wales derived at one or two divides
from a continental house, Savigny. Constitutionally they were held together by a
system of visitation and by an annual general chapter. However, as we have seen
there are indications that the system was under strain. This is suggested by the
passage quoted earlier, which gives evidence of Serlo's unwillingness to see more
colonies sent to England, and his reference to the problems of those who had
settled there. Robert of Torigny confirms that Abbot Serlo of Savigny encountered difficulties in controlling his English and Welsh houses. I am sure that
Davis was correct to point out that political difficulties after 1142 exacerbated
Serlo's task, and hampered access to the general chapter. As Davis astutely
pointed out, those three abbots who attended in 1147 all had patrons with
Angevin sympathies and presumably had no qualms about venturing into what
was by then Angevin territory.[25] However, the refusal – as early as 1138 – of the

---

21 Ibid., 148.
22 See, for instance, the detailed account of the merger of the two orders in C. Holdsworth,
    'The Affiliation of Savigny'.
23 This proposition would mean that we have to see a Cistercian abbot being elected as head of
    a non-Cistercian house, Savigny, which I find difficult to accept, and which would have
    gone counter to the *Carta Caritatis*. See Waddell, *Narrative and Legislative Texts*, 261–82
    and 441–50. Chapter 11 stated that abbots were not to be elected from non-Cistercian
    houses.
24 Burton, *History of Byland and Jervaulx*, 23, 45.
25 Davis, *King Stephen*, 100. The patrons of Neath and Quarr were, respectively, Richard de
    Granville, a knight of Earl Robert of Gloucester, half brother of the empress, and Baldwin
    de Redvers, earl of Devon. As Christopher Holdsworth remarks: 'For some Savigniac
    abbots … the prospect of attending the General Chapter between 1142 and 1147 meant that

Furness monks to readmit those of Calder I, and the rather chaotic foundation of Jervaulx, together hint at wider problems. After 1147 there was further trouble with Furness, and the attitude of the abbot and monks of Furness seems pivotal. In 1148 Pope Eugenius appointed Hugh, archbishop of Rouen, and Arnulf, bishop of Lisieux, as papal judges delegate to hear the case between the abbot of Savigny and Peter, abbot, and the monks of Furness. Archbishop Hugh wrote to Abbot Peter and the convent stating that Peter had failed to attend a meeting at Martinmas 1148, but that Abbot Serlo of Savigny had appeared and had offered convincing evidence that Furness was a daughter house of Savigny. The archbishop therefore ordered Peter to desist from rebellion.[26] It seems that Furness may have resisted the imposition of Cistercian customs and had been claiming independence from Savigny. It is instructive here to recall that Furness's patron was King Stephen, that in March 1147 a Cistercian pope had deprived Stephen's archbishop of York of his see, and that in December 1147 a Cistercian abbot, Henry Murdac, had been elected archbishop in his place. All this reinforces the point that monastic patronage and political loyalties were not easily separated.

Within a few years, in the aftermath of the merger, Furness renewed its claim to jurisdiction over Byland, and it is compelling to see in these episodes a royal abbey trying to break free from continental ties and establish its own northern family. The removal of Abbot Peter to the abbacy of Quarr around 1150 may have been part of a strategy of containment.[27] It was also in 1150 that we have a recorded visit to England of Abbot Serlo of Savigny for which the *Historia* is again the source, and letters ordering enforcement of Cistercian observances. On his visit to England in 1150 Serlo heard the renunciation by the abbot of Calder II of his claim to Byland. While he was in the country he confirmed Jervaulx as a daughter house of Byland, and he attested a further charter for Jervaulx, evidently issued in Richmondshire.[28] Serlo is also recorded at Crediton in Devon, where he received from Bishop Robert of Exeter a charter restoring land to Savigny's daughter house of Buckfast.[29] The abbot was clearly visiting his English and Welsh houses and bringing them into line to accept the merger and probably enforcing Cistercian observances. It was not always an easy task, for it was not until 1155 that Furness's claim over Byland was finally rejected, when Ailred of

---

they would be crossing into a part of the world controlled by a potentially hostile power' (Holdsworth, 'Affiliation of Savigny', 59).

[26] L. Delisle, 'Documents Relative to the Abbey of Furness, Extracted from the Archives of the Abbey of Savigny', *Journal of the British Archaeological Association*, 6 (1851), 419–24; Burton, *History of Byland and Jervaulx*, xxviii and 45.

[27] For the renewed claims of Furness, see Burton, *History of Byland and Jervaulx*, 28–32. On Peter's removal, see *The Heads of Religious Houses: England and Wales I, 940–1215*, ed. D. Knowles, C. N. L. Brooke, and V. C. M. London (2nd edn, Cambridge, 2001), 134, 139; Holdsworth, 'Affiliation of Savigny', 85 and note 100.

[28] Burton, *History of Byland and Jervaulx*, 26, 44.

[29] Ibid., 44; *EYC*, v, no. 308; *EEA XI: Exeter 1046–1184*, ed. F. Barlow (Oxford, 1996), no. 29.

Rievaulx, to whom the chapter delegated investigation of the conflicting claims, decided in favour of Savigny.[30]

The evidence for the English Savigniac congregation in the reign of King Stephen argues that the development of the order was greatly influenced by wider political events. Most of the English and Welsh houses had been founded directly from Savigny. The contacts between the mother house and its daughters seem to have become strained and fragmented, particularly those houses whose founders and patrons took the side of the king in the civil war, and as a result lost contact with their Norman lands which gradually fell into the hands of Geoffrey of Anjou. Historians have tended to ascribe the difficulties that Abbot Serlo experienced in controlling his English congregation both to his own personal shortcomings and to weakness in the structure of the order.[31] A re-reading of the sources would suggest that the political situation in England and Normandy was a significant factor in creating those difficulties and in pushing Serlo towards the rather more secure constitution of the Cistercian order in which the relationship among houses was, perhaps, more clearly defined and less subject to political pressures.

It was in the period 1135 to 1154 that the White Monks experienced their most dramatic expansion.[32] Constance Berman has raised the question of how far, before the mid-twelfth century, there was a Cistercian order in the accepted meaning of the word, and it has been useful to have been forced to re-examine the evidence for the nature of the wider Cistercian family in this formative period. This in turn invites us to question the extent of contacts between the English Cistercian houses and the nerve centre of the order. Indeed, questions about the nature of the Cistercian settlement still abound. How far were contacts maintained in the period after the initial foundation, when in those houses colonized from overseas a founding abbot and convent had gradually been replaced by men from the locality? The two mechanisms that underpinned the whole notion of 'order' were the annual visitation by a father abbot of all his daughter houses, and the annual general chapter, which brought together Cistercian abbots from across the congregation. Detailed and systematic records of the general chapter do not begin until 1180.[33] However, there is evidence of its functioning in relation to the

---

[30] Burton, *History of Byland and Jervaulx*, 28–32; Delisle, 'Documents', 423–4.

[31] D. Knowles, *The Monastic Order in England* (2nd edn, Cambridge, 1966), 250–1, also notes Serlo's own leanings towards the Cistercians.

[32] For comment see J. Burton, 'The Foundation of the British Cistercian Houses', in *Cistercian Art and Architecture in the British Isles*, ed. C. Norton and D. Park (Cambridge, 1986), 24–39, and *The Monastic Order in Yorkshire 1069–1215* (Cambridge, 1999), 98–124; C. Holdsworth, 'The Church', in King, *Anarchy*, 207–29, especially 215–28. See also P. Dalton, 'Churchmen and the Promotion of Peace in King Stephen's Reign', *Viator*, 31 (2000), 79–119, especially 94–109, for a suggestion that the increase in the number of Cistercian foundations between 1146 and 1148 may have owed some of its dynamic to attempts at peace making.

[33] *Statuta Capitulorum Generalium Ordinis Cisterciensis*, ed. J. M. Canivez, 8 vols. (Louvain, 1933–41); *Twelfth-Century Statutes from the Cistercian General Chapter*, ed. C. Waddell, *Cîteaux: Commentaria Cisterciensia*, Studia et Documenta, 12 (Turnhout, 2002).

English houses well before that. Indeed, according to the Annals of Waverley the first abbot of that house, the earliest Cistercian abbey in England, died during his return from the chapter in 1128, the very year of foundation.[34] In 1149 Abbot Roger of Byland called at Savigny on his way to Cîteaux, and journeyed to the chapter via Clairvaux in the company of the abbots of Savigny (his mother house) and St André de Gouffern (also a daughter house of Savigny).[35] The Byland *Historia* gives clear evidence that the general chapter appointed Ailred, abbot of Rievaulx, to investigate the affiliation of Byland, and contains a version of his judgement. The text is based on an original in the Archives Nationales, from the archives of the abbey of Savigny. It is witnessed by the abbots of Newminster, Louth Park, Basingwerk, Rufford, Jervaulx, Revesby, Kirkstall, Meaux and Ford, the prior and two monks of Rievaulx, two monks of Byland, three of Fountains and one of Revesby.[36] This suggests a fully fledged chapter, used to delegating cases to its abbots. It also shows the affairs of English houses being subject to regulation by the chapter.

Given the nature of the Cistercian expansion in England by the middle of the twelfth century, visitation would have been mostly internal. However – if fully observed – it would also have brought the abbot of Clairvaux to Rievaulx, Fountains, Margam and Boxley once a year, the abbot of L'Aumône to Waverley and Tintern, and the abbot of Savigny to his many English and Welsh daughters. But the practical problems of visitation are clear. St Bernard, father abbot of a family which spread widely, admitted the enormity of the task. At a date before 1143 he wrote to the abbots of Rievaulx and Fountains:

> I am obliged to go out of my house on visitations by the Rule of our Order, by the duty of our fraternity ... For this I wait and wait hoping to be given the strength to follow my ready will, but up to now I have been prevented. The way is hard and difficult, and my body is weak. ... Because of this, beloved, I am sending for your visitation my brother and dear friend Henry, Abbot of Vauclair. Hear him, I beg you, as if he were myself. He is an upright and reasonable man ... who ... shares my powers for the correction of faults and the maintenance of the Order.[37]

This is clear evidence that the system of visitation was well developed by the 1140s, and probably a lot earlier.[38] It reveals the practical difficulties that the

---

34 *Heads of Religious Houses I*, 147; *Annales Monastici*, ed. H. R. Luard, 5 vols. (RS, 1864–9), ii, 221.

35 Burton, *History of Byland and Jervaulx*, 46. St André may have been, like Byland, a Mowbray foundation, with which Roger lost contact until 1154 when he renewed certain grants: *Charters of Mowbray*, no. 162.

36 See above, note 30.

37 *S. Bernardi Opera, vols. 7–8: Epistolae*, ed. J. Leclerq and H. Rochais (Rome, 1974), no. 535; *The Letters of St Bernard of Clairvaux*, trans. B. S. James (repr. Stroud, 1998), no. 201.

38 Berman maintains that visitation, like the general chapter, was introduced much later than has been thought: *Cistercian Evolution*, 93–160. However, see the *Carta Caritatis Prior*, ch. 5, in Waddell, *Narrative and Legislative Texts*, 277–8 (translation, 445–6). *Carta*

system raised, but also that it was by then part of the ideology of the order. In terms of contacts between English houses and the continent one could also ask if we know anything of the origins of abbots, and this is an area ripe for research. But it raises difficult problems. The two volumes of *Heads of Religious Houses: England and Wales* are an invaluable guide to those monks who went on to hold the highest office, but a trawl through the Cistercian list for the period 1135 to 1154 reveals only a few who can be positively identified as coming from continental abbeys.[39] One was Thomas, second abbot of Boxley and a former monk of Fontenay.[40] Two other abbots promoted from continental houses, Henry Murdac and Richard III, held the office of abbot of Vauclair at the time of their election to the abbacy of Fountains. Both were native to Yorkshire. Moreover the election of Murdac was engineered by St Bernard, and Richard was appointed by Murdac as his suffragan in *c.* 1150.[41] These appointments have a wider significance. Abbot Richard II of Fountains died at Clairvaux on 12 October 1143, possibly on his way back from the general chapter at Cîteaux, which would have taken place in mid-September. Bernard seems to have been mindful of the clause in the *Carta Caritatis*, which dealt with the election of abbots, and required a father abbot to be present at the election of the head of a daughter house.[42] Given that Richard died at Clairvaux, Bernard would have been in a position to act quickly, but his letter to the prior and monks of Fountains hints at some delay:

> I would have sent someone to you long ago, but I have been waiting until I could do so conveniently and helpfully, because the venerable Abbot Henry, whom I had from the first destined for you, as he is capable and would, I believe, be very helpful to you in the present business, has been prevented by affairs from coming immediately. Receive him, dearest brothers, with the love and honour he deserves, and listen to him in all things, as you would to myself, in fact more than you would to myself for his virtue and judgement far exceed mine. I have given him full authority to act in the matter of this election and in anything that may need regularizing or correcting in your monastery or the others. I have sent with him William, a very dear son of mine.

Bernard urges that the election be conducted in an orderly manner:

Caritatis Posterior, the 'earliest recoverable version' of which Waddell identifies as the one issued by Pope Alexander III in 1165, allowed for the appointment of a proxy if a father abbot was unable to visit in person, ibid., 382, 498, 501. Christopher Holdsworth drew attention to no. 71 of the Institutes which appear in the revised customary of *c.* 1147; this indicates that proxies were already being used: Holdsworth, 'Affiliation of Savigny', 70; Waddell, *Narrative and Legislative Texts*, 358–9 and 488.

[39] *Heads of Religious Houses I*, 126–48.

[40] Ibid., 128.

[41] Ibid., 132–3; *Memorials of the Abbey of St Mary of Fountains*, ed. J. R. Walbran and J. T. Fowler, Surtees Society, 42, 67, 130, 3 vols. (1863–1918), i, 108, 131.

[42] Waddell, *Narrative and Legislative Texts*, 281–2 and 450.

And now I entreat you, dearest sons, to be all of one mind in this election and not to suffer factions to arise amongst you, but that you, one and all, with one mouth, glorify God ... May the enemy never be able to gloat over those whose master is the Holy Spirit in the school of Christ and glory in their dissensions because their souls are thereby endangered and all the labour of their penances rendered void, because the fair name of our Order is sullied and those whose especial duty is to glorify the name of Christ cause it to be blasphemed.

Bernard finishes by pointing out how discord can be avoided:

Rather, as befits holy men and servants of Christ, choose for yourselves with one voice, as I have every confidence you will, a worthy shepherd of your souls, in company with the Abbots of Rievaulx [William, d. 1145] and Vauclair [Henry Murdac], whose advice I wish you to follow as if it were my own.[43]

Bernard's confidence is even more clearly expressed in a letter written at about the same time to Henry Murdac: 'I charge you, Brother Henry, that you submit out of charity to the choice of our brothers at Fountains if, with the advice of the venerable Abbot of Rievaulx, they elect you as their abbot.'[44]

Certain phrases in these letters allude to the particular circumstances that surrounded what was clearly the grooming of Henry Murdac as third abbot of Fountains. The tortured events of the disputed York election have been rehearsed many times, and I do not propose to repeat them here.[45] However, it is worth emphasizing the political implications of the support of the reformed monastic orders – not just the Cistercians, but also the Augustinians – to the party that opposed William fitz Herbert, treasurer of York, elected to succeed Thurstan after a protracted period and confirmed by the king at Lincoln in February 1141. Although it has been questioned whether fitz Herbert was indeed a nephew of King Stephen, the newly elected archbishop did indeed enjoy royal support and his election took place under the watchful eye of William of Aumale, the king's earl of York.[46]

---

43 Bernard, *Opera*, no. 320; *Letters of St Bernard*, no. 173.

44 Bernard, *Opera*, no. 321; *Letters of St Bernard*, no. 174.

45 D. Knowles, 'The Case of St William of York', *Cambridge Historical Journal*, 5 (1936), 162–77, repr. in his *The Historian and Character* (Cambridge, 1963), 76–97; D. Baker, '*Viri Religiosi* and the York Election Dispute', in *Councils and Assemblies*, ed. G. J. Cuming and D. Baker, Studies in Church History, 7 (Oxford, 1971), 87–112; Burton, *Monastic Order in Yorkshire*, 112–16; Davis, *King Stephen*, 96–9. For the context of Cistercian intervention in disputed elections see M. G. Newman, *The Boundaries of Charity: Cistercian Culture and Ecclesiastical Reform 1098–1180* (Stanford, 1996), 191–218.

46 However, the most recent discussion – indeed the only full treatment – of William fitz Herbert's career accepts the relationship with the king. See C. Norton, *St William of York* (Woodbridge, 2006), 5–10 and 203–9.

What was the significance of the stance taken by the Cistercians, and in particular the abbots of Rievaulx and Fountains, against fitz Herbert? First, I think it has to be seen in the context of the Scottish connection cultivated by the Cistercians. Even before the crisis of 1141 the northern Cistercians had started to form contacts with Scotland.[47] It was while he was on a mission from the Scottish court to York in 1134 that Ailred entered Rievaulx Abbey;[48] and 1136 saw the foundation of a daughter house of Rievaulx by King David of Scotland at Melrose, to be followed by another at Dundrennan in 1142.[49] Bernard himself wrote to King David, in an often overlooked letter, praising his generosity to Rievaulx and asking him to be as open-handed to the newly founded monastery of Fountains, implying that David's patronage may have preceded Ailred's conversion.[50] David was a man of wide religious interests, but what might have been regarded, before 1135 or before 1141, as his pious endowment of a new order may have seemed more overtly political after the disputed election had gathered momentum.[51]

Also significant, surely, both for Stephen and for the English Cistercians would have been the blow to royal prestige and authority delivered by Bernard, abbot of the mother house of both Rievaulx and Fountains. Bernard entered into the controversy over the York election and weighed in against both Stephen and his brother Henry of Blois, bishop of Winchester. With Stephen's archbishop, William fitz Herbert – described by Bernard as a man who 'is rotten from the soles of his feet to the crown of his head'[52] and 'this vile and infamous person'[53] – and Stephen's brother, Bishop Henry of Winchester, criticized in strong terms,[54] the implications for the king's authority are clear. And Stephen did not escape personal censure from the abbot of Clairvaux.

> The King of kings has for long chastised your royal Majesty, for he is more powerful than you. Yet I believe that he has done it more in mercy than in fury because we know that he never forgets to be merciful in his anger. For this reason I humbly advise you and on bended knee implore you that on those matters for which above all God is especially chastising you and your realm, to wit the affairs of church and state, you give not the spouse of the church further cause for chastising you yet more harshly

---

47 Burton, *Monastic Order in Yorkshire*, 102–3, 114–16.
48 *The Life of Ailred of Rievaulx by Walter Daniel*, ed. and trans. F. M. Powicke (London, 1950, repr. Oxford, 1978), 14–16.
49 See the comments in Dalton, *Conquest, Anarchy and Lordship*, 222–7.
50 Bernard, *Opera*, no. 519; *Letters of St Bernard*, no. 172; J. Burton, 'Rievaulx Abbey: The Early Years', in *Reflections for an Architecture of Solitude: Essays in Honour of Peter Fergusson*, ed. T. Kinder, Medieval Church Studies, 11, and *Citeaux: Commentaria Cisterciensis*, Studia et Documenta, 13 (Turnhout, 2004), 47–53.
51 Dalton, *Conquest, Anarchy and Lordship*, 221–30; Burton, *Monastic Order in Yorkshire*, 114–15.
52 Bernard, *Opera*, no. 346; *Letters of St Bernard*, no. 187.
53 Bernard, *Opera*, no. 235; *Letters of St Bernard*, no. 202.
54 Bernard, *Opera*, no. 204; *Letters of St Bernard*, no. 204.

and even completely destroying you. Especially in the case of the church of York do I implore you with my whole heart to change your attitude and not attempt to hinder the termination of the affair according to the manner laid down by the Lord Pope. And if that man [William fitz Herbert] should fall, permit, I beg you, the canons to be left free lawfully to elect another, as not only the church of York but all the churches should be left free; then, if you do this, the Lord will be with you, he will render you glorious and exalt your throne.[55]

As is well known, Bernard applied pressure relentlessly until another protégé, the Cistercian pope, Eugenius III (1145–53), deposed William. His successor, consecrated by the pope, was the first archbishop of York since the Conquest to be elected without royal approval, and to rule his diocese – albeit without entering the cathedral city – for another four years without being reconciled to the king. That archbishop was Henry Murdac, and it was his election that brought to Fountains a succession of three suffragan abbots, the last of these Richard of York, like Murdac before him abbot of Vauclair, who outlived Henry and ruled Fountains until 1170.

I have argued elsewhere that the involvement of the Cistercians in the York election may have led to a loss of royal favour, and, conversely, a rise in the patronage offered to the Cistercians by those with pro-Angevin sympathies.[56] Henry of Anjou himself in 1149 granted land for the foundation of a daughter house of Quarr, which was itself, admittedly, a former Savigniac abbey.[57] However, such a divide must not be overstated: we only have to recall the foundation of two Cistercian houses, Vaudey (May 1147) and Meaux (January 1150), by Stephen's earl of York, William of Aumale.[58] The later of these must have been planned well before King Stephen granted the temporalities of the see of York to his Cistercian archbishop. In the mid-1140s three Cistercian houses were founded from continental abbeys, reversing the emerging trend of colonization from mother houses in England, that is, from Waverley, Rievaulx and Fountains and their daughters. These three were Boxley, Abbey Dore, and Margam. The first was founded by William of Ypres in 1143 or 1146 from Clairvaux, the second in 1147 by Robert of Ewyas from Morimond, and the third from Clairvaux in 1147 by Robert, earl of Gloucester. Of the two colonies sent by Bernard from Clairvaux, Boxley was founded by Stephen's mercenary leader, and Margam by

---

55 Bernard, *Opera*, no. 533; *Letters of St Bernard*, no. 197.
56 *Monastic Order in Yorkshire*, 115–24; Burton, 'The Foundation of the British Cistercian Houses'.
57 *Regesta*, iii, no. 666. The foundation at Loxwell was made 'ad faciendam ibidem capitalem abbatiam pro salute et incolumitate domini Gaufridi Normannie ducis et Andegavie comitis, necnon pro salute domine imperatricis matris mee et mea, et pro statu regni Anglorum et pro animabus Henrici regis avi mei et M(athildis) regine'.
58 Burton, *Monastic Order in Yorkshire*, 121–2. On William see P. Dalton, 'William Earl of York and Royal Authority in Yorkshire in the Reign of Stephen', *HSJ*, 2 (1990), 155–65.

the empress's half brother.[59] The Cistercians attracted patronage from both sides of the political divide.[60]

Other evidence has been taken to suggest that Stephen was indeed cooling towards the White Monks and that their stance in the York election may have cost them support in royal circles. The monks of Rievaulx had received routine charters of confirmation from Henry I, no doubt sought by their founder, the royal justice Walter Espec, and received one from Stephen on his visit to York in 1136. Christopher Holdsworth has suggested that Cistercian opposition to William fitz Herbert was the reason that Rievaulx received no charter from Stephen after 1136. The monks of Fountains also received one early charter of confirmation but their second had to wait until after the peace the king reached with Henry Murdac in 1151.[61] This seems to point towards a withdrawal of royal favour throughout the 1140s, when the election dispute was at its height. However, I would be cautious in drawing conclusions from the charter evidence. Stephen issued at least four charters for Rievaulx, only one of which has survived; their chronology is accordingly unknown.[62] Moreover, that the king was not overly hostile to Rievaulx is suggested by his confirmation of the foundation of a daughter house of Rievaulx at Rufford by Gilbert de Gant (Christmas 1146).[63] It may be that Stephen and his queen did not show any real enthusiasm for the Cistercians, and that their patronage of the order of Savigny waned once it and its continental estates had passed into Angevin hands, and the order had merged with that of Cîteaux. However, it is important not to read too much into this; by 1148, when they made their last great monastic foundation of Cluniac monks at Faversham, Stephen and his queen had, after all, a string of Savigniac foundations to their credit and may have wished, like so many other founders, to share their patronage among different orders.[64]

The development of the Cistercian order in England was in some respects quite clearly influenced by political events, and its continental connections ensured that the Cistercian voice was heard on occasions when ecclesiastical affairs took a political turn. There were always political overtones to monastic patronage, and these were heightened in times of political crisis. The virtual refoundation of Bordesley Abbey by the Empress Matilda is ample demonstration of this. Bordesley was founded in 1138 by Waleran, elder of the Beaumont twins, on

59 On William of Ypres, a bastard son of the count of Flanders, see, for example, Davis, *King Stephen*, 66–7; Matthew, *King Stephen*, 167.
60 This is the conclusion reached by Holdsworth, 'The Church', 220–7, which has caused me to modify the views I expressed in 'The Foundation of the British Cistercian Houses'.
61 *Regesta*, iii, no. 716 and nos. 335–6; Holdsworth, 'The Church', 226–7.
62 *Cartularium Abbathiae de Rievalle*, ed. J. C. Atkinson, Surtees Society, 83 (1889), 268 (notes from a cartulary extant in 1640); Burton, 'Rievaulx Abbey: the Early Years'.
63 *Regesta*, iii, no. 736.
64 Ibid., no. 300. As Christopher Holdsworth points out ('Affiliation of Savigny', 82) in founding a Cluniac house at Faversham and designating it as their place of burial they were emulating Henry I, who staffed Reading Abbey, intended as his mausoleum, with monks of Cluny.

royal demesne lands granted to him by King Stephen on his elevation to the earldom of Worcester.[65] As Marjorie Chibnall has demonstrated, after the battle of Lincoln in 1141 Matilda refused to recognize grants made by Stephen out of royal lands.[66] In many cases she made her point by issuing her own charter of confirmation, but in the case of Bordesley she was able to take a different tack.[67] In 1141, Waleran shifted his allegiance from Stephen to the empress. As part of the negotiations he was forced to hand over the patronage of Bordesley to Matilda, and her charters refer to it as her own foundation.[68] This was not the only time that the empress, the count, and the abbot of Bordesley came into contact. When Waleran sought to make a second Cistercian foundation near Lillebonne he planned to invite monks from Bordesley to colonize the new foundation. The empress, uneasy about bringing monks from an English house, engineered the staffing of the new monastery, La Valasse, from her own abbey at Mortemer rather than Bordesley.[69]

This paper has concentrated on the political implications of monastic patronage at a high level, and there is more to be investigated and known by looking in depth at how ideas cascaded down through networks and associations not only among the aristocracy but also the knightly class. However, it is impor-tant to recall that not all connections with the continent, whether with Normandy, Anjou or further afield, were dominated by political issues. The reign saw, for instance, the development of associations between English monastic houses and the French abbey of Arrouaise, a house of Augustinian canons in which there was an emphasis on liturgy and contemplation rather than pastoral work. A. G. Dyson showed many years ago how a common factor in the Arrouaisian houses estab-lished in the reign of Stephen was Bishop Alexander of Lincoln, founder of Dorchester (c. 1140), of which the empress was a benefactor, and where the regular canons replaced secular canons. In the same diocese under his rule were founded houses affiliated to Arrouaise at Missenden (1133), Bourne (1138) and the nunnery of Harrold (1138).[70] It was also in this period that the Yorkshire Augustinian house of Warter joined the congregation.[71] The nature of the contacts between the English houses and the French abbey is unclear, but the development of this monastic association is intriguing.

Other continental movements began to make their influences felt in England.

---

65 D. Crouch, *The Beaumont Twins: The Roots and Branches of Power in the Twelfth Century* (Cambridge, 1986), 39–40.

66 Chibnall, *Empress Matilda*, 129.

67 For what follows see ibid., 134–5, 182.

68 *Regesta*, iii, nos. 115–16, where Matilda refers to 'abbatia mea', which she founded ('Notum sit me pro dei amore … et pro pace et pro stabilitate regni Anglorum fundasse abbatiam quondam que dicitur Bordesleia, de ordine Cisterciensi …').

69 Chibnall, *Empress Matilda*, 182–7. On Mortemer see Holdsworth, 'Affiliation of Savigny', 63–8.

70 A. G. Dyson, 'The Monastic Patronage of Bishop Alexander of Lincoln', *Journal of Eccle-siastical History*, 26 (1975), 1–24, especially 11–14.

71 See Burton, *Monastic Order in Yorkshire*, 84–6.

Empress Matilda honoured the grants made by her father by confirming to the famous abbey of Fontevraud a pension of fifty silver marks from the farm of London, and in 1141 – as a mark of her political authority in the city – she ordered the barons and sheriff to make sure this was paid.[72] In the years before 1147, under the rule of Abbess Matilda, sister-in-law of Empress Matilda, plans were made for the first foundation from Fontevraud in England. Robert, earl of Leicester, a consistent royalist, granted land in Kintbury for the foundation of a house of nuns. This is another reminder that personal religiosity and a desire to patronize new monastic movements could be stronger than political affiliations and alliances. Sally Thompson suggested that the impetus that brought the order to England was the acquaintance between Abbess Matilda and the countess of Leicester, and that the abbess was planning to come to England to visit this, the first English daughter house, but was prevented by death. Certainly her successor, Audeburga, was present at the dedication of the permanent site of the nunnery at Nuneaton (c. 1155), a personal symbol of connections between the monastic order in England and the Angevin world.[73]

This paper began with William of Newburgh's assessment of the monastic expansion in the reign of Stephen. He, like so many since, was intrigued by the explosion of houses for men and women in this period of warfare, confused and changing alliances, and tenurial uncertainty. These new monastic establishments varied greatly in their size, composition, endowments, and nature, and much more could be said about them. For two congregations that sprang from the reforming ethos of the late eleventh and early twelfth centuries, the Savigniac and the Cistercian, events on either side of the Channel were highly significant for the direction in which those houses developed in this nineteen-year period.

[72] *Regesta*, iii, no. 328. Four years earlier Stephen had confirmed Henry I's pension to the nuns from the farms of London and Winchester, ibid., no. 327.

[73] S. Thompson, *Women Religious: The Founding of English Nunneries after the Norman Conquest* (Oxford, 1991), 123–4, 165.

7

Reeds Shaken by the Wind?
Bishops in Local and Regional Politics in
King Stephen's Reign

STEPHEN MARRITT

But they cowering in most dastardly fear, bent like a reed shaken by the wind, and since their salt had no savour they did not rise up or resist or set themselves as a wall before the house of Israel ... some bishops, made sluggish and abject by fear of them, either gave way or lukewarmly and feebly passed a sentence of excommunication that was soon to be revoked ...[1]

THIS WAS the *Gesta Stephani*'s assessment of episcopal conduct during the civil war. Similar, if more moderate, views were held until relatively recently.[2] Paul Dalton has now shown, however, that some bishops were committed to peace-keeping,[3] and it has also been argued that their relations with King Stephen were better and more constructive than is often allowed.[4] Here, another facet of the civil war bishops' office is explored which has been little addressed beyond the exceptional case of Durham: engagement and integration with local political, religious and social dynamics and networks.[5] Case studies are drawn from the three

---

1   *Gesta Stephani*, 157. I would like to thank the editors for their initial invitation to contribute to the conference, and for their care and patience thereafter. All errors of fact or interpretation remain my own.
2   C. Holdsworth, 'The Church', in King, *Anarchy*, 207–30, 215.
3   P. Dalton, 'Churchmen and the Promotion of Peace in King Stephen's Reign', *Viator*, 31 (2000), 79–119.
4   K. J. Stringer, *The Reign of Stephen: Kingship, Warfare and Government in Twelfth-Century England* (London, 1993), 72; H. R. Loyn, *The English Church 940–1154* (Harlow and New York, 2000), 133; S. Marritt, 'King Stephen and the Bishops', *ANS*, 24 (2002), 129–44.
5   Durham is not considered here, see A. Young, 'The Bishopric of Durham in Stephen's Reign', in *Anglo-Norman Durham 1093–1193*, ed. D. Rollason, M. Harvey and M. Prestwich (Woodbridge, 1994), 353–69. David Crouch has studied local Anglo-Norman earl-bishop relations, 'Earls and Bishops in Twelfth-Century Leicestershire', *Nottingham*

dioceses of Chester, Hereford, and Lincoln because bishops of all three are named in the *Gesta Stephani*. Bishop Robert de Bethune of Hereford exceptionally, 'manfully set himself like a shield of defence against the enemies of the catholic peace'.[6] Bishops Alexander of Lincoln and Roger de Clinton of Chester, however,

> (but it was no task for bishops) filled their castles full of provisions and stocks of arms, knights and archers, and though they were supposed to be warding off the evil doers who were plundering the goods of the church showed themselves more cruel and more merciless than those very evil-doers in oppressing their neighbours and plundering their goods.[7]

The place of bishops in local society during the civil war has perhaps been passed over because their traditional local political power has been considered as much reduced, and their dependence on central authorities as significantly increased, by 1135.[8] Work on aristocratic religious life has concentrated on the monastic orders, and bishops can appear peripheral in the private charters from monastic archives which historians use to analyse local society.[9] Episcopal *acta* can, further, seem only administrative, and Anglo-Norman bishops themselves have sometimes been portrayed as civil servants.[10] Bishops' charters are also only exceptionally attested by magnates.[11] Furthermore, episcopal peacemaking efforts possibly depended on bishops being outside secular political and social networks. In fact, in the civil war evidence, bishops' significance is most apparent in the expectations and reactions of others. It can thus be difficult to reconstruct the episcopate's local importance.[12] In developing the argument that bishops had considerable local significance during the war, this chapter will address each of these issues. In doing so, it will provide a context for analysis of the civil war evidence. It will also suggest that the significance of bishops at this time was due

---

Mediaeval Studies, 37 (1993), 9–20. See also H. R. Loyn, 'William's Bishops, Some Further Thoughts', *ANS*, 10 (1988), 223–35.

6   *Gesta Stephani*, 158.

7   Ibid., 159.

8   W. L. Warren, *The Governance of Norman and Angevin England* (London, 1987), 62; Holdsworth, 'The Church', 215; M. Brett, 'The English Abbeys, their Tenants and the King (950–1150)', in *Chiesa e mondo feudale nei secoli x–xii*, Miscellanea del Centro di Studi Medioevali, 14 (Milan, 1995 for 1992), 277–302, 297.

9   M. Brett, *The English Church under Henry I* (Oxford, 1976), 127, 146, 247; C. Harper-Bill, 'The Piety of the Anglo-Norman Knightly Class', *ANS*, 2 (1979), 63–77.

10 C. Morris, *The Papal Monarchy* (Oxford, 1989, repr. 1991), 222–3, 229, 289. V. H. Galbraith, 'Notes on the Career of Samson Bishop of Worcester (1096–1112)', *EHR*, 82 (1967), 86–101, 87; S. Mooers Christelow, 'Chancellors and Curial Bishops: Ecclesiastical Promotions and Power in Anglo-Norman England', *ANS*, 22 (1999), 49–69, 50, 54, 67, 69.

11 *EEA 20: York 1154–1181*, ed. M. Lovatt (Oxford, 2000), xlv. For example, *EEA V: York 1070–1154*, ed. J. E. Burton (Oxford, 1988), no. 63; *EEA XI: Exeter 1046–1184*, ed. F. Barlow (Oxford, 1996), nos. 22, 33.

12 For frustration see Brett, *English Church*, 233; J. A. Green, *The Aristocracy of Norman England* (Cambridge, 1997), 391.

as much to the pre-existing and well-established nature of their office as to anything resulting from the extraordinary circumstances of Stephen's reign.

I

Earls gradually disappeared as addressees from Henry I's charters, but bishops continued to be addressed, usually with the sheriff.[13] Early in his reign, for example, Henry ordered Bishop Robert of Chester and others not to summon the monks of Rheims to hundred or shire courts, while between 1115 and 1121 the shire court of Lincoln, including the bishop, was ordered not to hear a particular case before the king arrived.[14] Henry I also built up the military capacity of some of his bishops. Bishop's Stortford castle, built by the bishops of London with royal support, makes little sense with respect to their own estates, but much more in terms of Henry's domestic strategies.[15] It was Henry too, not the bishops of Lincoln, who developed the episcopal castle at Newark.[16] Both became the objects of magnate ambitions after 1139; the empress promised Geoffrey de Mandeville Bishop's Stortford and Earl Robert of Leicester seized Newark.[17] King Stephen, for his part, had expectations. Bishop Robert of Bath gave the king a tour of his city's defences in 1138, but when they were lost Stephen was furious with him.[18]

Quite how Anglo-Norman bishops held castles granted by the king was then, and is now, the subject of debate, but Archbishop Hugh of Rouen's 1139 judgement that they remained a royal resource fits with the material cited here.[19] Explicit evidence of bishops' use of their castles to pursue their private ambitions during Stephen's reign has yet to come to light.[20] The same applies to troops. Nigel of Ely did have an armed band for his protection, and Henry of Winchester his *milites episcopi*, but these were a civil war protagonist's army not a bishop's.[21] Episcopal resources could, nevertheless, potentially support locally significant military contingents. These might involve the bishops' tenants, although relations

---

[13] Warren, *Governance*, 62; J. A. Green, *The Government of England under Henry I* (Cambridge, 1986), 119; Marritt, 'Stephen and the Bishops', 136.

[14] *Regesta*, ii, nos. 900, 1374. For further examples, see Marritt, 'Stephen and the Bishops', 136.

[15] P. Taylor, 'The Military Endowment and Obligations of the See of London', *ANS*, 14 (1991), 287–313, 305–6, 309.

[16] *Regesta*, ii, nos. 1660–1, 1770, 1772, 1791.

[17] *The Registrum Antiquissimum of the Cathedral Church of Lincoln*, ed. C. W. Foster and K. Major, Lincoln Record Society, 10 vols. (1931–73), i, no. 283; *Regesta*, iii, no. 275.

[18] *Gesta Stephani*, 39–41, 43.

[19] C. Coulson, 'The Castles of the Anarchy', in King, *Anarchy*, 67–92, 74–5.

[20] Cf. I. Megaw, 'The Ecclesiastical Policy of Stephen, 1135–9', in *Essays in British and Irish History in Honour of J. E. Todd*, ed. H. A. Cronne (London, 1949), 24–46, 35–7; E. U. Crosby, 'The Organisation of the English Episcopate under Henry I', *Studies in Medieval and Renaissance History*, 4 (1967), 1–88, 57.

[21] *Liber Eliensis*, ed. E. O. Blake, Camden Society, 3rd ser., 92 (1962), 332; *John of Worcester*, ii, 266, 302; *Gesta Stephani*, 100.

with them were neither always straightforward nor necessarily militarized beyond royal service.[22] Most likely though, some bishops did develop defences and rely on their tenants to repel attacks, as the abbot of Evesham is known to have done.[23] Their extensive lands, lordship, jurisdictions and rights certainly gave them local significance whether they wished it or not. Reassessments of the civil war episcopate have, rightly, been influenced by continental episcopal peacemaking and dispute settlement, but another continental phenomenon was episcopal-comital conflict.[24] This might also be informative.

Powerful magnates did have to take episcopal authority into account. In 1140, Stephen's new earl of Worcester forced Bishop Simon of Worcester to come to an agreement about the distribution of the county's third penny and certain estates and rights the bishop had been holding.[25] Ecclesiastical governance could also be significant. In 1126 boundaries between the various jurisdictions of the earl of Gloucester and the bishop of Llandaff in south Wales were set out. Trial by water was to take place on the nearest episcopal land to Cardiff castle and trial by iron at Llandaff. The bishop's reeves were to be enrolled in his writ in the earl's court and he was to have a list of the comital officials.[26] The spiritual authority of bishops, as distinct from their administrative power, is more elusive. Orderic Vitalis has one magnate, on learning that his new estates lay outside episcopal jurisdiction, proclaim, 'heaven forbid that I should live without a spiritual shepherd or the yoke of ecclesiastical authority'. Both episcopal governance and a spiritual relationship are suggested here. Orderic also has another magnate advise his son, 'Fear and honour your bishop and your king as your protectors and never forget to obey their commands as far as you are able. Pray to God daily for their welfare so that through the care and merits of a good bishop you may obtain eternal salvation for your soul.'[27] It will be suggested in this chapter that the charter material, despite its limitations, can supplement these examples and yield evidence of bishops' ecclesiastical, political, and spiritual influence.

Edmund King once noted that bishops' inclusion in or absence from private charter address clauses was potentially significant.[28] In the case studies below, patterns become apparent which reflect magnates' recognition or avoidance of

---

22 S. E. Gleason, *An Ecclesiastical Barony of the Middle Ages: The Bishopric of Bayeux 1066–1204* (Cambridge, Mass., 1936), 51–2, 73, 81–2; E. U. Crosby, *Bishop and Chapter in Twelfth-Century England: A Study of the mensa episcopalis* (Cambridge, 1994), 187–9; N. E. Stacy, 'Henry of Blois and the Lordship of Glastonbury', *EHR*, 114 (1999), 1–33.

23 *History of the Abbey of Evesham*, ed. and trans. J. Sayers and L. Watkiss (Oxford, 2003), 20, 180.

24 Dalton, 'Churchmen', 81–4.

25 H. A. Cronne, 'An Agreement between Simon, Bishop of Worcester and Waleran, Earl of Worcester', *University of Birmingham Historical Journal*, 2 (1949/50), 201–7; D. Crouch, *The Beaumont Twins: The Roots and Branches of Power in the Twelfth Century* (Cambridge, 1986), 40.

26 *Regesta*, ii, no. 1466.

27 *Orderic*, ii, 27; iii, 195.

28 E. King, 'The Foundation of Pipewell Abbey, Northamptonshire', *HSJ*, 2 (1990), 167–78, 170.

episcopal authority (although this method is only valid where, as in these cases, a large proportion of extant charters retain address clauses). Episcopal confirmation was increasingly requested during the civil war as alternative repositories of legitimacy were sought in the absence of royal government, but it has not been emphasized that confirmation might be refused or politicized.[29] Lincoln episcopal agents refused to consent to one donation despite the king, the donor's lord, and the beneficiary's bishop having done so, because the gift had previously been granted elsewhere.[30] In another case, Bishop Ralph of Orkney, acting as the bishop of Lincoln's suffragan, rejected a compromise agreement between a priory and a baron because the former was in the right and the latter in the wrong.[31] William of Ypres gave a Kent church which had belonged to Hugh of Dover to St Bertin in the 1140s. Hugh, an Angevin supporter, was restored to his lands after 1154 and contested the donation. Pope Adrian IV ordered him to desist, but Archbishop Theobald of Canterbury wrote in his support admitting that,

> because ... William of Ypres ... threatened our existence we thought it necessary to dissemble ... if they [St Bertin] should produce a charter drawn up in our name we would have you to know (to confess our own imperfection) that it was wrung from us by force and by fear of the tyrant aforesaid.[32]

Perhaps the archbishop had been coerced, perhaps not. In any event, his confirmation legitimized William's possession and came to threaten Hugh's.

The archbishop influenced one donor who was,

> moved especially by the exhortation, the request and the counsel of the lord Theobald ... who showed me by the most reasonable and unanswerable arguments that a noble gentleman who has the fee of six knights should give not only the third part of a knight's lands to God and holy church for the soul's health of himself and his kin, but the whole of a knight's land or more than that ...[33]

This rare expansion of the common episcopal counsel and consent clause is a

---

29 Brett, *English Church*, 146; B. Thompson, 'Free Alms Tenure in the Twelfth Century', *ANS*, 16 (1993), 221–43, 224–6; J. Hudson, *Land, Law and Lordship in Anglo-Norman England* (Oxford, 1994), 228. Cf. *EEA VII: Hereford 1079–1234*, ed. J. Barrow (Oxford, 1993), lxxvi.

30 *EEA VII: Hereford*, nos. 42–3. Discussed in Brett, *English Church*, 147–8.

31 M. J. Franklin, 'The Secular College as a Focus for Anglo-Norman Piety: St Augustine's, Daventry', in *Minsters and Parish Churches: The Local Church in Transition 950–1200*, ed. J. Blair (Oxford, 1988), 97–105, 99.

32 *The Letters of John of Salisbury*, ed. and trans. W. J. Millor and H. E. Butler, 2 vols. (London, 1955), i, no. 24; R. Eales, 'Local Loyalties in Norman England: Kent in Stephen's Reign', *ANS*, 8 (1988), 88–108, 100–1.

33 F. Stenton, *The First Century of English Feudalism 1066–1166* (2nd edn, Oxford, 1961), 38–9, 259–60.

reminder that administrative survivals represent communal religious processes which involved bishops in local society. When Bishop Jocelin of Salisbury dedicated one chapel, local leaders swore that the parish church would suffer no loss. One of their sons remembered the oath twenty years later.[34] When a bishop symbolically transferred property between a donor and a monastery, he did so because both parties valued his involvement, not because of any legislative requirement to do so.[35] In the early years of Henry II's reign, Roger de Mowbray carried through his dealings with several religious houses in York Minster, often in the presence of the new archbishop. Both Roger and the representatives of the religious houses had to travel sometimes considerable distances, which suggests that York had significance for them.[36]

The *Gesta Stephani*'s comments on the episcopate were guided by a strict, reform model of the office of bishop, but John of Worcester, a contemporary chronicler, was informed by an alternative model.[37] The *Gesta* sympathized with Bishop Robert of Bath on the loss of his city, but John of Worcester castigated him and thought the king's anger justified. For the *Gesta*, the legacy of the 1139 arrest of the bishops was one of division and distrust between king and bishops, but for John, one of a renewed commitment and vigour in cooperation between the two for the better government of the kingdom in the localities.[38] John's model better fits the evidence cited here and it allows for more episcopal engagement in local society. Bishops' ecclesiastical authority and spiritual influence gave them then an important place in local networks in 1139, and they were still prominent figures in royal and shire government. Some held military resources to be used in the king's interests. This complex of roles must have affected bishops' conception of their office and actions, and informed magnate society's expectations of and attitudes towards them during the civil war.

II

Hereford's bishops, Robert de Bethune and Gilbert Foliot, had been local religious superiors, at Llanthony and Gloucester respectively, before their election. In a *Life* of Robert and in Gilbert's collected letters, the diocese offers unique material for the civil war period.[39] Hereford was considerably disrupted in the civil war. Miles of Gloucester (d. 1143), constable of Gloucester and sheriff of

---

34 *EEA 18: Salisbury, 1078–1217*, ed. B. R. Kemp (Oxford, 1999), no. 92.
35 Others, laity included, could do so, sometimes as bishops looked on, for example *EEA 18: Salisbury*, nos. 97, 112; *EEA 20: York*, nos. 65, 81. Cf. J. Barrow, 'From the Lease to the Certificate: The Evolution of Episcopal Acts in England and Wales (c. 700–c. 1250)', in *Die Diplomatik der Bischofsurkunde vor 1250*, ed. C. Haidacher and W. Köfler (Innsbruck, 1995), 529–43, 534.
36 *EEA 20: York*, nos. 26, 75, 76, 136.
37 *Gesta Stephani*, xxxiii–xxxviii.
38 Ibid., 39–41; *John of Worcester*, ii, 248, 266.
39 *Anglia Sacra*, ed. H. Wharton, 2 vols. (London, 1691), ii, 293–321; B. J. Parkinson, 'The Life of Robert de Bethune by William de Wycombe: Translation with Introduction and

Gloucestershire, was an early adherent of the empress, who made him earl of Hereford in 1141.[40] He, and his son Roger after him, sought to establish a 'principality' or 'regional hegemony' in Herefordshire.[41] Gilbert de Lacy fought them for family estates they had gained by marriage, while Hugh de Mortimer developed Wigmore in the north largely independently of the civil war. Both Lacy and Mortimer were also interested in Ludlow.[42] King Stephen made early efforts to reassert his authority, but had little direct influence thereafter.[43]

Bishop Robert owed his election to local leaders, Miles and Payn fitz John, and in 1137 he officiated at Payn's funeral in Gloucester Abbey with Miles and other marcher barons attending.[44] He had, then, a respected place in local society. Miles and he cooperated to re-house Llanthony's canons after Welsh raids in 1136, and Miles's father had retired there while Robert was prior. With war, however, the bishop was subject to Miles's expansionism.[45] Miles besieged Hereford castle in 1140 and his ally Geoffrey Talbot seized the cathedral.[46] Bishop Robert had to acknowledge Talbot's local power, but cannot have been happy doing so.[47] When Talbot died relations between the bishop and Miles may have improved,[48] but in 1143 they broke down again when the earl imposed a levy on churches and the bishop rejected it.[49] He placed an interdict on Hereford, blocked the cathedral doorways with thorns, had its crosses thrown down, and excommunicated Miles. Miles appealed against the bishop's jurisdiction, but died before the case was decided. For some of this period Bishop Robert was forced into exile, and Hereford castle was for him, *tumultus et sanguinum locus est*.[50]

Bishop Robert was loyal to Stephen and attended him on campaign in the region in 1139.[51] He granted Waleran of Meulan, Stephen's earl of Worcester, a

Notes', unpub. Oxford, B.Litt thesis (1951); *The Letters and Charters of Gilbert Foliot*, ed. A. Morey and C. N. L. Brooke (Cambridge, 1967).

[40] D. Walker, 'Miles of Gloucester, Earl of Hereford', *Transactions of the Bristol and Gloucestershire Archaeological Society*, 77 (1958), 66–84.

[41] Davis, *King Stephen*, 41; Crouch, *Reign of Stephen*, 112, 122.

[42] W. E. Wightman, *The Lacy Family in England and Normandy 1066–1194* (Oxford, 1966), 185–9; C. Hopkinson, 'The Mortimers of Wigmore 1086–1214', *Transactions of the Woolhope Naturalists' Field Club*, 46 (1989), 177–93, 183; B. Coplestone-Crow, 'From Foundation to Anarchy', in *Ludlow Castle, its History and Buildings*, ed. R. Shoesmith and A. Johnson (Little Logaston, 2000), 21–34, 21, 34.

[43] Crouch, *Reign of Stephen*, 79–80, 102, 112–17.

[44] *Anglia Sacra*, ii, 304–5; *EEA VII: Hereford*, xxxviii; *John of Worcester*, ii, 228.

[45] Walker, 'Miles', 66–8.

[46] *Gesta Stephani*, 108–10; *John of Worcester*, ii, 276–78; *Letters of Foliot*, nos. 1, 2.

[47] *EEA VII: Hereford*, no. 19.

[48] *John of Worcester*, ii, 290; *EEA VII: Hereford*, xxxix.

[49] 'The Anglo-Norman Chronicle of Wigmore Abbey', ed. and trans. J. C. Dickinson and P. T. Ricketts, *Transactions of the Woolhope Naturalists' Field Club*, 39 (1969), 413–46, 424; *Gesta Stephani*, 158–60; Walker, 'Miles', 75–6.

[50] *Anglia Sacra*, ii, 313–14; *EEA VII: Hereford*, no. 21.

[51] *John of Worcester*, ii, 276–8; D. Cox, 'Two Unpublished Charters of King Stephen for Wenlock Priory', *Transactions of the Shropshire Archaeological and Historical Society*, 66 (1989), 56–9; *EEA VII: Hereford*, xxxix.

castle in Worcestershire and attested an agreement between him and its bishop in which Waleran asserted his position in his new county in 1140 or 1141.[52] Miles had attacked Worcester in 1140.[53] To challenge Miles, Stephen also granted the title earl of Hereford to Waleran's brother, Earl Robert of Leicester.[54] In exile Bishop Robert stayed at Shobdon under Oliver de Merlimont's protection.[55] Oliver was steward to Hugh de Mortimer, to whom the bishop also granted a castle.[56] Oliver later deserted Hugh for Miles, and in response Hugh allied with Gilbert de Lacy, who attacked Shobdon. Bishop Robert then encouraged Hugh to become its patron, confirm Oliver's grants, and make further donations.[57] Hugh's action asserted his lordship over Oliver's estates and foundation. Bishop Robert's relationship with Miles's son, Earl Roger, is more opaque, but the Llanthony chronicle has Prior William forced to resign *c.* 1147, because Roger's hostility towards him was adversely affecting the priory. William, later the author of the *Life*, had criticized the earl's attitude towards Bishop Robert.[58] Earl Roger was committed to the Angevin cause,[59] while the bishop remained loyal to Stephen.[60]

Gilbert Foliot was closely related to Miles and had been appointed abbot of Gloucester at Miles's request in 1139.[61] Relations between them were difficult in 1143, but otherwise excellent, and even in that year Gilbert wrote to Bishop Henry of Winchester on the earl's behalf.[62] His willingness to plead for his patron contrasts with his attitude towards those who damaged or seized Gloucester's property: five times he wrote to bishops asking them to take action.[63] As vicar of vacant Hereford in 1148, he imposed an interdict against Earl Roger, but relations were, again, otherwise close.[64] He also supported the Angevin cause.[65] Gloucester received numerous grants from both earls in Gilbert's time as abbot, and

---

52 *Letters of Foliot*, no. 80; Crouch, *Beaumont Twins*, 40 and note 57; Cronne, 'Agreement'.
53 *John of Worcester*, ii, 272–6. The text reads '*urbs Glaona*', but Miles's power there makes it likely that this was his force, not the town's or Robert of Gloucester's. For Miles and Gloucester see *Gesta Stephani*, 94; *Historia Novella*, 62.
54 *Regesta*, iii, no. 437; Walker, 'Miles', 79–80; Crouch, *Beaumont Twins*, 48–9, 85.
55 'Chronicle of Wigmore', 424.
56 *Letters of Foliot*, no. 80.
57 'Chronicle of Wigmore', 420, 424–6.
58 *Monasticon*, vi, part 1, 133; C. H. Talbot, 'William of Wycumbe, Fourth prior of Llanthony', *Transactions of the Bristol and Gloucestershire Archaeological Society*, 76 (1957), 62–9, at 62–3.
59 Crouch, *Reign of Stephen*, 218, 242–3, 262–3, 256–7.
60 *Anglia Sacra*, ii, 320; *Regesta*, iii, nos. 460, 511–13, 760, 787; A. Saltman, *Theobald Archbishop of Canterbury* (London, 1956), 25–9. He did, however, confirm some grants to St Guthlac's at the empress's request, *EEA VII: Hereford*, no. 23.
61 *John of Worcester*, ii, 264; C. N. L. Brooke and A. Morey, *Gilbert Foliot and his Letters* (Cambridge, 1965), 35–7, 78–9.
62 *Historia et cartularium monasterii sancti Petri de Gloucestria*, ed. W. H. Hart, 3 vols. (RS, 1863–7), ii, no. 565; *Letters of Foliot*, no. 24.
63 *Letters of Foliot*, nos. 3, 5, 27, 32, 69.
64 Ibid., no. 77.
65 *John of Worcester*, ii, 294–5; *Letters of Foliot*, no. 26; Brooke and Morey, *Gilbert Foliot*, 105–22.

Roger acted as surety for him.[66] As bishop, Gilbert appeared in the address and attestation clauses of Roger's charters and Roger witnessed his.[67] Roger is *illustri comite* in the episcopal confirmation of a grant he made through the bishop's hands.[68] A Gloucester confirmation records some ceremony, *Hanc sententiam dedit dominus Gilbertus Hereford(ensis) episcopus pulsantibus campanis et candelis accensis in ecclesia cathedrali Hereford(ie) ad instantiam predicti Rogeri comitis.*[69] Only following Gilbert's appointment as bishop did Roger recognize some Hereford rights, and, perhaps, make reparations.[70] Bishop Robert, in contrast, had received nothing from the family beyond a confirmation of a tenant's grant to the cathedral.[71] Few of Miles's or Roger's charters address him, and he cannot be found in their religious lives after 1136.[72] Abbot Gilbert seems not to have required his services very often, and, with only two exceptions (one of which confirms a much earlier grant), neither Gloucester nor its benefactors requested his confirmation of their transactions.[73]

Gloucester had accepted Geoffrey Talbot's body in 1140 and bid for that of Miles in 1143.[74] By 1135 it had long been a regional focus for magnate piety, but it had no major patron. By 1144, Earl Roger was its advocate. Miles had perhaps held a similar position.[75] This complemented their control of Gloucestershire and furthered their place in regional society. Gilbert's predecessor as abbot was a Lacy, and the Lacys were the earls' main opponents. Gloucester developed St Guthlac's chapel in Hereford into a priory in the early 1140s with Miles's cooperation and Roger continued to support it.[76] It too offered an alternative social and spiritual focus to the bishop and had earlier owed much to the Lacys. Roger de Port, who had held Hereford castle against Miles in 1140, also had to concede his claims to its constituent parts.[77] Gloucester was thus backing the earls' ambitions.

---

[66] *Letters of Foliot*, no. 284; 'Charters of the Earldom of Hereford 1095–1201' [hereafter 'Hereford Charters'], ed. D. Walker, in *Camden Miscellany XXII*, Camden Society, 4th ser., 1 (1964), 1–76, nos. 6, 12, 21, 22.

[67] *Letters of Foliot*, nos. 302, 317, 338; 'Hereford Charters', nos. 11, 17, 18, 25, 26.

[68] *Letters of Foliot*, no. 332.

[69] Ibid., no. 302.

[70] 'Hereford Charters', nos. 19 (spurious), 20.

[71] *Charters and Records of Hereford Cathedral*, ed. W. W. Capes, Cantilupe Society (1908), 9; 'Hereford Charters', no. 13; *EEA VII: Hereford*, no. 28.

[72] *EEA VII: Hereford*, no. 13A.

[73] *Historia et cartularium*, i, cclxxviii; *EEA VII: Hereford*, no. 20. For pre-war examples, see nos. 15, 16, 17, 18, and for St Guthlacs, nos. 19, 21, 22, 24–7.

[74] *John of Worcester*, ii, 290; *Historia et cartularium*, i, app. to intro., no. ii.

[75] *Historia et cartularium*, i, no. 344; E. Cownie, *Religious Patronage in Anglo-Norman England* (Woodbridge, 1998), 24, 55, 64; Crouch, *Reign of Stephen*, 158.

[76] 'Hereford Charters', nos. 17, 18, 32–3, 40–2.

[77] The foundation's history is complex, *Historia et cartularium*, i, 16; iii, nos. 995–7; *Monasticon*, iii, 623; *EEA VII: Hereford*, xxxix, nos. 19, 21, 22, 24–7; Wightman, *Lacy Family*, 168; Cownie, *Religious Patronage*, 61; B. Coplestone-Crow, 'Payn fitzJohn and Ludlow Castle', *Transactions of the Shropshire Archaeological and Historical Society*, 70 (1995), 171–83, 181.

Bishop Robert refused Gloucester leave to dig a fishpond in Hereford, perhaps because he feared its expanding influence.[78] Earl Roger made a number of military alliances against Gilbert de Lacy in the late 1140s, and the bishop was present when one of them, with William de Braose, was agreed. He also attested and appended his seal to the agreement.[79] This was no Chester-Leicester *conventio*. First as abbot and then as bishop, Gilbert was a considerable political and religious support to Miles and Roger.

When Roger broke sanctuary to attack Lacy's knights, however, Bishop Gilbert had to hear the case on a mandate from King Stephen.[80] Despite his Angevin loyalties and regional political realities, both he and Lacy must have understood that his office entailed certain duties to the king. Royal absence did not negate the episcopal relationship with royal government. Bishop Robert's loyalty to Stephen likely contributed to his difficulties with the earls. Other Angevin supporters did, however, seek his confirmation, and the conflict may have been over authority in the city and shire.[81] Abbot Gilbert's 1143 letter on behalf of Miles implies as much. Miles perhaps considered his levy of the same year an earl's legitimate right. If so, Bishop Robert's opposition was not just that of a principled churchman, but also that of the earl's co-governor of the shire.[82] Bishop Robert also maintained his place in what remained of the shire community. He was part of *une grante congregacion* which met at Leominster, and a banquet was held in his honour at the dedication of Shobdon priory church.[83] His place in the shire, political connections, loyalty to Stephen, and spiritual influence constrained Miles's and Roger's attempts to create 'regional hegemony', but also helped him resist them.

III

Bishops Roger de Clinton of Chester and Alexander of Lincoln were criticized in the *Gesta Stephani*, but their successors, Walter Durdent and Robert de Chesney, have been cited in work on peacemaking because they guaranteed the Chester-Leicester *conventio*.[84] Much of the civil war history of the two dioceses remains obscure, but in their northern parts both were dominated by Earl Ranulf II of Chester, and the bishops of Chester are therefore considered first here.

The see of Lichfield was transferred to Chester in 1075, but, c. 1102, was

---

78 *Letters of Foliot*, no. 6; Brooke and Morey, *Gilbert Foliot*, 20–3, 86.
79 Z. N. L. Brooke and C. N. L. Brooke, 'Hereford Cathedral Dignitaries in the Twelfth Century – Supplement', *Cambridge Historical Journal*, 8 (1944–6), 179–85, 185; Crouch, *Reign of Stephen*, 79–80, 239, 257, 274, 306.
80 *Letters of Foliot*, nos. 94–6; Brooke and Morey, *Gilbert Foliot*, 123.
81 *EEA VII: Hereford*, nos. 45, 47.
82 Walker, 'Miles', 75–6.
83 'Chronicle of Wigmore', 422–4, 436. For an earlier date for the dedication, see G. Zarnecki, 'The Priory of Shobdon and its Founder', in *Studies in Medieval Art and Archaeology presented to Peter Lasko*, ed. P. Buckton and T. A. Heslop (Stroud, 1994), 211–20.
84 Stenton, *First Century*, 250–3, 286–8.

removed to Coventry. 'Chester' remained the bishops' title and their new church there was left unfinished, so they may have left unwillingly.[85] The last earl of Mercia had worked closely with the Anglo-Saxon bishop of Lichfield, but the earls of Chester did not dominate the whole diocese and the bishops were not their clients.[86] In Cheshire, they did have considerable autonomy, and the only other tenant in chief in 1086 was the bishop, but by 1135 episcopal estates in Chester were much reduced and in 1166 the bishop did not know the knights' service owed by his manors, although he did elsewhere.[87] The first earl perhaps saw advantages in a resident bishop, but his successors gradually restricted them, much as David Crouch has shown happened at Leicester, and Earl Ranulf may have closed Cheshire to them during the civil war. Bishop Roger last appears (with the earl) at the 1134 foundation of Combermere.[88] None of the earl's wartime Cheshire charters incorporate the bishops before he lay on his deathbed in 1153, and neither bishop nor archdeacon appear in material from St Werburgh's Chester, the earls' family foundation, or elsewhere.[89] St Werburgh's was seeking exemption from its bishops, and Ranulf contributed to its local ecclesiastical authority.[90] His son Hugh II succeeded to the earldom as a minor in 1153, and, with his mother, did address the bishop, while in 1157 the new abbot of St Werburgh's sought his blessing.[91] Episcopal involvement in Cheshire ecclesiastical issues followed.[92] Hugh II's minority made him vulnerable, St Werburgh's less confident, and episcopal support valuable.

Earl Ranulf II received a charter from Duke Henry in 1153, which gave him much of Derbyshire, Staffordshire, and northern Warwickshire.[93] It represents his civil war ambitions. Episcopal estates were exempt, but Ranulf's attitude towards

---

85 *Willelmi Malmesbiriensis Monachi de Gestis Pontificum Anglorum*, ed. N. E. S. A. Hamilton (RS, 1870), 310; *Annales Monastici*, ed. H. R. Luard, 5 vols. (RS, 1864–9), ii, 223; *VCH, Staffordshire*, iii, 7; *EEA 14: Coventry and Lichfield, 1072–1159*, ed. M. J. Franklin (Oxford, 1997), xxxii–vi.
86 N. J. Higham, 'Patterns of Patronage and Power: The Governance of Late Anglo-Saxon Cheshire', in *Government, Religion and Society in Northern England, 1000–1700*, ed. J. C. Appleby and P. Dalton (Stroud, 1997), 1–13.
87 *Domesday Book*, i, fols. 262c, 263a; *The Great Register of Lichfield Cathedral known as Magnum Registrum Album*, ed. H. E. Savage, William Salt Archaeological Society (1926), no. 262; 'Liber Niger Scaccarii Staffordscira', ed. G. Wrottesley, in *Collections for a History of Staffordshire* [hereafter *CHS*], 1st ser., 1 (1880), 145–240, 147; G. Barraclough, *The Earldom and County Palatine of Chester* (Oxford, 1953).
88 *Monasticon*, v, 323, no. 1.
89 *The Chartulary or Register of the Abbey of St Werburgh, Chester*, ed. J. Tait, Chetham Society, 79, 82 (1920–3); *The Charters of the Anglo-Norman Earls of Chester, c. 1071–1237* [hereafter *Chester Charters*], ed. G. Barraclough, The Record Society of Lancashire and Cheshire, 126 (1988).
90 *St Werburgh's Chartulary*, nos. 1, 61, 63; *Chester Charters*, nos. 13, 23, 61.
91 *Chester Charters*, nos. 119–21, 124, 157; *Annales Cestriensis*, ed. R. Copley, The Record Society of Lancashire and Cheshire, 14 (1916), entry for 1157.
92 *EEA 16: Coventry and Lichfield 1160–1182*, ed. M. J. Franklin (Oxford, 1998), nos. 14–21.
93 *Regesta*, iii, no. 180.

the bishops beyond Cheshire seems also to have been to exclude them where possible. Forty-six of his 103 charters concern the diocese, but Bishop Roger was addressed three times and witnessed twice, while Bishop Walter occurs only at Ranulf's deathbed.[94] Prior to the civil war relations had been better. Archbishop William de Corbeil addressed both bishop and earl with regard to St Werburgh's surrender of rights at Calke in Derbyshire.[95] Ranulf, further, did recognize the bishop on occasion in Stephen's reign. For instance, in the Chester-Leicester *conventio*. It is likely, therefore, that where the bishop was absent from Ranulf's lordships and charters, but active in neighbouring areas and noticed in charters originating in them, that Ranulf had chosen not to recognize his diocesan.

In northern Warwickshire Ranulf sought to consolidate his already strong presence.[96] He was a benefactor of Coventry priory, the major religious house, and buried a son there.[97] Coventry itself was seeking exemption from Bishop Roger and the return of resources he had taken with him when he had moved the see back to Lichfield.[98] No evidence survives of episcopal activity in northernmost Warwickshire until late in the civil war when Ranulf's authority was in decline.[99] Further south, in the earl of Warwick's sphere, episcopal *acta* and requests for episcopal confirmation are extant, and the archdeacon cooperated with the earl at his Warwick college.[100] Roger de Mowbray, who was not resident in the shire but had large estates there, also made use of the bishop, as did his tenants.[101] In Cheshire and in Warwickshire, bishops' ecclesiastical effectiveness depended on local political and religious powers.

Bishop Roger could not generally compete with Ranulf and Coventry, but at Combe, founded in 1147, he was more prominent. Combe's founder, Richard de Camville, was new to the region and loyal to Stephen, who had challenged Ranulf in 1146. Early donors such as the earl of Derby and Henry of Rugby were also

---

94 *Chester Charters*, nos. 34, 45, 63, 68, 82, 84, 100, 118.

95 *EEA 28: Canterbury, 1070–1136*, ed. M. Brett and J. A. Gribbin (Oxford, 2004), no. 63.

96 *Gesta Stephani*, 199–201; *Huntingdon*, 744; *Annales Monastici*, ii, 230; H. A. Cronne, 'Ranulf de Gernons, Earl of Chester, 1129–1154', *TRHS*, 4th ser., 20 (1937), 103–34, 127–8. For Coventry, see most recently, R. Goddard, *Lordship and Medieval Urbanisation: Coventry, 1043–1355* (Woodbridge, 2004), 21–49.

97 W. Dugdale, *Antiquities of Warwickshire*, 2nd edn rev. W. Thomas (London, 1730), i, 136; *The Early Records of Medieval Coventry*, ed. P. R. Coss and T. R. John, Records of Social and Economic History, ns, 11 (1986), no. 2.

98 *Magnum Registrum Album*, nos. 262, 454; *Regesta*, iii, no. 246; *Records of Coventry*, xviii; *EEA 14: Coventry and Lichfield*, xlvii–l.

99 *Monasticon*, v, 581.

100 Kenilworth Cartulary, BL Harley MS, 3650, fols. 17, 37, 44; Saltman, *Theobald*, no. 81; D. Crouch, 'Geoffrey de Clinton and Roger Earl of Warwick: New Men and Magnates in the Reign of Henry I', *Bulletin of the Institute of Historical Research*, 55 (1982), 113–24, 121; *The Cartulary of St Mary's Collegiate Church, Warwick*, ed. C. R. Fonge (Woodbridge, 2004), xli.

101 *Charters of the Honour of Mowbray 1107–1191* [hereafter *Mowbray Charters*], ed. D. E. Greenway, Records of Social and Economic History, ns, 1 (London, 1972), xxvi–xxviii, nos. 77–9, 175–7.

royalists.[102] Ranulf and his tenant Robert Basset were also donors, and their charters, unusually, addressed the bishop.[103] It has been suggested that the bishop had brought enemies together to neutralize disputed lands through the foundation, but Ranulf's charter probably dates to his deathbed, and his donation is not mentioned in later confirmations.[104] It may have been a restoration, and Basset's certainly was. He restored land he had seized from Warwick tenants. Following Stephen's attempts to push back Ranulf in 1146 and the establishment of a royalist magnate in the region, local powers with similar loyalties and facing similar pressures may have backed the foundation through which he affirmed his presence. If so, the bishop was not necessarily acting as peacemaker in this instance.

Derbyshire too was the object of Ranulf's ambitions.[105] Earl Robert de Ferrers was a Stephen loyalist as late as 1153, and so, while he was Ranulf's connection in the Chester-Leicester *conventio*, their alliance may have been brief.[106] It is only in 1147 x 1148 that his connections appear at Ranulf's court.[107] Ranulf expanded aggressively in the south-west where the Ferrers' estates were concentrated, and brought the Gresley family, tenants in chief, but also Ferrers' tenants, into his orbit.[108] The Gresleys themselves gained a presence at the heart of the Ferrers' honour when they married into the Bubendon family. Stephen de Beauchamp seized nearby Burton Abbey lands.[109] Earl Robert was under pressure. In the north, Ranulf was promised the honour of the Peak and he was also active in the east.[110] Bishops of Chester do not appear in Ranulf's Derbyshire charters, but can be found in Earl Robert's.[111] They too were lords of the Gresleys and of Bubendon. Earl Robert gave the bishops land during the civil war, and two of his clerical relatives appeared in their household.[112] Bishop Roger allowed Tutbury priory, the Ferrers' family house, to appropriate a church because the *status regni*

---

102 Combe Cartulary, BL Cotton MS, Vitellus, A I, fols. 42v, 43r, 45r; *EEA 14: Coventry and Lichfield*, no. 49; Dugdale, *Antiquities of Warwickshire*, i, 22–3.

103 Combe Cartulary, fol. 42v; *Chester Charters*, no. 100; *EEA 14: Coventry and Lichfield*, li, no. 46.

104 Dalton, 'Churchmen', 104–7.

105 Davis, *King Stephen*, 108, 146; M. Jones, 'The Charters of Robert de Ferrers, Earl of Nottingham, Derby and Ferrers', *Nottingham Mediaeval Studies*, 24 (1980), 7–27, 11.

106 *Gesta Stephani*, 234.

107 *Chester Charters*, nos. 45, 85.

108 Ibid., nos. 45, 68, 115; F. Madan, 'The Gresleys of Drakelow', in *CHS*, 1st ser., 19 (also titled ns, 1) (1898), 6–29.

109 'The Burton Chartulary', ed. G. Wrottesley, in *CHS*, 1st ser., 5 (in two parts) (1884), part i, 11, 50–1.

110 *Gesta Stephani*, 236; Jones, 'Charters of Robert de Ferrers', 9–11.

111 *Magnum Registrum Album*, no. 687; *The Cartulary of Darley Abbey*, ed. R. R. Darlington, Derbyshire Archaeological Record Society, 2 vols. (1945), ii, nos. H46, K16, N2–3, p. 548 (Gough cartulary, fol. 25).

112 *EEA 14: Coventry and Lichfield*, nos. 43, 60. Ex Ferrers land at *Bradestune* is included in an 1152 papal confirmation for the see, but not one of 1139, *Magnum Registrum Album*, nos. 262, 452.

tumultuosus had much diminished it, and Archbishop Theobald ordered all its possessions returned, singling out Ferrers' tenants for especial criticism.[113] Earl Robert himself stated that anyone who disrupted a grant to Darley would be answerable to the bishop.[114] Episcopal support shored up his lordship and status.

Northern Shropshire charters are also suggestive. The royalist Belmeis family and their foundation at Lilleshall often incorporated the bishops of Chester in their documents, but the fitzAlans, who supported the empress, and their house at Haughmond, did so only rarely.[115] The Belmeis were loyal to Stephen, the fitzAlans to Matilda. All but one of Stephen's charters addressed the bishop; of the empress's charters, only one did so. The empress's charters addressed William fitz Alan, Stephen's did not.[116] With the coming of peace, Duke Henry addressed the bishop.[117] Royalist Hamo Peverel died in the 1140s and was succeeded by Walchelin Maminot, an Angevin supporter. Both made grants to Shrewsbury Abbey: Hamo addressed the bishop, Walchelin did not.[118] The bishops were considered loyal to Stephen and had represented him in some way. Nevertheless, the fitzAlans as well as the Belmeis made grants to the new episcopal foundation of Buildwas during the civil war.[119] No conflict between the families broke out, and their donations may imply episcopal influence. In Shropshire, too, beyond his own power, Earl Ranulf addressed the bishop.[120]

Bishop Roger moved his see to Lichfield in Staffordshire before 1139, and brought the service of Coventry's knights.[121] His estates ran in a thick band across the centre of the county, concentrated around Lichfield and Eccleshall at either side.[122] Stephen granted him two royal chapels in 1136, and a third in 1139, at Wolverhampton.[123] This, as bishop and king must have known, had long been Worcester's, and it eventually had to be returned.[124] In the meantime, it gave Bishop Roger a considerable presence in south Staffordshire, and he quickly

113 *The Cartulary of Tutbury Priory*, ed. A. Saltman, *CHS*, 4th ser., 4 (1962), nos. 3, 6, 33; *EEA 14: Coventry and Lichfield*, no. 42A.
114 *Darley Cartulary*, ii, no. N3.
115 E.g. for the Belmeis, *Monasticon*, vi, pt. i, 261; *Regesta*, iii, no. 460. For the fitzAlans, *The Cartulary of Shrewsbury Abbey*, ed. U. Rees, 2 vols. (Aberystwyth, 1975), i, nos. 285, 307–8; *The Cartulary of Haughmond Abbey*, ed. U. Rees (Cardiff, 1985), nos. 272, 288, 583, 888, 925, 960, 1370; *EEA 14: Coventry and Lichfield*, nos. 23–4, both probably pre war.
116 *Regesta*, iii, nos 132, 376–8, 46–1, 820.
117 *Shrewsbury Cartulary*, ii, no. 311.
118 Ibid., i, nos 15, 28; Crouch, *Reign of Stephen*, 79, 184.
119 *EEA 14: Coventry and Lichfield*, no. 11; *The Cartae Antiquae Rolls 11–20*, ed. J. Conway Davies, Pipe Roll Society, ns, 33 (1960), no. 552; *VCH, Shropshire*, ii, 51.
120 *Chester Charters*, no. 61.
121 *Magnum Registrum Album*, no. 454.
122 *Domesday Book*, i, fols. 246a–247c.
123 *Regesta*, iii, nos. 451–3; J. H. Denton, *English Royal Free Chapels 1000–1300* (Manchester, 1970), 72–3.
124 *Regesta*, iii, no. 969; *The Cartulary of Worcester Cathedral Priory*, ed. R. R. Darlington, Pipe Roll Society, ns, 38 (1968), nos. 263, 266–7; Denton, *Royal Chapels*, 41–4.

enfeoffed tenants there.[125] During the civil war the bishops also picked up churches in two royal manors and, late on, Bishop Walter was granted a mint at Lichfield.[126] It confirmed him as a secular authority and royal representative in Staffordshire, but, to receive it, he must have been considered in this way already.

Staffordshire had no earl, but Robert II de Stafford had large estates in the north-west and was sheriff and constable at Stafford castle.[127] Dudley, to the south, was Angevin, but its civil war history is obscure.[128] Earl Ranulf had lands in the south-east, and when he and the king tried to reach a settlement in 1146 he was permitted a castle at Newcastle under Lyme in the north-west.[129] By 1163 there was also a castle at nearby Trentham, and on his deathbed he had made recompense to its canons.[130] Presumably he had led fighting there. Duke Henry's charter promised him the whole county, with the Staffords holding from him. Robert de Stafford is unlikely to have been his ally and may have been loyal to Stephen.[131] Robert had good relations with both bishops and his and his tenants' charters often address them.[132] He enfeoffed two episcopal tenants, and two important members of the bishops' household held his church at Bradley in succession.[133] Bishop Walter set up his steward on ex-Stafford land.[134] When three archdeacons judged a case involving lands over which Robert was lord, he issued a certificate in support of their findings.[135]

Bishop Roger fortified Lichfield and perhaps Eccleshall during the civil war, and Coventry's knights gave him, potentially, a significant military force.[136] The dean's prebend and the estates of the common fund were badly damaged, and William de Ridware, one of the episcopal tenants enfeoffed by Robert de Stafford, lost estates. Henry II would later order sheriffs to hear Lichfield's complaints.[137] Earl Ranulf was also much less successful in Staffordshire than

---

125 'Liber Niger', 147.
126 *Regesta*, iii, no. 457; M. Blackburn, 'Coinage and Currency' in King, *Anarchy*, 145–205, 161. The churches appear in Lichfield's 1152 papal confirmation, but not that of 1139, *Magnum Registrum Album*, nos. 262, 452.
127 *Domesday Book*, i, fols. 246a, 248d–249d; *VCH, Staffordshire*, iv, 49–53; J. A. Green, *English Sheriffs to 1154* (London, 1990), 75.
128 J. Hunt, *Lordship and the Landscape: A Documentary and Archaeological Study of the Honour of Dudley c. 1066–1322* (Oxford, 1997), 32.
129 *Regesta*, iii, no. 178; T. Pope, *Medieval Newcastle under Lyme* (Manchester, 1928), 2–3.
130 *PR 15 Henry II*, 72; *Chester Charters*, nos. 117–18.
131 Green, *Aristocracy*, 313; 'Liber Niger', 147–8.
132 E.g. Kenilworth Cartulary, fol. 26; *The Stone Cartulary*, ed. G. Wrottesley, *CHS*, 6, part 1 (1885), 3; 'The Staffordshire Cartulary', ed. G. Wrottesley, in *CHS*, 1st ser., 2 (1881), 178–276, 195–209, 217–20, 238–40.
133 'The Staffordshire Cartulary', 219–20; *Magnum Registrum Album*, nos. 67, 168–9.
134 *EEA 14: Coventry and Lichfield*, no. 63.
135 'The Staffordshire Cartulary', 233–8.
136 *Anglia Sacra*, i, 434; 'Liber Niger', 147. King John granted Bishop Hugh de Nonant licence to fortify his castle at Eccleshall, which may therefore have already existed, *Magnum Registrum Album*, no. 21.
137 'Liber Niger', 147; *Magnum Registrum Album*, nos. 351, 497; *Regesta*, iii, no. 715; *EEA 16: Coventry and Lichfield*, nos. 59, 64–5, 70–1.

elsewhere. This suggests, although there is no explicit evidence, that Bishop Roger at least, and probably in cooperation with Robert de Stafford, held off Ranulf's expansion by, sometimes, military means. Earl Ranulf threatened not only the bishops' estates, but also their ecclesiastical authority and autonomy. He excluded them where he was powerful, abetted by St Werburgh's, Chester and Coventry priory. Magnates who looked to their bishops were, like them, under pressure from Ranulf, often loyal to Stephen and had a role in shire government. Sometimes, too, there was a spiritual connection.

IV

In the diocese of Lincoln, Henry I's involvement in Newark's development was noted above.[138] Stephen early gave the bishops two fees of the Honour of Poitou and two in Kent, the castleguard duty of the latter being transferred from Dover to Newark.[139] The bishops also still owed castleguard at the royal castle and Bishop Alexander was justiciar for Lincolnshire until his arrest in 1139. His replacement, William II de Roumare, was made earl soon after.[140] Bishop Alexander was soon reconciled with the king, and was granted the Condet family wardship and tower in Lincoln, further gifts in 1146, and attended the king on campaign in 1143.[141] Bishop Robert regained the justiciarship and was given a mint at Newark.[142] The civil war bishops of Lincoln were thus loyal to the king, involved in royal governance, and possessed of considerable resources in Lincolnshire.

Civil war Lincolnshire was dominated by Earl Ranulf of Chester and his half brother William de Roumare, who sought, 'independent tenurial, governmental and military domination'.[143] Among their claims were the Poitou lands. Gilbert II de Gant was their main opponent, and was made Stephen's earl of Lincoln in 1148.[144] Ranulf of Bayeux in the north-east also came under pressure.[145] The bishops too: in Well wapentake they had a monopoly of justice and their estates linked Lincoln with Newark, but Earl Ranulf took control of the area. When Stephen granted the bishop the Poitou fees and the Condet wardship, he must have been aware that the half brothers claimed them, and his grant of the wapentake centre of Torskey to Earl Ranulf and its church to Bishop Alexander created more tension. Relations between the bishops and the half brothers were

---

138 *Regesta*, ii, no. 1791.
139 *Regesta*, iii, nos. 470, 485.
140 Ibid., nos. 490, 493; Davis, *King Stephen*, 134–5.
141 *Regesta*, iii, nos. 125, 290, 399, 471, 482, 486, 605–6, 655.
142 Ibid., nos. 489, 490.
143 P. Dalton, 'Aiming at the Impossible: Ranulf II Earl of Chester and Lincolnshire in the Reign of King Stephen', in *The Earldom of Chester and its Charters: A Tribute to Geoffrey Barraclough*, ed. A. Thacker, Chester Archaeological Society, 71 (1991), 109–34, 111. The remainder of this paragraph depends on this reconstruction, except where otherwise noted.
144 Davis, *King Stephen*, 135.
145 Dalton, 'Churchmen', 96–7.

not good. Bishop Alexander's role in the prelude to the battle of Lincoln is well known, but Stephen's 1143 campaign also moved against Earl Ranulf.[146] Stephen had to repeat the Poitou grant in 1146 which suggests that the half brothers had prevented it.[147] In 1153, Duke Henry found it necessary to resolve Bishop Robert's difficulties with Earl Ranulf to bring him on side, and had to guarantee the earl's considerable reparations.[148] It was probably not coincidence that Bishop Robert received the justiciarship and the mint in the same year that Gilbert de Gant was made earl.[149]

Bishops are rare in Earl Ranulf's and William de Roumare's civil war Lincolnshire charters. Twenty-six survive for Ranulf, of which only six incorporate bishops of Lincoln. All six, none of which were issued at Lincoln, have been dated to after 1149, by which time Ranulf's power was in decline.[150] The present writer is aware of twenty-one of William's charters; the bishops appear in six.[151] In contrast, ten of Gilbert de Gant's seventeen civil war charters for his family house at Bardney include the bishops (and episcopal confirmation charters survive for another three), while at Ranulf de Bayeux's Newhouse the bishops are almost ubiquitous.[152] Bardney lay isolated from Gant estates in a wapentake the half brothers sought to control, and Gilbert looked to the bishops to buttress its position. Elsewhere where he was under pressure he also sought episcopal confirmation.[153] He later made recompense to Norwich through Bishop Robert's hands, and he is the only great magnate to be found at Lincoln cathedral during the war.[154]

Recent work has suggested that Bishop Alexander tried to limit conflict in Lincolnshire and, 'deliberately orchestrated religious patronage to promote peace between many powerful laymen', including Earl Ranulf and William de Roumare.[155] It has focused on Newhouse and William's Cistercian foundation at

---

[146] *Gesta Stephani*, 111; *Huntingdon*, 732; *Regesta*, iii, nos. 125, 290, 605–6, 655.

[147] *Regesta*, iii, nos. 480, 486.

[148] Ibid., nos. 491–2.

[149] Davis, *King Stephen*, 134–5.

[150] *Chester Charters*, nos. 16–17, 44, 48, 53–5, 58–9, 66, 69, 76–80, 92–3, 96, 104, 107–8, 111, 117.

[151] Kirkstead Cartulary, BL Cotton MS, Vespasian, E 18, fo. 142v; Bardney Cartulary, BL Cotton MS, Vespasian, E 20, fos. 123v–124r; BL Harleian Charters, 55 E 10, 55 E 12; Crowland Cartulary, Spalding, Spalding Gentleman's Society, fos. 193r–v; *Documents Illustrative of the Social and Economic History of the Northern Danelaw*, ed. F. M. Stenton (London, 1920), nos. 185, 499–501, 512–13, 515–16, 518; *Facsimiles of Early Charters from Northamptonshire Collections*, ed. F. M. Stenton, Northamptonshire Record Society, 4 (1930), no. 1.

[152] Bardney Cartulary, fos. 63r–75v, 86r–v, 89r, 91v, 104r, 105r, 111r–112r, 113v–114v, 120r, 123v–4r, 197v, 231r–v; Dalton, 'Churchmen', 99; *EEA I: Lincoln 1067–1185*, ed. D. Smith (Oxford, 1980), no. 51.

[153] *EEA I: Lincoln*, nos. 85–6.

[154] Ibid., no. 200; *Registrum Antiquissimum*, ii, no. 315.

[155] A. G. Dyson, 'The Monastic Patronage of Bishop Alexander of Lincoln', *Journal of Ecclesiastical History*, 26 (1975), 1–25, 9–10; Dalton, 'Churchmen', 95.

Revesby, founded from Rievaulx and a beneficiary of magnates of different loyalties. Alexander attested the foundation charter and advised Ailred of Rievaulx, the first abbot, to accept contested land to further peace. Ailred was close to King David of Scotland who also used Rievaulx as a mother house.[156] So did others, loyal to Stephen. The Cistercians were keen on initial episcopal consent, but this did not entail continuing connections. No Revesby cartulary survives, but at nearby Kirkstead the bishop witnessed the foundation charter but was little involved thereafter.[157] The contemporary Cistercian expansion meant that some houses provided monks for, and some received donations from, magnates on both sides of the civil war, but it did not necessarily mean the creation of relationships between them. Earl Simon of Northampton, loyal to Stephen, was a benefactor of Revesby and founded Sawtry from Rievaulx, but he held his earldom because the king had taken it from the Scots, and Sawtry was built on lands of tenants loyal to King David.[158] Newhouse's benefactors were lesser barons whose lords, the civil war rivals, confirmed their gifts. Bishops appeared in almost all their charters. Lincolnshire barons, however, in fact witnessed each other's charters regardless of their respective overlords, and a shire community existed autonomously of the great magnates.[159] Overlords may have confirmed their tenants' grants, but did not necessarily take great interest in the donation or the house.[160]

Indeed, the bishops' involvement with Newhouse may represent instead their importance to that shire community. Newhouse's founders made donations to it at Lincoln cathedral, and Ranulf of Bayeux separated from his wife there to enter the religious life, before the bishop.[161] A number of local lords made donations to houses in the cathedral, sometimes, again, in the bishops' presence. Other barons attested their charters.[162] In the absence of legitimate or undisputed secular

---

[156] Dyson, 'Monastic Patronage', 10; Dalton, 'Churchmen', 97.

[157] Dyson, 'Monastic Patronage', 7; Holdsworth, 'The Church', 216–17. Kirkstead Cartulary, fos. 2r–v, 19r, 32r–33r, 71r, 73v–4r, 99r–100v, 142v, 158r, 179r.

[158] J. Burton, *Monastic and Religious Orders in Britain, 1000–1300* (Cambridge, 1994), 69–77.

[159] For example, BL Cotton Charters, xi 26; Kirkstead Cartulary, fos. 99r–100v; *Danelaw Documents*, nos. 19, 216, 500. For Lincolnshire's political geography see Dalton, 'Aiming at the Impossible', 125, 127–8.

[160] Earl Ranulf's grant to Bishop Alexander's Louth Park and both half brothers' attendance at his Haverholme foundation have also been cited, but the first was founded before the war, while the second was founded 1139 x 1140 when Alexander was in disgrace and the two magnates ruled Lincolnshire for Stephen. Neither made a donation. *EEA I: Lincoln*, no. 50; *Calendar of the Charter Rolls Preserved in the Public Record Office, III* (London, 1908), 247; Dyson, 'Monastic Patronage', 9; Dalton, 'Churchmen', 96–8. Anathema and 'Amen' clauses in episcopal *acta* have been considered significant, but were quite common, *EEA: I Lincoln*, lvii, nos. 47, 52, 53; Dalton, 'Churchmen', 96, 98.

[161] BL Harleian Charters 45 F 17, 50 H 58; Dalton, 'Churchmen', 98.

[162] BL Harleian Charters 46 B 3, 52 G 21, 55 G 25; BL Additional Charters 11292 (6); Kirkstead Cartulary, fos. 17r, 99r; *Danelaw Documents*, nos. 2, 58, 303; *Transcripts of Charters relating to the Gilbertine Houses of Sixle, Ormsby, Cately, Bullington and*

government, and with their own lords in conflict, the giving of gifts in the cathedral offered some guarantee for both donor and monastery, but it may also have been a neutral space where the community could gather.

Cathedral chapters, further, had considerable resources of their own, and might be politically significant.[163] The great magnates, excepting Gilbert de Gant, cannot be found at Lincoln, but it was important to them.[164] Earl Robert of Leicester had got Philip de Harcourt made dean c. 1133.[165] During the civil war Gilbert contributed to the prebend of Nassington, Earl Ranulf tried but failed to found one based on Scamblesby, William de Roumare was in dispute with the chapter over Asgardby, and Earl Simon of Northampton made a grant direct to the cathedral. King Stephen founded three prebends and attempted two more.[166] One, for his keeper of the seal, he hoped to fund jointly with the bishop to their mutual benefit, partly from the revenues of the city. He had to repeat the foundation, probably because the half brothers had prevented the first attempt because it would have given him a presence in their city. Earl Ranulf's castle and the cathedral faced each other. Considerable work was done on the latter's magnificent west front in the 1140s, and it represents, indeed it may have been intended to represent, an assertion of episcopal spiritual authority against the earl's military power.[167]

In Leicestershire, David Crouch has shown that the earls gradually pushed the bishops out of Leicester before 1135. They rarely appear in Earl Robert's civil war charters, or those of his foundation at St Mary's, Leicester.[168] No representative of the diocese had been among the shire notables gathered at its foundation.[169] Earl Robert also granted St Mary's every church in Leicester save the bishops' and gained for it the right to bury excommunicates, thus making provision to evade the sanction.[170] He may not have incorporated the bishops in his Leicestershire charters, but he did elsewhere. In north-west Buckinghamshire, he disseised Robert of Meppershall and transferred the estates to his steward, Ernald de Bosco. He and Ernald founded Biddlesden there because their actions were of doubtful legitimacy.[171] Both Ernald's foundation charter and Earl Robert's

Alvingham, ed. F. M. Stenton, Lincoln Record Society, 18 (1922), Alvingham ser. no. 3, Sixle ser. no. 54.

163 Crosby, *Bishop and Chapter*, passim.

164 *Registrum Antiquissimum*, ii, no. 315; *EEA I: Lincoln*, no. 200.

165 *Registrum Antiquissimum*, i, nos. 130–3, 252, 310, 315; *Fasti Ecclesie Anglicanae 1066–1300, III, Lincoln*, compiled by D. Greenway (London, 1977), 8, 78, 94; Crouch, *Beaumont Twins*, 130.

166 *Regesta*, iii, nos. 477–80, 484–6.

167 P. Kidson, 'Architectural History', in *A History of Lincoln Minster*, ed. D. M. Owen (Cambridge, 1996), 14–46.

168 *EEA I: Lincoln*, nos. 146–8. The St Mary's register does not preserve address clauses.

169 *Monasticon*, vi, pt. i, 463–8, no. 21; *EEA I: Lincoln*, no. 39; Crouch, *Beaumont Twins*, 201–2.

170 *Papsturkunden in England*, ed. W. Holtzmann, 3 vols. (Berlin and Göttingen, 1930–52), iii, no. 75.

171 BL Harleian Charters, 85 G 48; *Monasticon*, v, 367; Crouch, *Beaumont Twins*, 79–82.

confirmation addressed the bishop, and other early documents incorporated him.[172] Bishop Robert issued two early confirmations himself, and insisted Robert of Meppershall remit his claims.[173]

In the north-west, Earl Robert consolidated his power by founding Garendon Abbey on Chester lands.[174] William Gerbert, the tenant, later granted the same land as it had been unjustly taken away from his father and given by Robert.[175] He promised to increase the endowment if he recovered the land, and made his grant to the mother house, thus denying the foundation. His charter addresses the bishop, one of only three to do so of the twenty-two civil war charters in the Garendon register. Chester tenants, like their lord, rarely looked to the bishop, but in Leicestershire he was the only alternative to Earl Robert. In the north-east, Earl Ranulf himself pushed into the Honour of Belvoir at Redmile. He issued two charters for Belvoir priory, in one of which he admitted that the land had been William d'Aubigny's, the lord of the honour, who had already made the same grant. Here Ranulf addressed the bishop and his archdeacon, but there is no extant confirmation, and instead the bishops confirmed d'Aubigny's charters.[176] Ranulf also moved into Belvoir in neighbouring Northamptonshire where d'Aubigny founded Pipewell in the early 1140s, but Ranulf later granted the same endowment to the abbey. D'Aubigny reaffirmed his foundation in 1148. Both lords' charters addressed the bishops, but they confirmed d'Aubigny's not Ranulf's.[177]

In Huntingdonshire and Northamptonshire the Scottish royal family held the earldom until 1139, when Stephen granted it to Simon II de Senlis.[178] Simon must have struggled to establish his authority because there was substantial disruption to monastic and royal estates and he was forced to make a marriage alliance with the Mauduit family to end their expansion at his expense.[179] He also had problems on his own estates where there was residual loyalty to the Scots.[180] In response, he

---

172 BL Harleian Charters 84 H 18, 84 H 45; Biddlesden Cartulary, BL Harley MS 4714, fo.1; *Monasticon*, v, 367.

173 *EEA I: Lincoln*, nos. 81–4; Stenton, *First Century*, 255–6.

174 E. King, 'Mountsorrel and its Region in King Stephen's Reign', *Huntington Library Quarterly*, 44 (1980), 1–10, 5, 9.

175 Garendon Cartulary, BL Lansdowne MS 415, fo. 15r.

176 *Chester Charters*, nos. 50, 52; 'Belvoir Cartulary', in *Historical Manuscripts Commission 12th Report, Appendix, Part IV: The Manuscripts of the Duke of Rutland preserved in Belvoir Castle*, 4 vols. (London, 1880–1905), iv, 140, 147; *EEA I: Lincoln*, nos. 78–9; E. King, 'The Origins of the Wake Family: The Early History of the Barony of Bourne in Lincolnshire', *Northamptonshire Past and Present*, 5 (1975), 167–77, 173.

177 Pipewell Cartulary, BL Additional MS 37022, fo. 8r; *Chester Charters*, no. 85; *EEA I: Lincoln*, nos. 222–3; King, 'Foundation of Pipewell', 172–6.

178 *Regesta Regum Scottorum Volume I: The Acts of Malcolm IV King of Scots 1153–1165*, ed. G. W. S. Barrow (Edinburgh, 1960), nos. 18, 100–3.

179 *The Peterborough Chronicle of Hugh Candidus*, ed. and trans. W. T. and C. Mellows (Peterborough, 1941), 66; *Regesta*, iii, nos. 167, 581; *The Beauchamp Cartulary Charters 1100–1268*, ed. E. Mason, Pipe Roll Society, ns, 43 (1980), iv, xxvi, xxxiv.

180 BL Additional Charters 6037; J. A. Green, 'Henry I and David I', *Scottish Historical Review*, 75 (1996), 1–19, 21–4.

took over Scottish foundations at St Andrews in Northampton and at Daventry. The bishops confirmed both.[181] At Fotheringay in Northamptonshire and Sawtry in Huntingdonshire, Simon established new foundations on lands belonging to the Olifard family who were in exile in Scotland.[182] One of the earliest Sawtry charters noted the bounds of the estates and local consultation with more than usual care, and thanked the earl's steward and the bishop for their work.[183] This suggests that Simon knew his actions were dubious. After the civil war King Malcolm IV regained the earldom, but his early Sawtry charters treat the abbey as his foundation and are for its mother house. They do not incorporate the bishop. Contemporary charters do, and Bishop Robert was then Henry II's government agent in the county.[184]

Both bishops of Lincoln had also been active in royal government in Northamptonshire and Huntingdonshire in cooperation with the earl, but also independently of him, during the civil war.[185] Episcopal administration was also prominent. Both bishops held full synods, Alexander's suffragan was active, and Bishop Robert issued up to twenty four *acta* for Northamptonshire and settled a number of disputes in Huntingdonshire.[186] Relations between the bishops and the earl were harmonious, with the bishops buttressing the earl's authority and contributing to the stability of the two counties through their involvement in secular as well as ecclesiastical government.

Evidence for episcopal activity in Lincoln's southern counties is more limited. Missenden's cartulary (Bucks.) does not preserve charter address clauses, but neither Dunstable's nor Harrold Priory's (both Beds.) civil war charters regularly incorporate the bishop.[187] King Stephen and Earl Simon often included the

---

[181] *EEA I: Lincoln*, no. 192; *The Cartulary of Daventry Priory*, ed. M. J. Franklin, Northamptonshire Record Society, 35 (1985), nos. 5, 6, 8; Franklin, 'The Secular College', 98, 101–2.

[182] Fotheringay: *Monasticon*, v, 208–13, nos. 1, 2, 5, 9; K. Stringer, 'The Early Lords of Lauderdale, Dryburgh Abbey and St Andrews Priory at Northampton', in *Essays on the Nobility of Medieval Scotland*, ed. K. Stringer (Edinburgh, 1985), 44–72, at 45. Sawtry: BL Cotton Charters VII 3; *Regesta Regum Scottorum I*, no. 305.

[183] *Monasticon*, v, 522–3, no. 3.

[184] *Regesta Regum Scottorum I*, nos. 128, 142–3, 208–10, 285, 305. Bishop included: BL Harleian Charters 85 B 5, 85 B 6. For Henry II, see for example *Cartulariam Monasterii de Rameseia*, ed. W. H. Hart and P. A. Lyons, 3 vols. (RS, 1884–93), i, no. 97; ii, nos. 139, 140 (6); *Registrum Antiquissimum*, i, nos. 158, 184.

[185] Marritt, 'Stephen and the Bishops', 135.

[186] Northants: Pipewell Cartulary, BL Cotton MS Caligula A XII, fos. 3r, 8r, 8v, 11r, 27r, 36v, 37r; *EEA I: Lincoln*, nos. 85, 107, 131, 156, 167, 185–95, 198–9, 220–3, 247i–ii, 278, 280; *Monasticon*, vi, part 2, 1018, no. 1; *Facsimiles of Northants. Charters*, Boughton ser., nos. 46–7; *Daventry Cartulary*, nos. 5, 6, 8, 667, 701, 815. Hunts.: *Registrum Antiquissimum*, i, nos. 134, 226–7, 236, 238, 267.

[187] *The Cartulary of Missenden Abbey*, ed. J. G. Jenkins, 3 vols., Buckinghamshire Archaeological Society, Record Branch (1938–62); *Digest of Dunstable Cartulary*, ed. G. H. Fowler, Bedfordshire Historical Record Society Publications, 10 (1926), nos. 106–8, 126; *Records of Harrold Priory*, ed. idem, Bedfordshire Historical Record Society Publications, 17 (1935), no. 2.

bishops in their charters for Northamptonshire and Huntingdonshire, but did not for Bedfordshire or Buckinghamshire.[188] Fewer episcopal *acta* are extant than for elsewhere and ecclesiastical governance may have been devolved to the archdeacons.[189] Both counties were also somewhat disrupted.[190] Bishops' authority in magnate society perhaps had geographical limits in time of war.

Things should have been different in Oxfordshire, where the bishops were prominent landholders and patrons before the civil war began. Fully a quarter of their knights were enfeoffed in the county, Bishop Robert was a canon of St George's in Oxford castle, and his brother William was Stephen's captain there.[191] Material also survives from a number of monasteries. Episcopal engagement seems, nevertheless, to have been limited. Eynsham, where the bishops were patron, has left thirty civil war charters, but only two address them, both issued by a far distant donor.[192] Bishop Alexander had dedicated Godstow on the eve of the war in the presence of king, queen, archbishop and court, and had made an enormous donation, but he appears in only one civil war charter.[193] Bishop Robert can only be shown to have used his authority to back his brother once, when he attested Stephen's 1149 confirmation of the transfer of St George's to Oseney Abbey. The donors were royalists, the bishop's brother and Richard de Camville, but in the empress's earlier confirmation her allies are named instead, John de St John and Henry d'Oilly.[194]

Oxfordshire episcopal *acta* relate mainly to internal issues at houses where the bishops were patron and include few confirmations.[195] Monasteries were keen, though, on confirmations from King Stephen, Empress Matilda and Duke Henry.[196] The bishops' possessions were concentrated in the north, which was relatively peaceful, but further south there was much heavy fighting between the

188 'Honour of Wardon, Potton and Halstead Charters', ed. G. H. Fowler, Bedfordshire Historical Record Society Publications, 11 (1927), nos. 1a, 1b; *Regesta*, iii, nos. 683, 745–6, 861–2, 919–20, 960.
189 *EEA I: Lincoln*, nos. 108–9, 171–2, 242–3. Biddlesden Cartulary, BL Harley MS 4714, fo. 1r; *Monasticon*, vi, part 1, 950; *Dunstable Cartulary*, nos. 106, 108, 161; *Missenden Cartulary*, ii, no. 272; *Registrum Antiquissimum*, ix, no. 256; *Letters of Foliot*, no. 371; *Twelfth-Century English Archidiaconal and Vice-Archidiaconal Acta*, ed. B. R. Kemp, Canterbury and York Society, 92 (2001), nos. 69–72.
190 *Gesta Stephani*, 184; *Historia Ecclesie Abbendonensis: The History of the Church of Abingdon*, ed. J. Hudson, 2 vols. (Oxford, 2002–7), ii, 278; *Regesta*, iii, nos. 456, 487; *The Red Book of the Exchequer*, ed. H. Hall, 3 vols. (RS, 1896), i, 312; Crouch, *Reign of Stephen*, 206, n. 50.
191 *Domesday Book*, i, fos. 154, 155; *Regesta*, iii, no. 366; *EEA I: Lincoln*, xxxv, nos. 25, 34–5, 232, 251; E. Amt, *The Accession of Henry II in England: Royal Government Restored, 1149–1159* (Woodbridge, 1993), 5, 50–5. For civil war Oxfordshire see ibid., 48–64.
192 *The Eynsham Cartulary*, ed. H. E. Salter, 2 vols., Oxford Historical Society (1907–1908), i, nos. 34, 46.
193 *The English Register of Godstow Nunnery near Oxford*, ed. A. Clark, 3 vols., Early English Text Society, 129, 130, 142 (1904–11), iii, 848.
194 *Regesta*, iii, nos. 632–3.
195 For example *EEA I: Lincoln*, nos. 27, 28, 59, 116–18, 122, 232, 259, 261–2, 264.
196 *Regesta*, iii, nos. 643–4, 679–80, 697, 853–4.

'official' parties to the civil war.[197] Episcopal authority was limited there, either because the bishops chose not to assert themselves or because when they did, they made little impact. In Oxfordshire, the *Gesta Stephani*'s comment that bishops' 'salt had no savour' perhaps has some basis. It may not be coincidence that it was the only county in which the 'official' civil war dominated events.

V

Beyond Oxfordshire, the six bishops of Hereford, Chester, and Lincoln were all engaged in local politics and society, and, at times, partisan. Bishop Robert de Bethune, the *Gesta Stephani*'s holy man, also had secular connections, while Bishops Alexander and Roger de Clinton had spiritual as well as political relationships with magnates. The effectiveness of ecclesiastical administration, and bishops' political and spiritual authority, could be dependent on local secular and religious powers, but could also be significant enough for those same powers, sometimes in cooperation, to seek to exclude them. It was these authority figures building their own power, not out of control mercenaries, who caused the bishops most trouble. All were excommunicated, but episcopal administration could also have effect. Confirmation charters buttressed and legitimized claims to lands and rights or ignored them, thus impacting on political developments. Other magnates, such as the earls of Derby and Northampton, Robert de Stafford and Gilbert de Gant, looked to their bishops for support, and received it in ecclesiastical, political, spiritual, and perhaps military forms.

The bishops for their part, and not always successfully, opposed attempts to constrain their authority and dominate their dioceses. The patterns, and there are such patterns in these dioceses, of who looked to them and who did not, who they supported and who they did not, suggest that they also strove to maintain and further local political and tenurial stability, and legitimate local government. It seems too that they opposed the aggressor and supported the victim. Their connections tended to be at least ostensibly loyal to King Stephen. Common political interests coincided with moral imperatives and spiritual relationships, because those who were most aggressive and disruptive of secular government were often those who most transgressed ecclesiastical law and victimized those they sought to dominate. Bishop Gilbert Foliot might seem the exception, but as an Angevin loyalist his support of Miles's and Roger's efforts can, to some extent at least, be considered in the same light. If the *Gesta Stephani* is correct and Bishops Roger and Alexander did engage in military activity, then this was the context, and their actions were not far removed from John of Worcester's conception of their office.

Both bishops' civil war authority and motivation were grounded in a combination of their ecclesiastical authority and spiritual influence, their place in shire government, their association with the king and, sometimes, their own resources:

197 Amt, *Accession*, 11, 55.

all traditional rather than extraordinary. The three case studies offered here are neither intended as representative of every diocese nor as implying an alternative episcopate to that put forward by others. They do, however, open an additional facet of a very complex office, and there are parallels elsewhere.[198] Two broader points are perhaps justifiable. Civil war bishops could be active and partisan in local politics and society as well as peacemakers, and their ecclesiastical and spiritual activity ought not to be considered independently of local political contexts, while those contexts cannot be fully outlined without incorporating the episcopate.

[198] For example, early conflict between Reginald fitz Roy and the Bishop of Exeter, *Gesta Stephani*, 102–3; an allegation that Bishop Simon of Worcester failed to censure William de Beauchamp because they were friends, 'La Chronique de Sainte-Barbe-en-Auge', ed. R. N. Sauvage, *Mémoires de l'Academie Nationale des Sciences, Arts et Belles Lettres de Caen: documents* (Caen, 1906), 1–69, 29, 41–2, 45; and Bishop Hilary of Chichester's assertion of episcopal authority against the Sussex rapeholders, and appointment as sheriff after 1153, *The Chartulary of the High Church of Chichester*, ed. W. D. Peckham, Sussex Record Society, 46 (1942–3), nos. 94, 297–9; H. Mayr-Harting, 'Hilary, Bishop of Chichester (1147–1169) and Henry II', *EHR*, 78 (1963), 209–24, 213.

8

Violent Disorder in King Stephen's England: A Maximum Argument

HUGH M. THOMAS

RECENT WORKS on Stephen and his reign have added great depth and nuance to our understanding of England's history from 1135 to 1154.[1] They give us a better sense of Stephen's abilities and the difficulties he faced, the degree to which his government remained functioning, and the role of the magnates in the civil war that engulfed his reign. Unfortunately, the scholars responsible have also sanitized the reign, unduly minimizing the amount of violence and disorder in their efforts to prove that Stephen was not such a bad king, that magnates were not mindless feudal anarchists, and that the reign should not be labelled 'the Anarchy'.[2] Though I accept many of their arguments, I believe that they are far too eager to dismiss or downplay contemporary accounts of disorder, violence and suffering because these accounts seem to support outdated historiographic approaches to the reign. In contrast, I would argue that recent work on military history suggests that a prolonged civil war could lead directly to the kind of wide-spread suffering and the sorts of atrocities that the sources describe. There were exaggerations in the lamentations about the reign, but recent scholarship has badly overcorrected for such excesses. It is time to restate and improve the case for viewing Stephen's reign as a deeply violent and disorderly period.

The arguments against the bleak picture of the reign are not entirely new, but

[1] I would like to thank Patricia Rosario Thomas and Andrew Lowerre for creating the maps. Marlon Joseph also helped immensely. Jennifer Paxton read through the article and made a number of helpful suggestions. Several members of the Haskins society made useful comments on an earlier version, as did the organizers and attendees of the Liverpool conference.

[2] K. J. Stringer, *The Reign of Stephen: Kingship, Warfare and Government in Twelfth-Century England* (London, 1993), 4, 86; G. J. White, *Restoration and Reform, 1153–1165: Recovery from Civil War in England* (Cambridge, 2000), 13; G. J. White, 'The Myth of the Anarchy', *ANS*, 22 (2000), 323–37; J. Bradbury, *Stephen and Matilda: The Civil War of 1139–53* (Stroud, 1996), 190–3; Crouch, *Reign of Stephen*, 1–7, 161; Matthew, *King Stephen*, 123, 127–33, 149, 154, 192–3, 230.

have been stated with particular force in recent years. Some of these arguments draw on evidence showing that not *everything* was doom and destruction. Many individual churches flourished and royal government did not completely collapse in Stephen's reign.[3] These are important subjects in their own right, but their main significance here is the implication that if churches flourished and government survived in some diminished capacity, perhaps England's state was not so dismal after all. More broadly, any sign of normality can be taken to cast doubt on the traditional picture.[4] Scholars also sometimes point to violence in other reigns or periods, suggesting that Stephen's reign may not have been unusual.[5] The main arguments, however, involve undermining the credibility of the sources. Above all, there is a simple reluctance to accept the descriptions of the reign as plausible. Donald Matthew has written, 'Conditions cannot have ever become as bad as they have been painted', and frequently argues that writers tended to make statements full of hyperbole.[6] He and others have pointed to biases in the sources.[7] Several scholars maintain that the famously bleak descriptions are based on local conditions and that the chroniclers or modern scholars have misleadingly generalized from isolated events to create laments covering all of England for all of the reign.[8]

It is no surprise that 'minimalist' scholars focus on undermining the sources, for the sources provide plentiful evidence about violence and disorder that needs to be explained away if one is to adopt a relatively benign picture of Stephen's reign. The evidence does not consist only of a few jeremiads, but includes many references to specific acts of violence. In Map 1, I have marked a large number of recorded incidents from the reign, either at the places where they occurred or, if that is not specified, at the places they were recorded. Some individual dots represent more than one incident, such as the multiple sieges of Wallingford. Map 1 does *not* include the problematic evidence of pipe roll waste (see Map 10) or of land seizures (see Map 9). Even with these subtractions, the map shows that practically every area of England felt the impact of war and violence at some point in Stephen's reign.[9]

3   White, *Restoration*, 12–76; White, 'Myth', 323, 331–3; Crouch, *Reign of Stephen*, 305–7, 312, 327–39; Matthew, *King Stephen*, 32, 133–40, 216–20, 236–7; Stringer, *Reign of Stephen*, 5, 28–60; Bradbury, *Stephen and Matilda*, 191–2.
4   Matthew, *King Stephen*, 32–4, 223–4, 234–6.
5   Ibid., 133, 148–9; Crouch, *Reign of Stephen*, 136–7.
6   Matthew, *King Stephen*, 123, 127, 130, 133, 192–3.
7   Stringer, *Reign of Stephen*, 4, 83–4, 86; White, 'Myth', 323–31; White, *Restoration*, 2–3; Matthew, *King Stephen*, 41–2, 132, 153–63; C. Coulson, *Castles in Medieval Society: Fortresses in England, France, and Ireland in the Central Middle Ages* (Oxford, 2003), 118–19.
8   Stringer, *Reign of Stephen*, 86; Matthew, *King Stephen*, 127–33, 230; Crouch, *Reign of Stephen*, 5, 161; White, 'Myth', 326.
9   The author may be contacted at h.thomas@miami.edu for tables and a bibliography showing the sources of this material. Most of the material there is already known. Sources that I have not seen noted elsewhere include documents from Thorney Abbey (Cambridge University Library Additional MS 3020, fos. 22v, 41r; MS 3021, fo. 207r) and some later legal cases: *Rotuli Curiae Regis*, ed. F. Palgrave (London, 1835), i, 93, 440–41; ii, 162; *Curia Regis Rolls*, ii, 234; viii, 18–21.

To place Stephen's reign in perspective, I have made a comparison, using more limited data, with the reigns of Henry I and Henry II. In Maps 2–3 I have compared incidents recorded in eight major chronicles of Stephen's reign with any remotely comparable incidents (even including the murder of Becket) recorded in the major chronicles for the surrounding reigns.[10] The comparison includes few 'ordinary' acts of violence such as murders, assaults, and land seizures; comparable data does not exist, given the growth in records for the three reigns. This may be a disabling shortcoming to those who would argue that the existence of violence in other reigns or periods meant that there was little special about Stephen's reign. However, the jeremiads about Stephen's reign do not complain about an upsurge in murders or seizures of land but about raiding, plundering, kidnapping, torture, and warfare. The events marked in Maps 1–3 do not concern what might be called ordinary crime, but record more serious acts of violence and warfare. What a comparison of the maps shows is that similarities can be found between the early years of all three reigns, and between the revolt of 1173–4 and Stephen's reign, points to which I will return. But the maps also indicate that in terms of violence dramatic enough to warrant recording in chronicles, the bulk of the reigns of Henry I and Henry II differed markedly from Stephen's reign. Only if the chroniclers sharply and consistently distorted the evidence can these comparisons be ignored.

I intend to discuss biases and problems in the sources in a separate article.[11] Certainly, clerical anti-war biases and biases in favour of the Angevins could and did lead to exaggeration, though I would argue for a royalist more than a specifically Angevin bias since chroniclers were perfectly willing to record mayhem in the reign of Henry II. Indeed, nearly all the types of violence and atrocity discussed later in this article for Stephen's reign were also recorded for the short civil war of 1173–4.[12] Overall, however, the impact of bias on the chronicling of Stephen's reign was quite complex, and I believe the revisionists fall short of proving that bias was sufficiently standardized or common to give a consistently distorted picture of Stephen's reign across a range of sources, including not just

---

[10] For Stephen's reign, the chronicles are *Historia Novella*; *Huntingdon*; *John of Worcester*; *Orderic*; Richard of Hexham, *De Gestis Regis Stephani et de Bello Standardii*, in Howlett, *Chronicles*, iii, 139–78; John of Hexham, *Historia Regum*, in *Symeonis Monachi Opera Omnia*, ed. T. Arnold, 2 vols. (RS, 1882–5), ii, 284–322; *Gesta Stephani*; *ASC*. For Henry I's reign, I have used *ASC*, *Huntingdon*, *John of Worcester*, *Orderic*, *Gesta Regum*, and the history of the kings of England attributed to Simeon of Durham. For Henry II's reign, I have used *Torigni*; *Jordan Fantosme's Chronicle*, ed. R. C. Johnston (Oxford, 1981); Howden, *Gesta Regis*; Howden, *Chronica*; *The Historical Works of Gervase of Canterbury*, ed. W. Stubbs, 2 vols. (RS, 1879–80); *Newburgh*; and *Diceto*.

[11] I hope to address this issue more fully in a future article entitled 'Divine Intervention, Biases, and the Chronicling of King Stephen's Reign'.

[12] These include plundering, wasting, burning, kidnapping, killing of non-combatants, and violations of churches: *Torigni*, 261, 264; *Jordan Fantosme's Chronicle*, 42–5, 52–3, 58–9, 70–3, 84–9, 124–7; Howden, *Gesta Regis*, i, 64, 66, 69–71; Howden, *Chronica*, ii, 47, 57–8, 60; *Gervase of Canterbury*, i, 247–8; *Newburgh*, 177–8, 182–3; *Diceto*, i, 376, 381.

chronicles, but also saints' lives, collections of miracle stories, letter collections, charters, the early pipe rolls of Henry II's reign, the *Cartae Baronum* of 1166, and legal cases. Moreover, I argue that the Christian historiographic framework of the chroniclers, which caused them frequently to speak in terms of evil, devils, and madness, makes modern historians overly prone to dismiss their claims; for modern scholars, scepticism sells and elaborate moralizing passages do not. Therefore, I reject any claim that the grim overall picture of the reign merely stems from distortions in the sources.

Coin hoards provide a category of evidence that is untainted by bias and Map 4 illustrates known hoards from the three reigns.[13] Between the reigns of Henry I and Stephen the number of known hoards jumps from approximately one for every three and a half years of the reign (10/35) to just under one per year (19/20). For Henry II's reign, the number dips somewhat to just under one for every year and a half (22/35). Unfortunately, the evidence of coin hoards has its own problems. First, there is no way of knowing what percentage of hoards was abandoned due to violence or unrest rather than other causes. Martin Allen has found a correlation between the Scottish wars of the early fourteenth century and a jump in coin hoards in the north, and a similar rise in the number of hoards after the Norman Conquest also shows the impact of war.[14] However, the impact of war on numbers of hoards remains impossible to measure. Second, precise dating remains very difficult and a shift of just a few hoards from one reign to another can make a big difference in the picture given the small sample. Third, the big jump from Henry I's reign is not matched by an equally large decline from Stephen's reign to that of Henry II. Some scholars have argued for a link between some of the hoards from Henry II's reign and the 1173–4 revolt, but dating methods are insufficiently exact for certainty.[15] If coin hoards from that revolt could be factored out, the number of hoards per year for Henry II's reign might look a lot more like those for Henry I's reign; or they might not. Overall, however, the evidence of coin hoards provides at least some support for the picture of Stephen's reign as an unusually warlike and disorderly period.

Returning to the written evidence, it is important to stress how much the revisionist picture relies on extensive, if often implicit, reliance on arguments from silence. When scholars write that the famous jeremiads built on exceptional local

13 The evidence on coin hoards may be found in M. Allen, 'English Coin Hoards, 1158–1544', *British Numismatic Journal*, 72 (2002), 24–84; M. Allen, 'The Volume of the English Currency, c. 973–1154', in *Coinage and History in the North Sea World c. AD 500–1200*, ed. G. Williams and B. J. Cook (Leiden, 2006), 485–523. One hoard from Stephen's reign and one from Henry II's reign are not noted on the map because their place of origin is unknown. There are also three hoards within the period 1158–1247 and six in the period 1180–1247. I would like to thank Martin Allen for sending me the latter work in advance of publication and for providing some cautionary advice to a novice in the field of numismatics. I would like to thank Chris Lewis for suggesting the use of coin hoard evidence.
14 Allen, 'English Hoards, 1158–1544', 22.
15 T. C. R. Crafter, 'A Re-examination of the Classification and Chronology of the *Cross-and-Crosslets* Type of Henry II', *British Numismatic Journal*, 68 (1998), 42–63 at 52–4.

conditions to over-generalize about England during the reign as a whole, they necessarily rely on silences in the sources to discount the evidence of contemporary writers. Scholars sometimes cite the finding of Thomas Callahan that only 10 per cent of religious houses suffered *recorded* damage or losses. This figure seems correct, but raises the question of how good a picture the records give.[16] Arguments from silence can sometimes be useful despite their dangers, but to be convincing there needs to be silence where we would expect information, and there needs to be a reasonable certainty that existing sources provide a full picture. Neither condition applies to the evidence for Stephen's reign.

First, the sources that one would expect to discuss violence and disorder do consistently discuss it. Of over thirty national and local chronicles containing good information on Stephen's reign, most of them written at or near to the time, only two make no obvious mention of troubles related to the civil war. One of these is focused on a specific land dispute.[17] Although saints' lives concentrate on the sanctity of individuals, not political and military affairs, every *vita* of a saint active during Stephen's reign, except for the life of Christina of Markyate, records or comments on the violence of the time. Many collections of miracle stories written in the decades following Stephen's reign also refer to troubles in the reign or to specific incidents.[18] Every existing collection of letters provides evidence for violence and disorder.[19] Many of Gilbert Foliot's letters do seem to show life going on as normal, but of 106 letters from Gilbert Foliot's collection that can be clearly dated to Stephen's reign, more than two dozen refer to violence and its consequences, while of the 147 letters from Henry II's reign, only one does.[20]

Where arguments from silence might seem strongest is with charters. Over one hundred survive that give reasonably clear evidence for violence and its impact, but these represent a tiny percentage of the charters from the reign. Given the problems with any argument from silence in the chronicles, many of which do refer to damages to specific monasteries, Callahan's argument on the limited effects of violence on religious houses must rest primarily on the silence of most charters.[21] But charters were generally preserved or copied into cartularies only if they had long-term evidentiary value. Thus, charters preserving grants of land made as reparations would be likely to be preserved. But only the wealthiest

---

16 T. Callahan, 'The Impact of Anarchy on English Monasticism, 1135–1154', *Albion*, 6 (1974), 218–32; Bradbury, *Stephen and Matilda*, 191; Crouch, *Reign of Stephen*, 336.

17 *Monasticon*, v, 568–74; J. Hunter, *Ecclesiastical Documents* (London, 1840), 1–48.

18 H. M. Thomas, 'Miracle Stories and the Violence of King Stephen's Reign', *HSJ*, 13 (2004), 111–24.

19 *The Letters and Charters of Gilbert Foliot*, ed. A. Morey and C. N. L. Brooke (Cambridge, 1967), nos. 1–3, 5, 9–11, 13, 19–20, 24, 26–7, 29–32, 35, 50–2, 61, 65, 69, 79, 85, 93–6; *The Letters of Osbert of Clare, Prior of Westminster*, ed. E. W. Williamson (London, 1929), 120–6, 130–1; *The Letters of John of Salisbury*, ed. and trans. W. J. Millor, H. E. Butler, and C. N. L. Brooke (2nd edn, Oxford, 1986), i, nos. 23–4, 40, 65.

20 *Letters of Foliot*, no. 131. I have ignored here references to Becket's murder.

21 Callahan, 'Impact of Anarchy', 218–32.

plunderers were likely to make reparations in land, and there is no guarantee that the charters involved would record the fact. Many plunderers must have made reparations in the form of movable property, as did one Robert son of Odo of Loxley. We know about him only because land he leased to the priory of Stone in return for the stock needed for reparations remained permanently with the priory.[22] Many plunderers surely made no reparations at all. Thus, Callahan's figure of 10 per cent of houses having *recorded* damages proves little about the level of violence. Overall, the sources we might expect to record violence and disorder in Stephen's reign do in fact reveal these phenomena.

Moreover, there are good reasons to think that our picture of violence in Stephen's reign is very incomplete when it comes to specifics. After all, we know of three local wars only from later sources.[23] How many more happened that we do not know about? Stephen is the figure whose campaigns were most closely followed by the chroniclers, and yet two of the sieges he engaged in are known only through references to them in his charters.[24] How good is our record of the reign when knowledge of sieges by the king himself survives by chance references? When the author of the most detailed chronicle of the reign, the *Gesta Stephani*, outlined several local incidents at one point, he stated he would not go on with countless others for fear of boring the reader. Why should we not believe him?[25] Clearly none of the chroniclers was willing or able to give a complete picture and we should be wary of assuming that apart from major battles and campaigns we have a good picture of military operations in the reign.

Maps 5 and 6 illustrate important geographic gaps in what contemporary chronicles reveal. Map 5 shows how regionally biased or limited in coverage many major chronicles were, and Map 6, which compares events shown in the major chronicles with those shown in minor chronicles and other sources, indicates that much activity occurred in areas covered only lightly by our best sources.[26] Bradbury has argued that the major writers happened to be based in areas at the centre of the troubles, but he may have matters reversed; we may consider these the major areas of trouble *because* there were chroniclers nearby to describe how bad local conditions were.[27] Had major chronicles been written in other areas, our picture of violence in the reign might be substantially fuller. For

---

[22] BL Additional MS 47677, fo. 252b.

[23] *History of William Marshall*, ed. A. J. Holden, S. Gregory, and D. Crouch (London, 2002), i, 8–11, 18–21; *The Chronicle of Pierre de Langtoft in French Verse from the Earliest Period to the Death of King Edward I*, ed. T. Wright, 2 vols. (RS, 1866–8), i, 484–5; 'The Anglo-Norman Chronicle of Wigmore Abbey', ed. and trans. J. C. Dickinson and P. T. Ricketts, *Transactions of the Woolhope Naturalists' Field Club*, 39 (1969), 413–46, at 428–9.

[24] *Regesta*, iii, nos. 1, 138, 456.

[25] *Gesta Stephani*, 166–71.

[26] The northern chroniclers are Richard and John of Hexham. The western chroniclers are John of Worcester, William of Malmesbury, and the author of the *Gesta Stephani*. The general chroniclers are Henry of Huntingdon, Orderic Vitalis, and the author of the *Anglo-Saxon Chronicle*.

[27] Bradbury, *Stephen and Matilda*, 190.

instance, there are few points on the maps in the far south-west, but the *Gesta Stephani* states that there were important and devastating campaigns there.[28] The composite map shows that, taking the reign as a whole, there was nothing regional or local about violence in the reign.

One must also be wary of a temporal bias in the sources, especially the chronicles. Recent scholarship has tried to determine relative periods of disorder and tranquillity in the reign. Matthew and Crouch have both suggested the early years were not too bad, and the former has suggested they were comparable to those of Stephen's predecessors.[29] Map 7, which breaks down violence into four periods within the reign, *does* support these arguments. Davis spoke of a magnates' peace beginning in 1150, and Crouch has dated it slightly earlier.[30] A key to Crouch's belief that the excesses described by the chroniclers were temporally limited comes with his argument that violence expanded with the need for magnates to secure regional control after central control had deteriorated, and then contracted once they had achieved dominance. This would suggest a steep rise in violence and then a sharp drop off.[31] However, Map 7 indicates that although the pace of recorded violence slackened after 1141, it remained high. This was true of the period 1142–8, which approximately corresponded to the later years of struggle between Stephen and Matilda, and of the period 1149–54, during which the future Henry II took up his mother's struggle.

More important, the number and quality of chronicles dropped sharply after the early 1140s. *Half* of the major chronicles ended in the late 1130s or early 1140s.[32] Moreover, the fullest source for the reign, the *Gesta Stephani*, became much less detailed as time went on. Not enough events from other sources can be dated sufficiently closely to provide a check on the major chronicles, but we need to be wary of assuming that the apparent decline of activity later in the reign, and therefore the magnates' peace, are more than illusions of the sources. To cite a concrete example of the problem, Crouch depicts the years 1150–1 as very quiet.[33] Yet the author of the *Gesta Stephani* assures us that Stephen was busy from 1150 to 1152 with many raids and battles, even though he specifically notes only two sieges.[34] Should we assume from this lack of detail that his general statement is false? Overall, it would be dangerous to place too much faith in the apparent slackening of violence before the peace settlement of 1153.

The problem of temporal bias raises doubts about the reality of the magnates' peace and about arguments that nobles successfully imposed order in local areas.

---

28 *Gesta Stephani*, 80–3, 102–3, 150–1, 210–13, 222–3.
29 Matthew, *King Stephen*, 73–4, 82–3; Crouch, *Reign of Stephen*, 52–4, 135–6.
30 Davis, *King Stephen*, 108–24; Crouch, *Reign of Stephen*, 234–9.
31 Crouch, *Reign of Stephen*, 146–61. See also Stringer, *Reign of Stephen*, 28–60, 81–5; White, 'Myth', 332–5; White, *Restoration*, 13–14, 55–68; E. King, 'The Anarchy of King Stephen's Reign', *TRHS*, 5th ser., 34 (1984), 133–53.
32 Richard of Hexham's chronicle ended in 1138, Orderic Vitalis and the continuation of John of Worcester in 1141, and William of Malmesbury in 1142.
33 Crouch, *Reign of Stephen*, 255.
34 *Gesta Stephani*, xviii, 226–9.

Space does not permit a full discussion of this issue, but some points may be raised. No doubt magnates often tried to impose local hegemony and order out of self-interest, public spiritedness, or a mixture of both. But the only clear example in contemporary sources of one who succeeded was Earl Robert of Gloucester, though there is also a significant silence in the sources about violence in the far north under King David of Scotland.[35] In contrast, the abbot of Ramsey faced the problem of satisfying many competing local authorities.[36] Given the geographic spread of noble estates in England and the decline of honorial ties, there must be serious *a priori* questions about how easily magnates could gain hegemony in any given area without continual fighting. Moreover, even for magnates, the temptations of military gains could offset the benefits of peace, and they were not the only actors on the scene. Stephen, Matilda, and the future Henry II all pushed for complete triumph. Lower down, mercenaries, opportunistic landholders of the second rank and poor warriors could profit from the war and had an interest in prolonging it.[37] Even the agreements between the magnates that form the basis for arguments about the magnates' peace suggest deep distrust, sometimes even between supposed allies, indicating that they were fragile affairs. In my view, the widespread success of magnates in achieving local hegemony must remain doubtful.

If arguments from silence remain problematic and the successful hegemony of magnates an unproved theory, then the idea that the jeremiads of the chroniclers only concerned local and temporary conditions can be treated at best as a possibility, one which directly contradicts the claims of the chroniclers that they described conditions generally. Therefore, the case for minimizing the horrors of the reign comes down largely to the plausibility or otherwise of the descriptions of the sources. To restate my argument on this point, I believe that, allowing for hyperbole, the sources describe the kinds of events one would expect in a civil war.

The starting point for this argument is that war in the medieval period, as in others, created horrible suffering. Recent work stresses the destructive practices of medieval warfare. One therefore does not need to see Stephen's reign as unique to believe the core descriptions of the jeremiads. I have already noted that chroniclers described most of the same phenomena in the civil war of 1173–4 as in Stephen's reign, and a comparison of Maps 1 and 3 will underline the similarities. The main difference with Stephen's reign is that the civil war was so long. It is time, therefore, to set the civil war between Stephen and Matilda in the context of what we know generally about the impact of war in the period, with special

---

35 Ibid., 148–51.
36 *Chronicon Abbatiae Rameseiensis*, ed. W. Dunn MacRay (RS, 1886), 334.
37 *Historia Novella*, 32–3; *Gesta Stephani*, 154–5; John of Ford, *Wulfric of Haselbury*, ed. M. Bell (Frome, 1933), 68–9; *The Book of the Foundation of Walden Monastery*, ed. and trans. D. Greenway and L. Watkiss (Oxford, 1999), 14–17; Crouch, *Reign of Stephen*, 161–5; P. Dalton, *Conquest, Anarchy and Lordship: Yorkshire, 1066–1154* (Cambridge, 1994), 185–92; Thomas, 'Miracle Stories', 120.

reference to the war of 1173–4. I will start with Map 8, which summarizes different kinds of military operations during the reign. This map indicates that few if any areas escaped military activity over the course of the reign.

Part of the reason war had such a harmful impact was that it created a constant and often desperate need for money. 'In war', wrote Richard fitz Nigel, '[money] is lavished on fortifying castles, paying soldiers' wages, and innumerable other expenses.'[38] Henry II's pipe rolls allow us to follow much of it pouring out during the 1173–4 revolt.[39] The royal government, during that revolt, raised money through seizing the lands and goods of enemies and merchants from enemy lands, special taxes on the royal demesnes and seized lands, and even through plunder and the ransoming of prisoners, but almost all business unrelated to war stopped, depriving the government of other traditional forms of revenue. Just two years of fighting clearly strained Henry II's government and finances. Stephen's reign involved nearly two decades of civil war, a decade and a half of it intense. We know little about expenditures on warfare in Stephen's reign, but an entry on the first pipe roll of Henry II, revealing payments of over £150 for knights left in the castle of Worcester after Stephen's death, shows the cost of garrisoning just one castle.[40] A major preoccupation for every military commander must have been to find the resources to keep his forces going. Matthew and others have suggested that Stephen maintained a healthy financial situation throughout the reign.[41] He *had* to or he would have lost the war. However, the question is how he and others obtained their money and how disruptive their techniques might have been.

Ordinary revenues rarely sufficed to finance wars, either for kings or nobles. Map 9 shows some of the extraordinary measures that could be taken. Seizing the land of one's enemies, even temporarily, decreased their resources and increased one's own. Land disputes and seizures were common enough in peacetime, so in Map 9 I have only depicted instances that our sources link to the war or where circumstances (often uncovered by modern scholars) make it likely that such a link existed. Map 9 gives a deeply understated picture of the seizure of land in the reign. If Henry of Huntingdon was right that the second of three rebel lines at the battle of Lincoln was made up of men disinherited by Stephen, then royal confiscation at least must have been quite extensive.[42] As Map 9 shows, the well known practice of levying *tenseries* and other demands on non-combatants, including peasants, townspeople, and the religious, was also common.

Such practices were not necessarily violent; the pipe roll evidence for the 1173–4 revolt shows royal officials simply stepping in to collect the farms and

---

38 Richard fitz Nigel, *Dialogus de Scaccario*, ed. C. Johnson, F. E. L. Carter, and D. E. Greenway (Oxford, 1983), 2.
39 For instance, *PR 21 Henry II*, 7, 164.
40 *The Red Book of the Exchequer*, ed. H. Hall, 3 vols. (RS, 1896), ii, 656.
41 Matthew, *King Stephen*, 147. For Stephen's finances, see J. Green, 'Financing Stephen's War', *ANS*, 14 (1992), 91–114.
42 *Huntingdon*, 724–7.

renders from confiscated lands and placing tallages on such lands.[43] However, even peaceful seizures bore hard on the dispossessed and extra taxation of any kind weighed heavily on a peasantry that struggled in the best of times. More important, these practices could often lead to disruption and violence. The vast majority of instances in Map 9 did not take the form of government confiscation, and most were likely to have been disputed. Though lords may have abandoned some lands without a struggle, many seizures probably met active resistance. Moreover, breakdowns of order must have made it easier for ordinary claimants to pursue claims with force and for the opportunistic to grab land, resulting in further violence. One later Bedfordshire lawsuit linked the seizure of land in Stephen's reign to the killing of the plaintiff's father.[44] As Henry of Huntingdon's evidence for the battle of Lincoln suggests, land seizures also left a pool of impoverished warriors with a grudge and motivation to fight. Levies, too, could provoke threats and violence. On one occasion, royalist magnates only obtained money from the abbey of St Albans after they threatened to burn down the adjacent town.[45] Extortion could easily shade into plundering. Though Abingdon was paying protection money to the constable of Wallingford, he plundered one of the abbey's villages anyway.[46] The Anglo-Saxon Chronicle, in its famous lament, claimed that castellans levied *tenseries*, and then, when people could pay no more, raided and burned their settlements.[47] In a long civil war, peaceful levies for military purposes could easily turn violent, leading to more disorder.

Plundering the lands of enemies was another frequent way of financing armies.[48] In a civil war, every landholder was potentially someone's enemy and thus every piece of the countryside was potentially a legitimate target from someone's perspective. Gilbert Foliot's letters show the kind of losses landholders could suffer from raiding in the reign, even if one makes allowances for possible exaggeration. Gilbert complained in one letter that John of Marlborough and Walter de Picquigny had taken coin and goods worth more than 200 marks, and, in another letter, he revealed that he hoped to recover more than 300 marks taken by Welsh raiders.[49] Plundering could have long-term and indirect impacts; pipe rolls entries written in the aftermath of the 1173–4 revolt show that estates could lose value in subsequent years because of the seizure of stock and also reveal fairs

43 For example, *PR 19 Henry II*, 20–1, 28, 37–8, 49, 66–7, 75–6, 78.
44 *Rotuli Curiae Regis*, i, 440–1.
45 Thomas Walsingham, *Gesta Abbatum Sancti Albani*, ed. H. T. Riley, 3 vols. (RS, 1867–9), i, 93–4.
46 *Historia Ecclesie Abbendonensis: The History of the Church of Abingdon*, ed. J. Hudson, 2 vols. (Oxford, 2002–7), ii, 314–15.
47 *ASC* 1137.
48 M. Strickland, *War and Chivalry: The Conduct and Perception of War in England and Normandy, 1066–1217* (Cambridge, 1996), 260–8; S. Morillo, *Warfare under the Anglo-Norman Kings, 1066–1135* (Woodbridge, 1994), 101.
49 *Letters of Foliot*, nos. 32, 65.

losing value and guilds suffering due to the disruption of trade.[50] The plundering of merchants, for instance by Brian fitz Count, must have disrupted trade even more in Stephen's reign, which may explain the complaints of the Londoners about their losses of revenue when the empress tried to tax them.[51] While landlords and merchants faced a loss of revenues, peasants stripped of their goods could face starvation, especially if plough beasts or seed corn were taken. Map 9 shows that plundering was a common part of military action in Stephen's reign, and this indicates that the economic consequences of many years of war must have been severe. Plundering also fuelled the cycle of violence created by the civil war. One miracle story, concerning villagers who attacked a band of raiders that had plundered them, suggests that if peasants thought they could successfully resist looters they might try to do so.[52] Many of the castles about which the chroniclers complained must have been designed to prevent plundering as well as facilitate it. Thus, widespread plundering resulted from standard military practices, but created great suffering and encouraged more violence.

Even more disruptive was another common practice of warfare in the time, the deliberate wasting of the lands of opponents to weaken them.[53] The most efficient way to do this was with fire. One passage in the *Gesta Stephani* describes how Stephen decided to 'attack the enemy everywhere, plunder and destroy all that was in their possession, set fire to the crops and every other means of supporting human life', in order to force them to surrender. According to this source, Stephen considered this a necessary evil to end the worse evil of continuing war, and the author went on to describe how the king carried out his intentions.[54] The king and his supporters were not alone in their use of wasting; Gilbert Foliot wrote to the pope on behalf of Reading Abbey and described how the armies of both sides had frequently passed through Reading's lands, 'whence [the monks] are weakened by burnings and slaughter of their men, and plundering of their possessions.'[55] Map 10 (which distinguishes the pipe roll evidence from other evidence) shows

---

[50] *PR 20 Henry II*, 39, 57, 63; *PR 21 Henry II*, 4, 108, 110; *PR 23 Henry II*, 126; *PR 24 Henry II*, 21, 74–5.

[51] H. W. C. Davis, 'Henry of Blois and Brian Fitz-Count', *EHR*, 25 (1910), 297–303 at 301; *Gesta Stephani*, 122–3.

[52] Reginald of Durham, *Libellus de Admirandis Beati Cuthberti Virtutibus*, ed. J. Raine, Surtees Society, 1 (London, 1835), 130–4. See also, *Gesta Stephani*, 116–17, 134–5, for fighting by 'rustici'.

[53] J. Gillingham, 'Richard I and the Science of War in the Middle Ages', in *War and Government in the Middle Ages: Essays in Honour of J. O. Prestwich*, ed. J. Gillingham and J. C. Holt (Cambridge, 1984), 78–91; J. Gillingham, 'War and Chivalry in the History of William the Marshall', *Thirteenth Century England*, 2 (1984), 1–13; J. Gillingham, 'William the Bastard at War', in *Studies in Medieval History Presented to R. Allen Brown*, ed. C. Harper-Bill, C. J. Holdsworth, and J. L. Nelson (Woodbridge, 1989), 141–8; Morillo, *Warfare*, 98–102; Strickland, *War and Chivalry*, 268–81; E. Amt, *The Accession of Henry II in England: Royal Government Restored, 1149–1159* (Woodbridge, 1993), 133–4.

[54] *Gesta Stephani*, 218–21.

[55] *Letters of Foliot*, no. 85.

that in the civil war between Stephen and Matilda, as in other wars of the time, wasting and burning were standard practices.

One purpose of wasting was to spread terror, and those painting a brighter picture of Stephen's reign underestimate the psychological impact of this widespread practice not just on its victims but on *potential* victims. Wasting also had a profound economic effect. Another letter of Gilbert Foliot indicates that a Welsh raid had done sixty marks of damage in one estate (doubtlessly including plunder), and a charter of Robert de Vaux reveals that his father had remitted a small rent in reparation for 'evils and damages' he had done to Malmesbury Abbey to the value of one hundred marks or more.[56] If one were to multiply these sums many times over for the wasting and plundering done throughout the kingdom, one could quickly gain a sense of the cumulative economic impact of the devastation of war.

The widespread independent evidence of wasting and burning lends credence to the belief that mentions of 'waste' in particular places and large exemptions for 'waste' in the collection of danegeld in the early pipe rolls of Henry II's reign do represent the impact of plundering and wasting (see Map 10). They also support Amt's argument that exemptions throughout most of England for the 'restoration' of individual royal estates, or of the royal demesne in entire counties, also resulted from the war.[57] However, a number of scholars have argued that this evidence (particularly of danegeld waste) is problematic.[58] These scholars raise valid points about anomalies in the records, and suggest reasonable alternative explanations such as disputes over liability and problems of outdated records. However Amt has, to my view, answered most of their points, and I believe that the balance of probabilities is that waste in the pipe rolls meant just that for the majority of cases.[59]

For reasons of space, I will not repeat Amt's views. I will note that my earlier argument about gaps in the evidence supports her arguments.[60] I will also note

56 Ibid., no. 13; *The Register of Malmesbury Abbey*, ed. J. S. Brewer, 2 vols. (London, 1879–80), i, no. 121.
57 Amt, *Accession*, 142–8. Map 10 uses Amt's figures for danegeld waste.
58 The fullest early argument that waste represented devastation comes from H. W. C. Davis, 'The Anarchy of Stephen's Reign', *EHR*, 18 (1903), 630–41. For criticism, see J. Green, 'The Last Century of Danegeld', *EHR*, 96 (1981), 241–58, at 251–2; King, 'Anarchy of King Stephen's Reign', 143–6; G. White, 'Were the Midlands "Wasted" during Stephen's Reign?', *Midland History*, 10 (1985), 26–46; E. King, 'Introduction', in King, *Anarchy*, 28–9; G. White, 'Damage and "Waste" in Yorkshire and the North Midlands in the Reign of Stephen', in *Government, Religion and Society in Northern England, 1000–1700*, ed. J. C. Appleby and P. Dalton (Stroud, 1997), 63–79.
59 Amt, *Accession*, 133–41. One important suggestion Amt makes is that danegeld exemptions did not necessarily represent the wasting of specific hides but rather more general tax relief. See J. Palmer, 'War and Domesday Waste', in *Armies, Chivalry and Warfare in Medieval Britain and France*, ed. M. Strickland (Stamford, 1998), 256–75, for a strong reaffirmation that waste entries in Domesday Book represented the direct impact of war.
60 To his credit, Graeme White, the chief proponent of the argument, recognizes the difficulty: 'Were the Midlands "Wasted"?' 36.

that the more detailed pipe rolls made during and after the 1173–4 revolt lend strong circumstantial evidence to the belief that waste in the earlier pipe rolls resulted largely from the devastation of war. There, respites from payment by sheriffs *were* sometimes given for accounting difficulties brought on by the war, but no money owed was written off for that purpose. However various respites and outright pardons were given 'for war', 'for waste in war', 'for waste that Earl Hugh (or the earl of Leicester) made', 'for grain burnt or carried off', and for the removal of stock.[61] There was no danegeld collection to compare with 1155–6, but in Cumbria, a similar tax called nutgeld was collected yearly. From the first year of the war, some 57 per cent of the nutgeld remained in respite 'for waste of the county through war'. The nutgeld owed for this year and large amounts for several subsequent years were lumped together with other sums owed, and eventually most was pardoned for the 'destruction of demesnes through war' or 'the destruction of lands through war'.[62] All this suggests that war could dramatically reduce the collection of a tax like danegeld, and that in the aftermath of the 1173–4 revolt, when exchequer officials and scribes thought about waste and about writing off money, they were concerned with the direct impact of war. There is no certainty that exchequer officials and scribes followed similar practice in compiling the earliest pipe rolls of Henry II's reign, but the later evidence strengthens the probability that sums written off for waste in those rolls did in fact largely reflect the direct impact of plundering and wasting. The debate over pipe roll waste will doubtlessly continue, but I would argue that the entries for waste in Henry II's early rolls probably do illustrate the dramatic economic (and social) impact of warfare in Stephen's reign.

One occasional practice of war in this time, as Strickland has shown, was the deliberate slaughter of non-combatants.[63] The sources refer to killing, homicide, slaughter, and depopulation reasonably often (see Map 11), particularly in overviews of the reign. Most instances probably referred to deaths in combat, incidental killings, and, in cases of depopulation, starvation or flight. Sources describing the Scottish invasions of the north early in the reign do, however, include detailed and macabre accounts of massacres.[64] These sources included an additional bias, namely the depiction of the various Celtic peoples as bloodthirsty barbarians, and descriptions of such deeds as slaughtering children and drinking their blood will obviously raise red flags. Nonetheless, given cultural differences in the rules of war, massacres in the north cannot be ruled out.[65] Elsewhere, a handful of sources refer or seem to refer to killings of non-combatants or

---

[61] *PR 19 Henry II*, 114; *PR 20 Henry II*, 38–9, 57, 58, 105, 140; *PR 21 Henry II*, 29, 89, 107–8, 110, 126, 165, 173, 183–4; *PR 22 Henry II*, 65, 70–1, 90, 137; *PR 23 Henry II*, 125–6, 143.

[62] *PR 19 Henry II*, 114; *PR 24 Henry II*, 125.

[63] Strickland, *War and Chivalry*, 270–3, 304–13.

[64] Richard of Hexham, *De Gestis*, 151–3, 156; John of Hexham, *Historia*, 290; *Huntingdon*, 710–11; *Orderic*, vi, 518–19; Ailred of Rievaulx, *Relatio de Standardo*, in Howlett, *Chronicles*, iii, 187–8.

[65] J. Gillingham, 'Conquering the Barbarians: War and Chivalry in Twelfth-Century Britain', *HSJ*, 4 (1993), 67–84; Strickland, *War and Chivalry*, 299–304.

prisoners, but such references are rare.[66] Overall, the sources seem mainly to reflect the obvious fact that war causes many deaths, both directly and incidentally.

A much more common practice was the kidnapping of non-combatants. In the far north, this involved enslavement by the Scots and Galwegians.[67] Elsewhere, soldiers kidnapped non-combatants for ransoms, responding to the insatiable financial demands of war. Recent historiography has ignored this phenomenon except to ridicule one piece of evidence for it.[68] Perhaps this phenomenon seems too 'anarchic' to fit in with current orthodoxy. In a recent article, I discussed kidnapping for ransom in the context of miracle stories set in the reign. There, I argued that despite the problematic nature of such evidence miracle stories provide plausible details, such as the giving of hostages to arrange ransoms and the need for castellans to consult with their lords. I also argued that kidnapping was an efficient way of raising the money commanders needed to compete in a civil war marked by many local struggles.[69] What I need to emphasize here is just how widespread the evidence for this practice was, despite the tendency of recent works to ignore it (see Map 12).

First, the practice is noted in the majority of important chronicles.[70] Likewise, in his letters Osbert of Clare speaks of those 'who like Nimrod, hunt men rather than animals', and refers to men hunting men for ransom.[71] One might dismiss Osbert's letters and the chronicle accounts as the hysterical reactions or rhetorical excesses of biased clerics, but John of Worcester provides compelling detail. John speaks of the kidnapping of townsmen during the looting of Worcester, where he was present, and describes how on another occasion Count Waleran, having taken 'much plunder of men, goods, and herds', mercifully chose to release the men.[72] Chronicles and miracle stories are not the only sources describing such activity. Frank Stenton uncovered a charter in which a local land-holder made arrangements for local monks to act as go betweens if he, his wife, or son were kidnapped.[73] A letter of Gilbert Foliot probably alludes to arrangements for ransoming as well, and the canons of a church council from the reign mandate the automatic excommunication of anyone holding the hostage of a kidnapped cleric and those holding the clerics themselves or receiving ransoms.[74] The Walden Chronicle's detailed account of how Geoffrey de Mandeville organized a

---

[66] *Gesta Stephani*, 94–5, 230–1; *John of Worcester*, iii, 272–3; *Liber Eliensis*, ed. E. O. Blake, Camden Society, 3rd ser., 92 (1962), 341.
[67] Richard of Hexham, *De Gestis*, 156–7; John of Hexham, *Historia*, 290–1.
[68] Matthew, *King Stephen*, 127.
[69] Thomas, 'Miracle Stories', 122.
[70] ASC 1137; *Historia Novella*, 70–3; *Huntingdon*, 724–5, 742–3; *Gesta Stephani*, 62–5, 80–1, 94–5, 156–7; *John of Worcester*, iii, 290–1.
[71] *Osbert of Clare*, 125, 130.
[72] *John of Worcester*, iii, 274–5, 282–5.
[73] F. Stenton, *The First Century of English Feudalism 1066–1166* (2nd edn, Oxford, 1961), 246, 284–5.
[74] *Letters of Foliot*, no. 9; *Councils & Synods*, ii, 803.

kidnapping ring, complete with spies, might be dismissed as implausible, but the jurors of an early thirteenth-century survey recorded how a minor local figure, Godebold of Writtle, had been taken by Geoffrey and forced to mortgage property to pay his ransom.[75] Gilbert Foliot complained about the imprisonment of his abbey's men by Baderon of Monmouth, and Henry de Lacy made a settlement with Nostell Priory for, among other things, the taking of their men.[76] The practice was found in later English wars as well, including that of 1173–4.[77] Overall, the evidence for widespread kidnapping of non-combatants for ransom is overwhelming.

Such ransoming had an economic impact that was uneven, but would have been disastrous for some individuals. Kidnapping also created disruption that at least on one occasion had a knock-on effect. One episode in the life of Godric of Finchale records how the head of a band of robbers, Elfere of Chester-le-Street, initially turned to robbery in order to pay a ransom after being kidnapped himself.[78] Fears of kidnapping must also have caused great psychological stress, particularly for its victims, but also for its potential victims, who included just about anyone. Any overall account of conditions in Stephen's reign that ignores this practice distorts the picture.

Even more distressing would have been the widespread and related use of torture described or noted by a number of sources, most famously the Anglo-Saxon Chronicle (see Map 12).[79] Most references are fairly vague, in terms that could refer to a range of suffering. But the Anglo-Saxon Chronicle is quite specific in describing a catalogue of tortures. So too is Lawrence of Durham's *Dialogi*, which provides an independent list.[80] Recent historiography has largely ignored these accounts of torture, intimating that at most they formed isolated incidents. This is probably wishful thinking. The *Gesta Stephani* and the chronicle of John of Hexham mention Earl Ranulf of Chester and Count Alan of Richmond being tormented in order to force them to surrender castles.[81] Even if one assumes that the torments were much milder than those described by the

---

[75] *Book of the Foundation of Walden*, 16–17; *The Book of Fees, Commonly Called Testa de Nevill*, ed. H. C. Maxwell Lyte et al., 3 vols. (London, 1920–31), i, 125.

[76] *Letters of Foliot*, no. 69; *EYC*, iii, no. 1497.

[77] *Jordan Fantosme's Chronicle*, 86–7; Howden, *Gesta Regis*, i, 69; Howden, *Chronica*, ii, 58; *Diceto*, 381; Strickland, *War and Chivalry*, 312.

[78] Reginald of Durham, *Libellus de Vita et Miraculis S. Godrici, Heremitae de Finchale*, ed. J. Stevenson, Surtees Society, 20 (1847), 102–3.

[79] *ASC* 1137; *Historia Novella*, 72–3; *Gesta Stephani*, 62–3, 80–1, 156–7; *John of Worcester*, iii, 236–7, 248–51, 270–3; *Huntingdon*, 724–5; Symeon of Durham, *Libellus de Exordio atque Procursu istius, hoc est Dunhelmensis, Ecclesie*, ed. D. Rollason (Oxford, 2000), 298–303, 314–17; 'Historia Selebeiensis Monasterii', in *The Coucher Book of Selby*, ed. J. T. Fowler, 2 vols., The Yorkshire Archaeological and Topographical Association, 10, 13 (1891–3), i, 41–3; *Liber Eliensis*, 328.

[80] *Dialogi Laurentii Dunelmensis Monachi ac Prioris*, ed. J. Raine, Surtees Society, 70 (1880), 23–6.

[81] *Gesta Stephani*, 116–17; John of Hexham, *Historia*, 308, 324; Strickland, *War and Chivalry*, 198–9.

Anglo-Saxon Chronicle and Lawrence of Durham, the torture of such powerful figures suggests how vulnerable ordinary people were. As I have written elsewhere, a number of miracle stories describe torture in the context of kidnapping and ransoming and provide straightforward motives for the use of torture on captives: to put pressure on relatives, to take revenge on hostages whose freed relatives had not paid up, or to get prisoners to pay up more quickly.[82] Sean McGlynn has highlighted a passage from Roger of Wendover showing later armies torturing captives to extract money.[83] Some historians may be reluctant to accept that English nobles and warriors ever resorted to torture, but the evidence is sufficiently strong that it must be taken seriously. I would argue that torture was far more widespread than those downplaying the horrors of the reign believe, and that it created profound psychological distress throughout the country, even among those who were not victims.

Although I have focused so far on the horrors of war, there were also rules of war, one of which was that, in theory, churches and cemeteries were places of refuge.[84] Map 12 reveals how often this rule was broken, and suggests the strains war put on contemporary norms. But rules about sanctuary did have some effect, and documents revealing the demand for sanctuary in the reign provide another neglected type of evidence of the impact of civil war on people's lives. John of Hexham wrote that during the Scottish invasions the ordinary inhabitants of Northumberland could survive only by fleeing into the wilderness or finding sanctuary in churches.[85] The *Liber Eliensis* makes a similar claim for England as a whole.[86] There is obviously exaggeration here, but the practical importance of ecclesiastical sanctuary is shown by the fact that people built chapels specifically to provide refuge in Stephen's reign. The Winchcombe cartulary records that William de Solers built a chapel at Postlep at the request of his men, so that they might have refuge from incursions of robbers.[87] A charter of Henry Murdac, archbishop of York, states that five chapels built after Archbishop Thurstan's death in 1140 in the parish of St Oswald, Gloucester, could remain standing until the end of war. A bull of Adrian IV for Reading Abbey forbade that the chapels erected within the abbey's parishes during the time of war should prejudice the rights of its parish churches, 'since what is done in time of emergency ought to cease when

---

82 Thomas, 'Miracle Stories', 122–3.
83 S. McGlynn, 'Roger of Wendover and the Wars of Henry III, 1216–1234', in *England and Europe in the Reign of Henry III (1216–1272)*, ed. B. K. U. Weiler and I. W. Rowlands (Aldershot, 2002), 183–206 at 196.
84 Thomas, 'Divine Intervention'. See also B. R. O'Brien, *God's Peace and King's Peace: The Laws of Edward the Confessor* (Philadelphia, 1999), 68–9; Strickland, *War and Chivalry*, 78–83, 86–97. One interesting absence in the sources is the lack of references to rape, particularly in comparison to the Norman Conquest. I suspect that upper class women, at least, were less likely to suffer rape in the conditions of civil war than of conquest.
85 John of Hexham, *Historia*, 298.
86 *Liber Eliensis*, 341.
87 *Landboc sive Registrum Monasterii Beatae Mariae Virginis et Sancti Cenhelmi de Winchelcumba in Comitatu Gloucestrensi Ordinis Sancti Benedicti*, ed. D. Royce, 2 vols. (Exeter, 1892–1903), i, 81, 84.

the emergency is over'.[88] Even more striking is the claim in the *Gesta Stephani* that people built their houses around churches for protection and another report from Winchcombe that the monastery itself was surrounded by the huts of peasants, who had taken long-term refuge there.[89] Such examples show that in certain areas, at least, raiding was simply a fact of life.

Finally, one must take into account the indirect but potentially severe impact of warfare on non-combatants. The peasants living in huts around Winchcombe were clearly refugees. *The History of William Marshal* records that the poor abandoned their land in Stephen's reign and the author of the *Gesta Stephani* also described the abandonment of land as a widespread phenomenon.[90] More specifically, the Abingdon chronicle noted that one of the abbey's estates, 'like many others', had been deserted because of fear of plunderers.[91] Where the displaced could find other livelihoods, only disruption was involved, but many may have died as a result. The famous passage in the Anglo-Saxon Chronicle referred to many thousands starving to death, the *Liber Eliensis* described a famine resulting from a lapse of cultivation for twenty or thirty miles around Ely, and the *Gesta Stephani* spoke of famine in every province.[92] In his letter to Henry of Blois, Brian fitz Count expressed fears that the poor would perish if peace could not be achieved soon, and Osbert of Clare, in a letter seeking help from Archbishop Theobald of Canterbury, wrote that many were dying of hunger, which he blamed partly on 'the iniquitous deeds of tyrants', described elsewhere as castellans and men of violence.[93] There is nothing implausible about these often matter-of-fact claims concerning displacement of peasants or resulting starvation. Though often localized, the cumulative impact of displacement and famine could well have been quite large, as the Anglo-Saxon Chronicle and the *Gesta Stephani* claimed (see Map 11).

In the end, are the bleak pictures of Stephen's reign drawn from twelfth-century writers plausible? I would argue that in the context of twelfth-century warfare, and with a certain allowance for hyperbole, they were. This argument, I might note, does not require accepting medieval caricatures of combatants as mere evildoers. Nor does it depend on a model of anarchic feudal barons running wild against a bad king, to oversimplify a traditional historiographic picture that has come under justifiable criticism.[94] It depends instead on political and military actors reacting rationally, albeit ruthlessly, to difficult and dangerous conditions created by a long civil war.

---

[88] *The Register of William Greenfield, Lord Archbishop of York, 1306–1315*, ed. W. Brown and A. Hamilton Thompson, Surtees Society, 5 vols. (1931–8), i, 205–6; *Reading Abbey Cartularies*, ed. B. R. Kemp, 2 vols. (London, 1986), i, no. 147.

[89] *Gesta Stephani*, 152–3; *Landboc de Winchelcumba*, i, 83.

[90] *History of William Marshall*, i, 34–5; *Gesta Stephani*, 152–5.

[91] *Historia Ecclesie Abbendonensis*, ii, 290–1.

[92] *ASC* 1137; *Liber Eliensis*, 328; *Gesta Stephani*, 152–3.

[93] Davis, 'Henry of Blois and Brian Fitz-Count', 302; *Osbert of Clare*, 126.

[94] Crouch, *Reign of Stephen*, 2–7; Matthew, *King Stephen*, 184–7.

What of the more positive evidence that the reign was not so bad? Recent claims that government did not entirely disappear in Stephen's reign are clearly correct.[95] Nonetheless, this new work does not entirely negate the old picture that Stephen's government functioned much less effectively. In a period when the number of surviving royal documents per year tended dramatically to increase with each reign, the average number from Stephen's reign declined slightly.[96] However much recent works attempt to downplay the numismatic evidence, the history of coinage in Stephen's reign shows anomalies that raise doubts about his government. The exchequer may have survived, but even White, one of the key figures in describing the survival of government in Stephen's reign, shows that much rebuilding needed to be done afterwards.[97] Royal government may not have completely collapsed in Stephen's reign, but even the most optimistic views indicate serious problems.

What of evidence that the church prospered?[98] Most of the evidence for this is anecdotal, and the very historians who cast so much doubt on the veracity of the chroniclers ignore the possibility that some of them may have exaggerated what their particular abbots had accomplished in order to flatter them or hold them up as models.[99] One area that is not simply anecdotal concerns the number of religious houses founded in the period.[100] However, the increase of foundations and of grants to existing foundations *stems* partly from the violence and disorder of the period. Walter Daniel's biography of Ailred of Rievaulx contains a famous passage in which generosity to Ailred's house is placed in the context of the violent disorders of Stephen's reign, and grants of land as reparation certainly resulted from violence.[101] Paul Dalton has described the role foundations and grants may have played in peacemaking.[102] How many other grants resulted from the religious concerns of lords and others forced to commit acts they considered sinful because of military necessity? Moreover, many of the foundations in this period required little initial investment. As for existing institutions, the situation of the church may have been atypical. William of Wycombe, John of Salisbury, and the author of the *Gesta Stephani* all wrote that combatants plundered or placed levies on the church only after they had targeted their enemies or

---

95 Matthew, *King Stephen*, 216–23; Crouch, *Reign of Stephen*, 327–39; White 'Myth', 331–3; White, *Restoration*, 17–64; Bradbury, *Stephen and Matilda*, 192–3.

96 M. T. Clanchy, *From Memory to Written Record: England 1066–1307* (2nd edn, Oxford, 1993), 60.

97 White, *Restoration*, 134–50, 158.

98 Callahan, 'Impact of Anarchy', 218–32; H. A. Cronne, *The Reign of Stephen 1135–54: Anarchy in England* (London, 1970), 14; Matthew, *King Stephen*, 32, 127–8, 137–40, 235–7; Crouch, *Reign of Stephen*, 336.

99 Thomas, 'Divine Intervention'.

100 C. Holdsworth, 'The Church', in King, *Anarchy*, 216–20.

101 *The Life of Ailred of Rievaulx by Walter Daniel*, ed. and trans. F. M. Powicke (London, 1950), 28.

102 P. Dalton, 'Churchmen and the Promotion of Peace in King Stephen's Reign', *Viator*, 31 (2000), 79–119.

exhausted other resources.[103] Though the surviving evidence highlights the suffering of the church, ecclesiastical institutions probably suffered less than secular lords and their peasants, who were unprotected by ideals of sanctuary. Though the number of foundations and the apparent prosperity of some churches must be taken into account when trying to estimate the overall impact of violence and disorder, this evidence should not trump the plentiful evidence for extensive violence and disorder. Set against it, moreover, must be Maurice Beresford's finding that the number of new towns founded dropped significantly during Stephen's reign and Christopher Dyer's suggestion that the violence of Stephen's reign contributed to the surprisingly slow growth of landed incomes in the twelfth century.[104]

Stephen's reign has been brought into the broader debate over the 'feudal revolution', through the work of Professor Bisson, and this article therefore has implications for that debate.[105] Since Stephen's reign lies on the fringes of the controversy, however, I will limit myself to suggestions. One subtext running throughout the debate concerns levels of violence and whether they could change. My basic argument here is that there is good reason to accept as reliable contemporary perceptions that Stephen's reign saw a dramatic rise in certain types of violence. This argument could be taken as support for the thesis of 'feudal revolution'. On the other hand, I argue for the plausibility of the chronicles not on the basis of aggressive lordship but by comparison to general practices of warfare in the period, often practices used by kings. Though Bisson argues that standard acts of warfare played a role in the kind of violence encompassed within the 'feudal revolution', he sees warfare, like feuding, as an insufficient explanation.[106] Thus, my findings represent only limited support for the concept of 'feudal revolution'.

What I would argue, however, is that my conclusions suggest that historians need to take a new look at an old subject, namely the importance of strong versus weak royal power. This suggestion will set off alarm bells in the minds of many readers. A major anxiety that runs throughout the debate on the 'feudal revolution' is that the thesis might reopen the way for old fashioned 'statist' history, which saw the rise of powerful kings as automatically a 'good thing'.[107] Historians of

---

103 William of Wycombe, 'De vita Roberti Betun, episcopi Herefordensis', in *Anglia Sacra*, ed. H. Wharton, 2 vols. (London, 1691), ii, 313; John of Salisbury, *Policraticus sive de Nugis Curialium et Vestigiis Philosophorum*, ed. C. C. I. Webb, 2 vols. (Oxford, 1909), ii, 394–5; *Gesta Stephani*, 154–5.

104 M. Beresford, *New Towns of the Middle Ages: Town Plantation in England, Wales and Gascony* (2nd edn, Wolfesboro, 1988), 336; C. Dyer, *Making a Living in the Middle Ages: The People of Britain, 850–1250* (London, 2002), 102–3.

105 T. N. Bisson, 'The "Feudal Revolution" ', *Past and Present*, 142 (1994), 6–42; D. Barthélemy and S. D. White, 'The "Feudal Revolution" ', *Past and Present*, 152 (1996), 196–223; T. Reuter, C. Wickham, and T. N. Bisson, 'The "Feudal Revolution" ', *Past and Present*, 155 (1997), 177–225; D. Crouch, *The Birth of Nobility: Constructing Aristocracy in England and France 900–1300* (Harlow, 2005), 194–200.

106 Bisson, 'Feudal Revolution', 14.

107 White, 'Feudal Revolution', 222–3; Reuter, 'Feudal Revolution', 180–1; Wickham,

England will also be concerned about a revival of the 'good king/bad king' paradigm of English history.[108] These anxieties are reasonable. The 'good king/bad king' approach leads to simplistic history and one has to be wary of modern biases towards centralization and of potentially anachronistic visions of the rise of the 'state'. I myself have argued that a relatively strong Angevin government did not prevent the gentry from using violence for local control and that the gentry also used the royal courts to enhance their own power, hardly a traditional 'statist' view.[109] But fears of 'statist' history may have prompted us to throw the baby out with the bathwater. One need not employ preconceived values (plunder and devastation by royal forces was a regrettable necessity but when baronial forces did the same the barons were mad, bad, and anarchic) to investigate what difference royal power might make. It is time to look again, from a neutral perspective, at the impact of major changes in royal power in England and in other medieval kingdoms.

Such an ambition lies beyond the scope of this paper, and I will finish with a narrower conclusion. Whatever the reasons for Stephen's failure to solidify his control early in his reign, the consequences for England were major. Among those consequences was the rise of the types of violence associated with any kind of warfare in the twelfth century. An understanding of the military context of Stephen's reign helps to reaffirm the broad validity of the laments of the chroniclers and of the traditionally bleak picture of the period of civil war. Though there is much that I admire in recent scholarship on Stephen's reign, I hope that this article will correct what I believe is an overcorrection concerning violence in the collective recent scholarly depiction of the reign.

'Feudal Revolution', 196–8. Bisson denies a 'statist' approach in his arguments about the 'feudal revolution', but also argues for the importance of royal government; 'Feudal Revolution' (1997), 216, 222–23. For an interesting example of a non-statist approach to government and violence, see D. Barthélemy, *La société dans le comté de Vendôme de l'an mil au XIVe siècle* (Paris, 1993), 724–35.

[108] Reuter, 'Feudal Revolution', 192.

[109] H. M. Thomas, *Vassals, Heiresses, Crusaders, and Thugs: The Gentry of Angevin Yorkshire* (Philadelphia, 1993), 59–85.

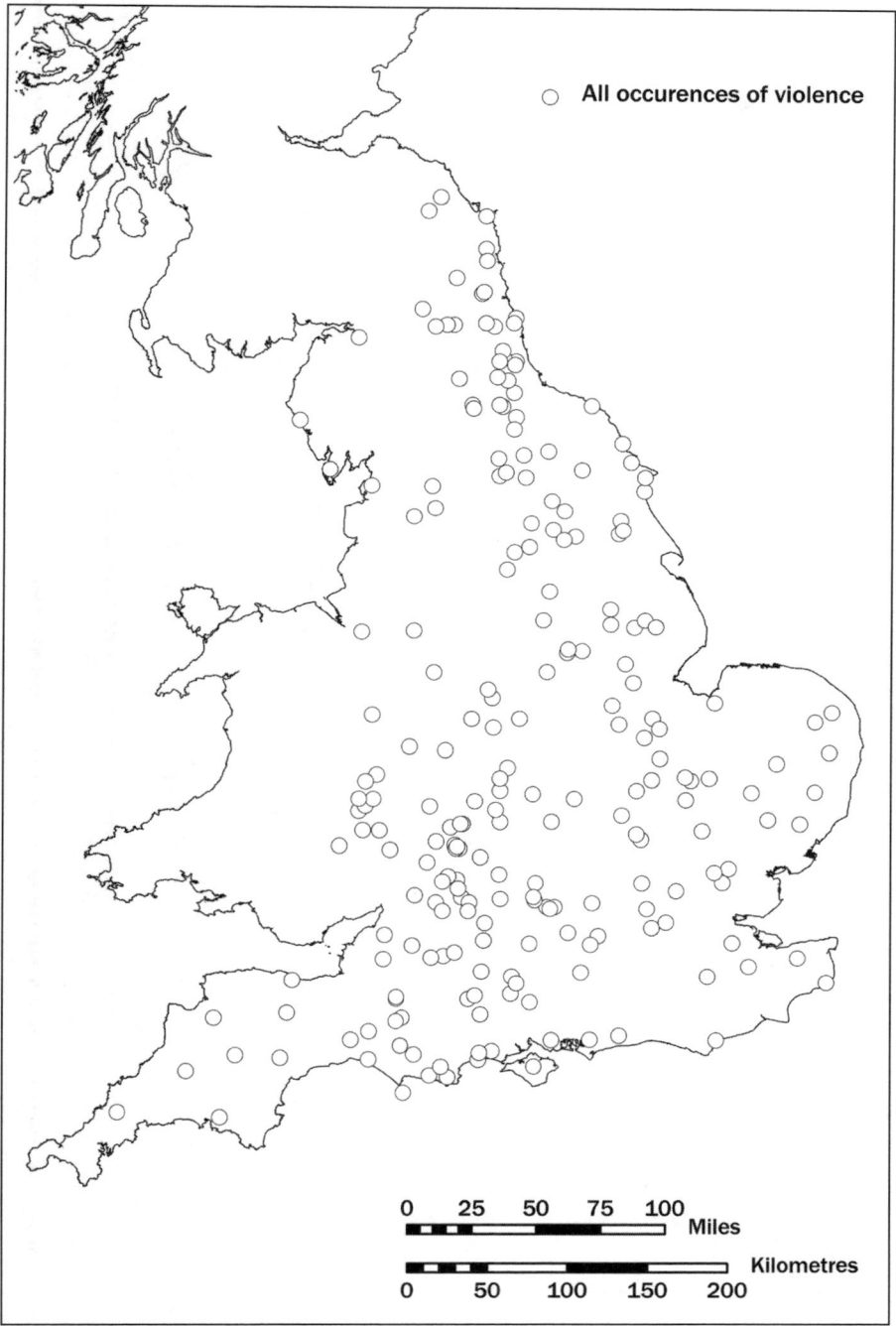

○ All occurences of violence

0   25   50   75   100
                        Miles

                        Kilometres
0   50   100   150   200

Map 1. Recorded incidences of violence during Stephen's reign

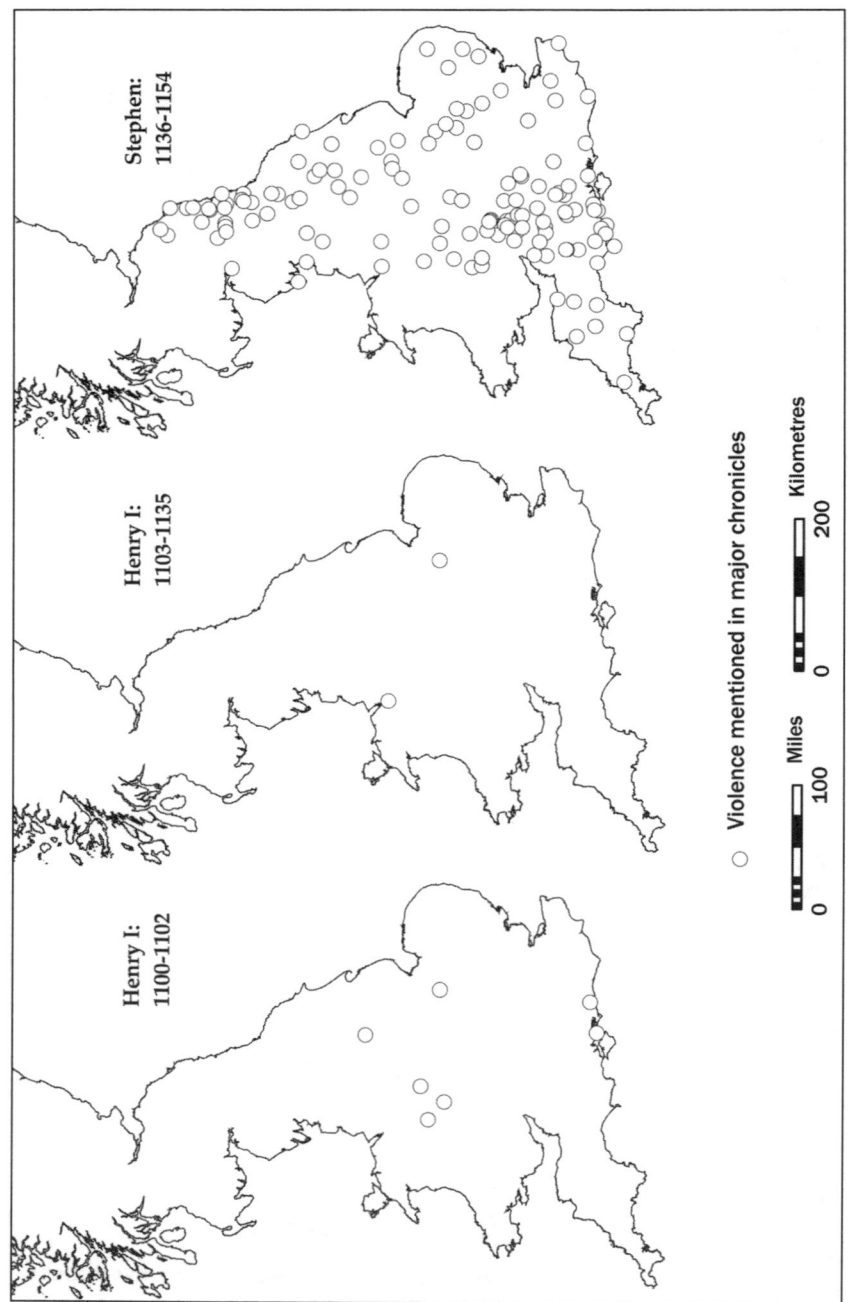

Map 2. Chronicled violence in the reigns of Henry I and Stephen

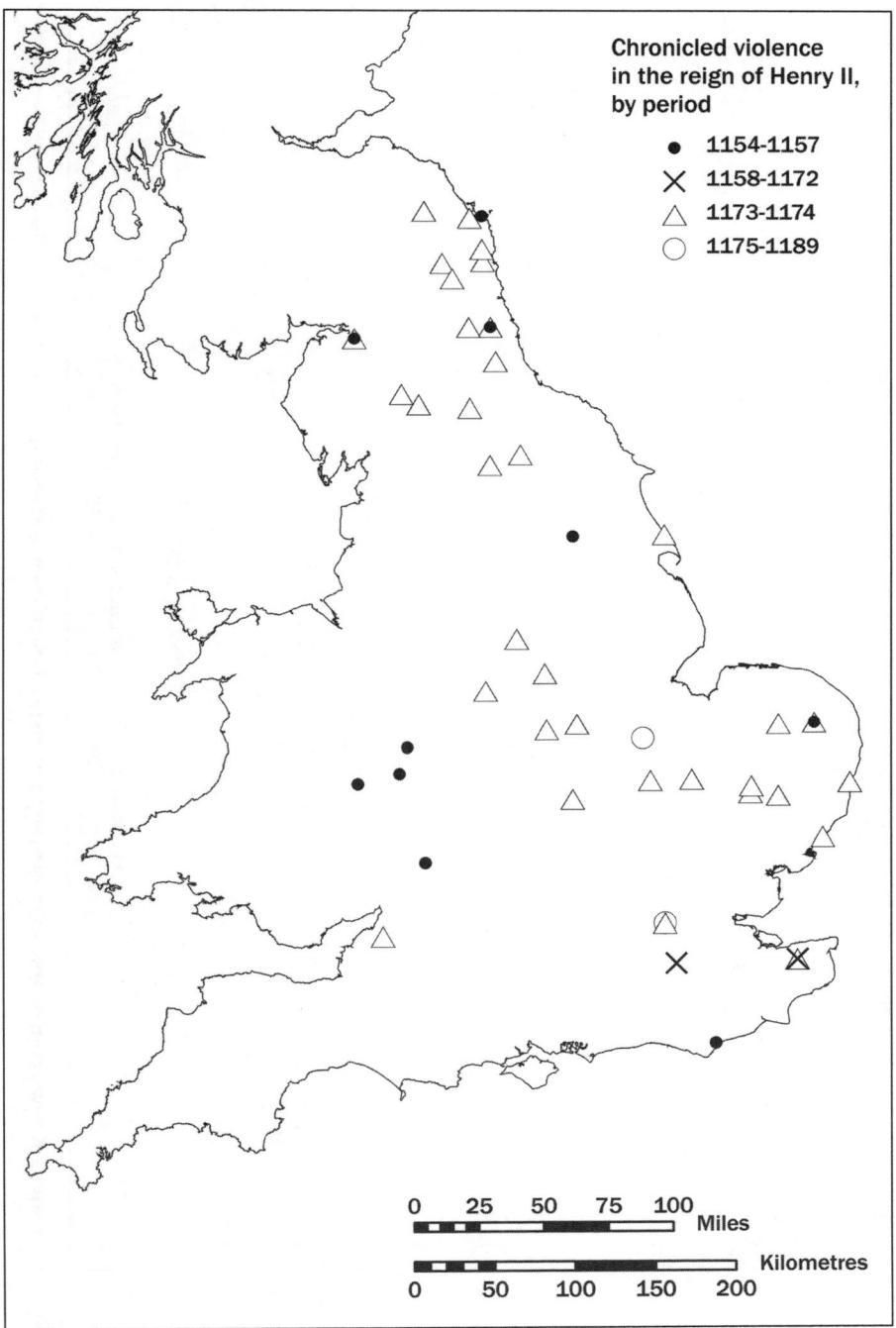

Map 3. Chronicled violence in the reign of Henry II, by period

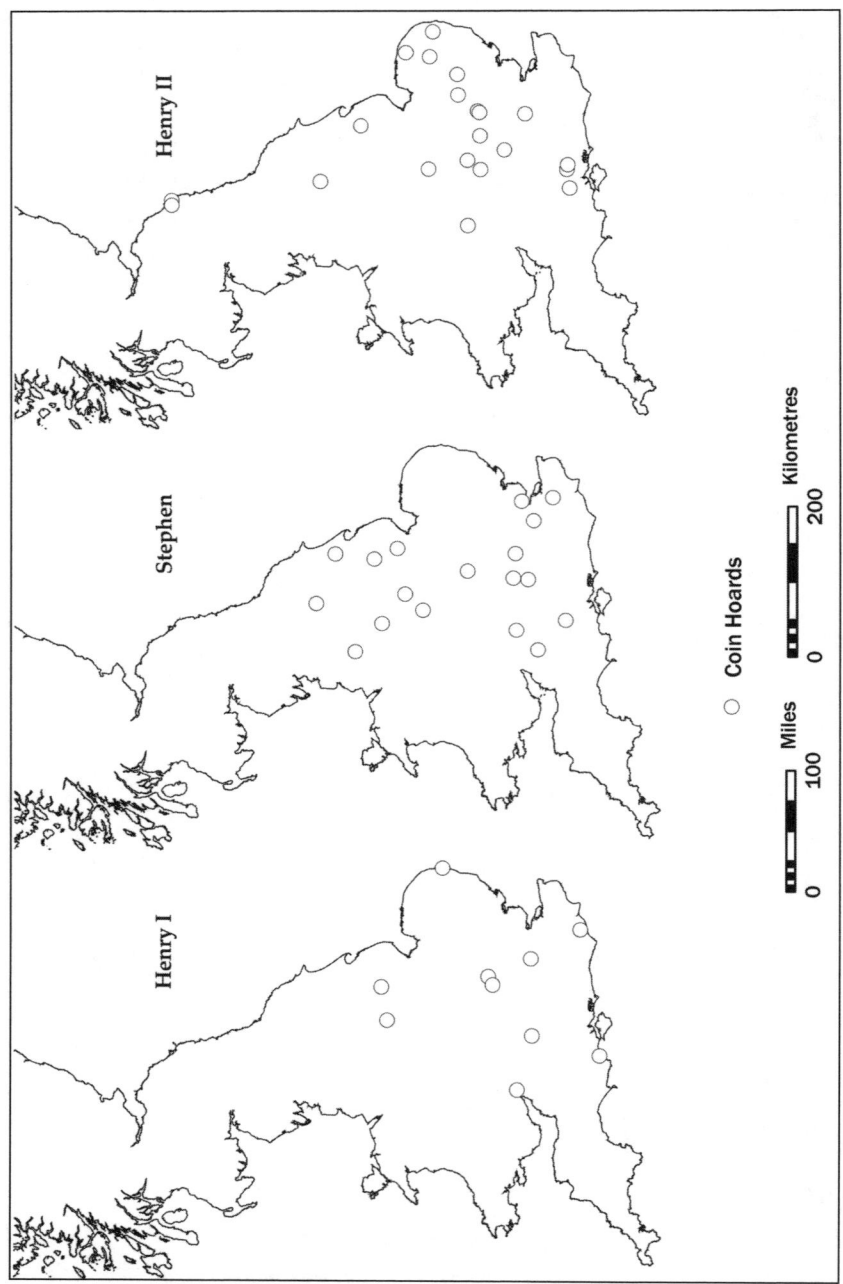

Map 4. Known coin hoards from the reigns of Henry I, Stephen and Henry II

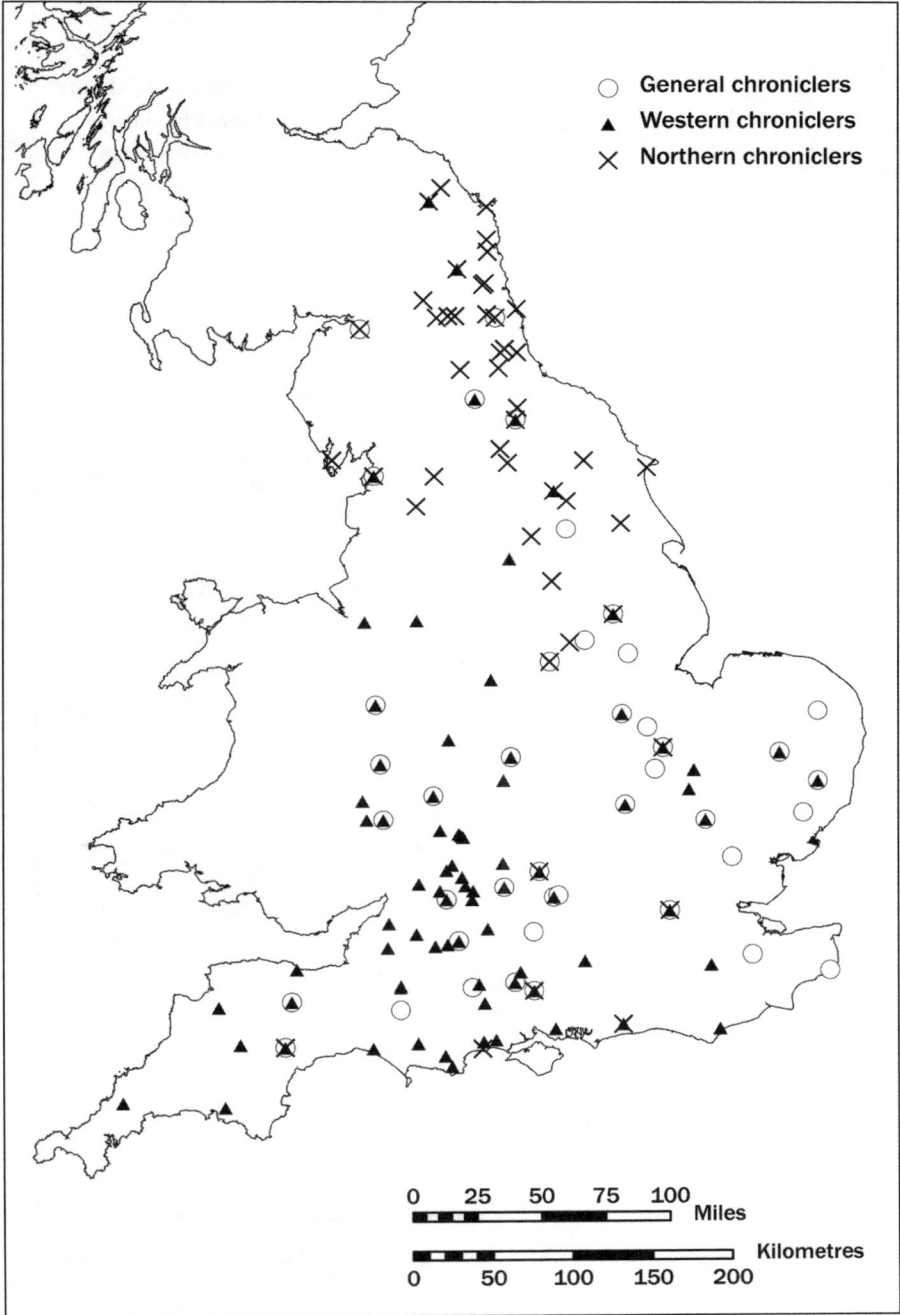

Map 5. Distribution of violence in Stephen's reign as recorded in regional chronicles

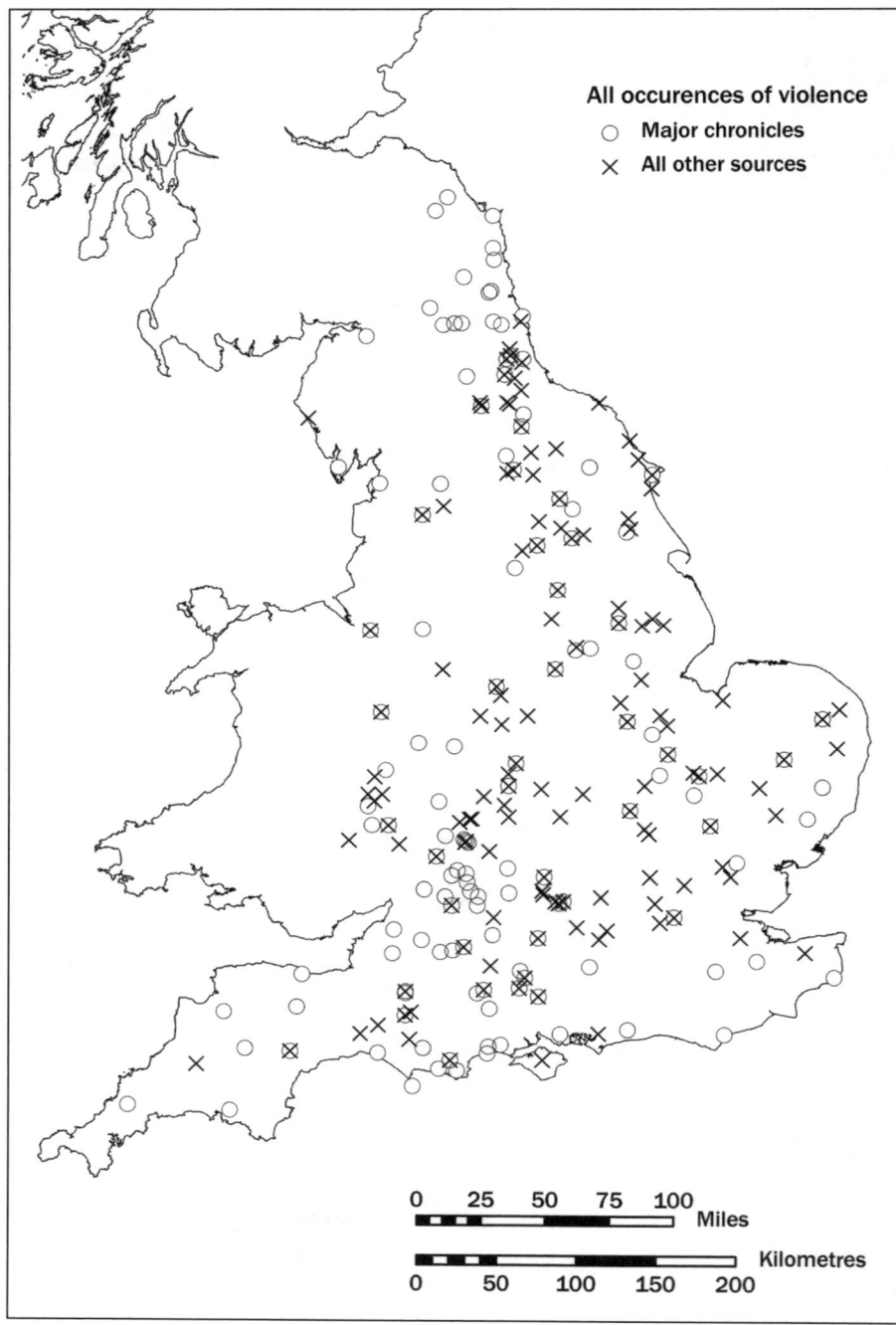

Map 6. Distribution of violent events in Stephen's reign as recorded by major and minor sources

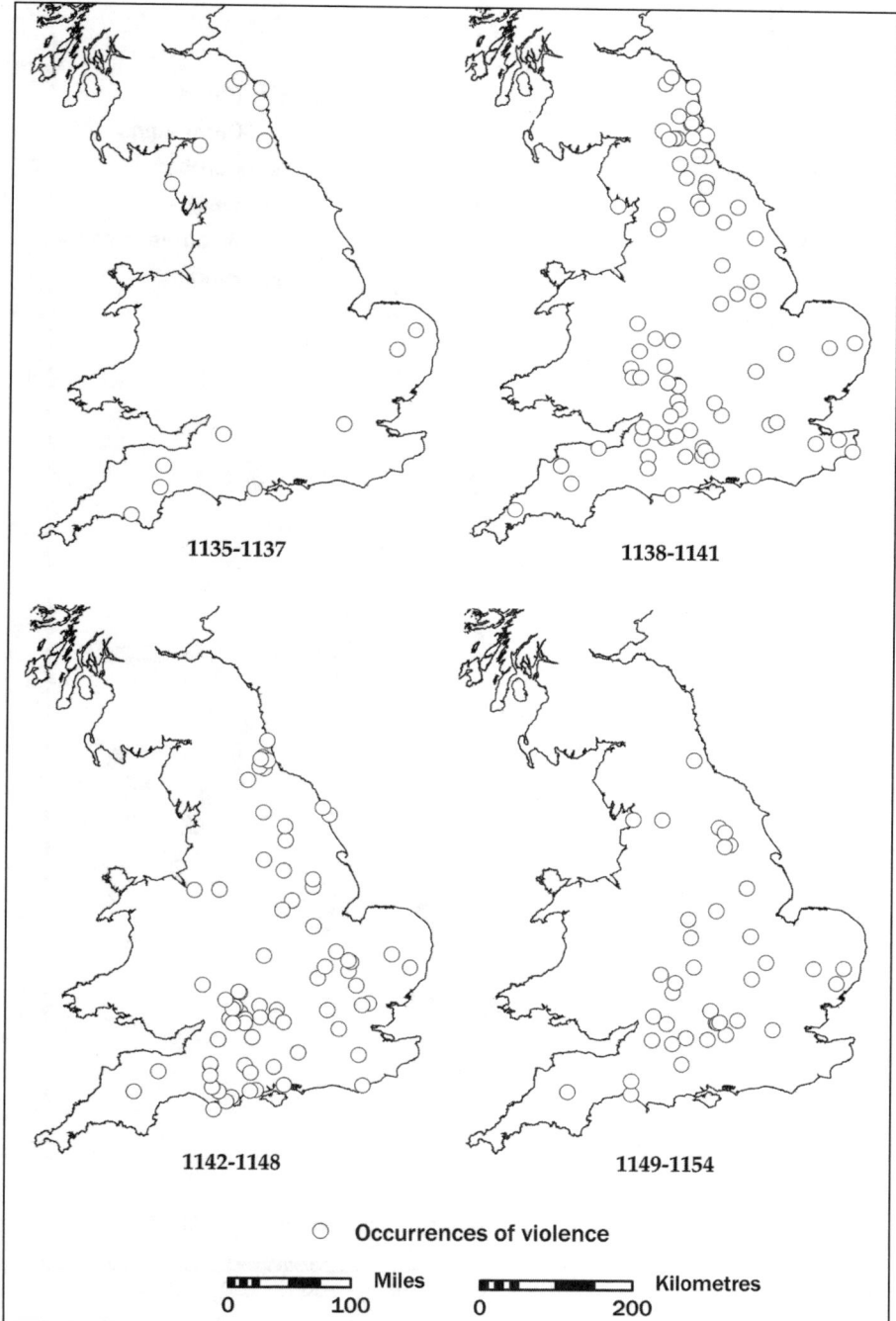

1135-1137

1138-1141

1142-1148

1149-1154

○ **Occurrences of violence**

Miles

0   100

Kilometres

0   200

Map 7. Occurrences of violence by period during Stephen's reign

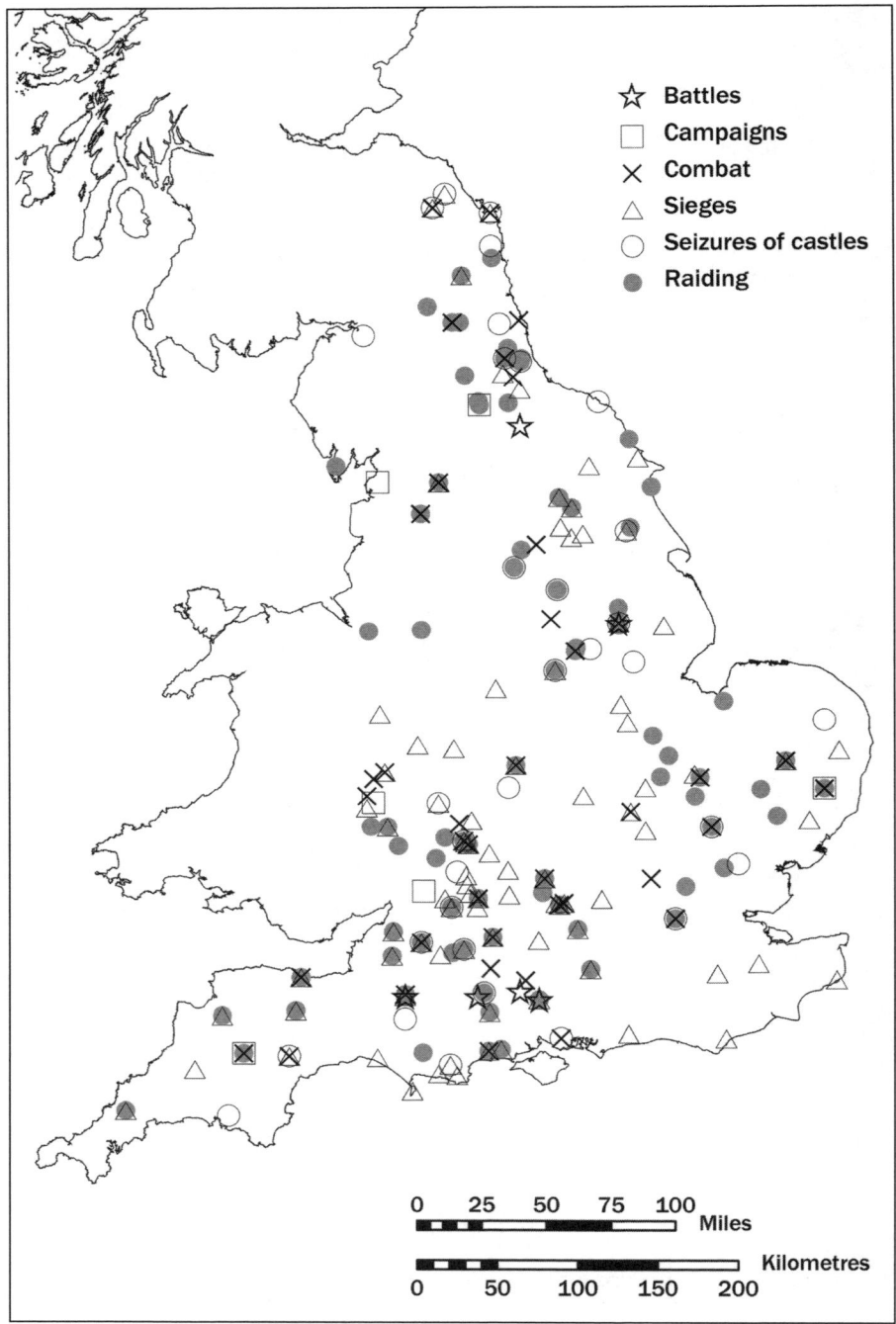

Map 8. Military operations in Stephen's reign, by type

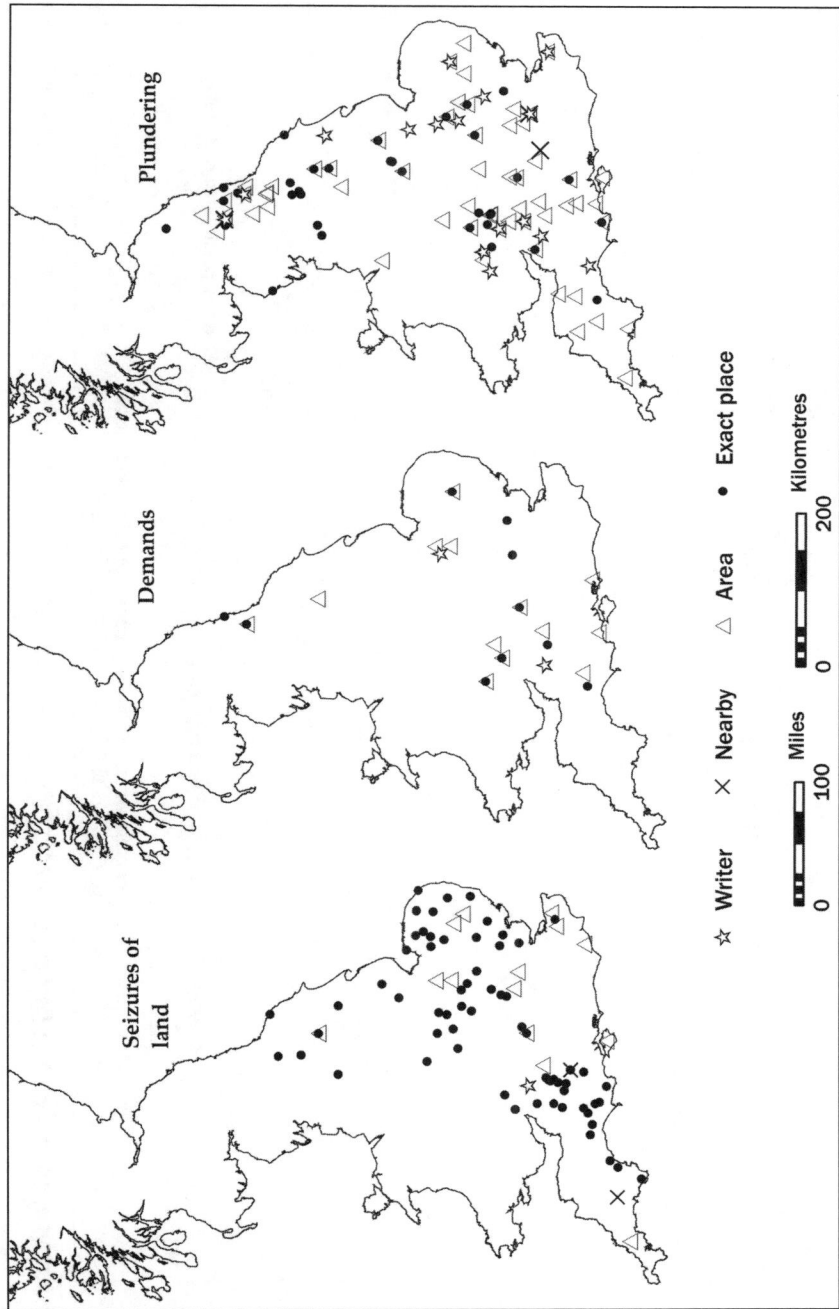

Map 9. Measures taken to finance military activity during the civil war between Stephen and Empress Matilda

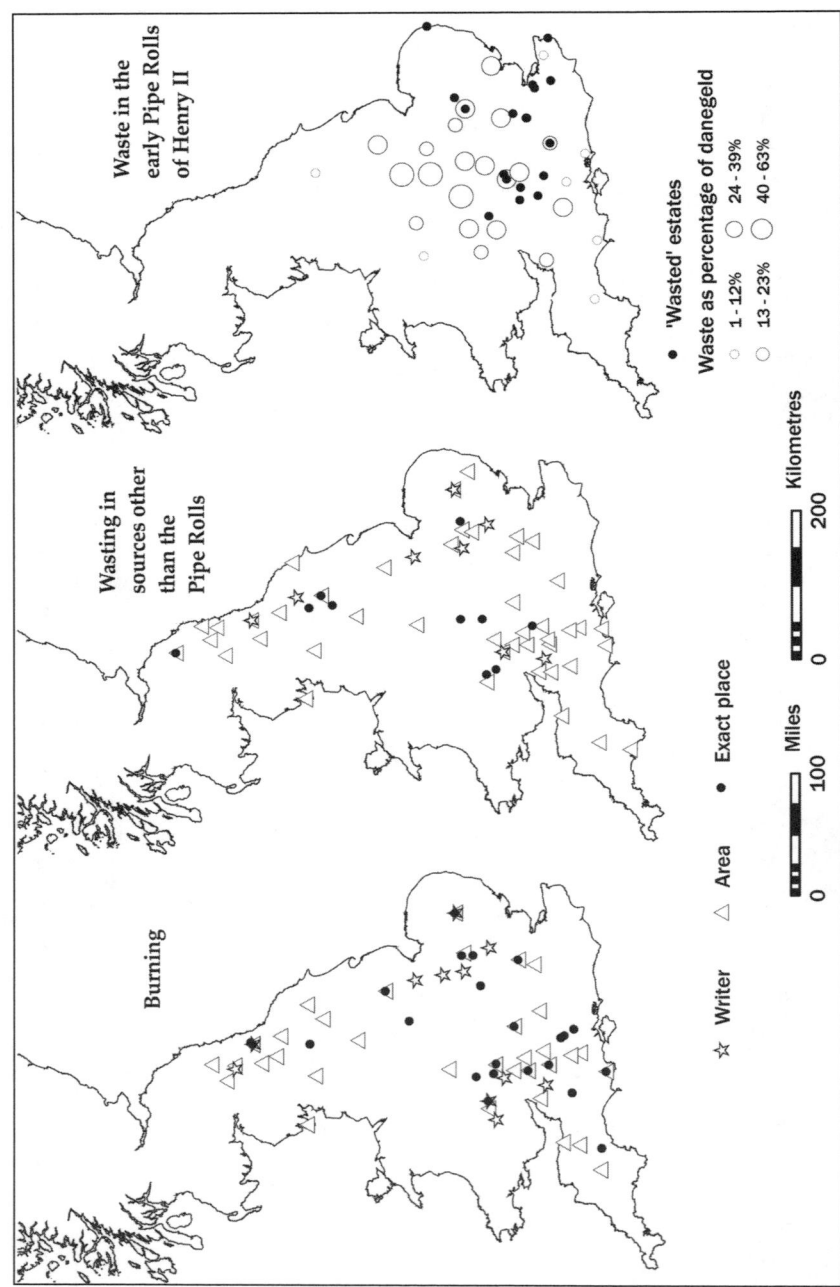

Map 10. Wasting of land in Stephen's reign

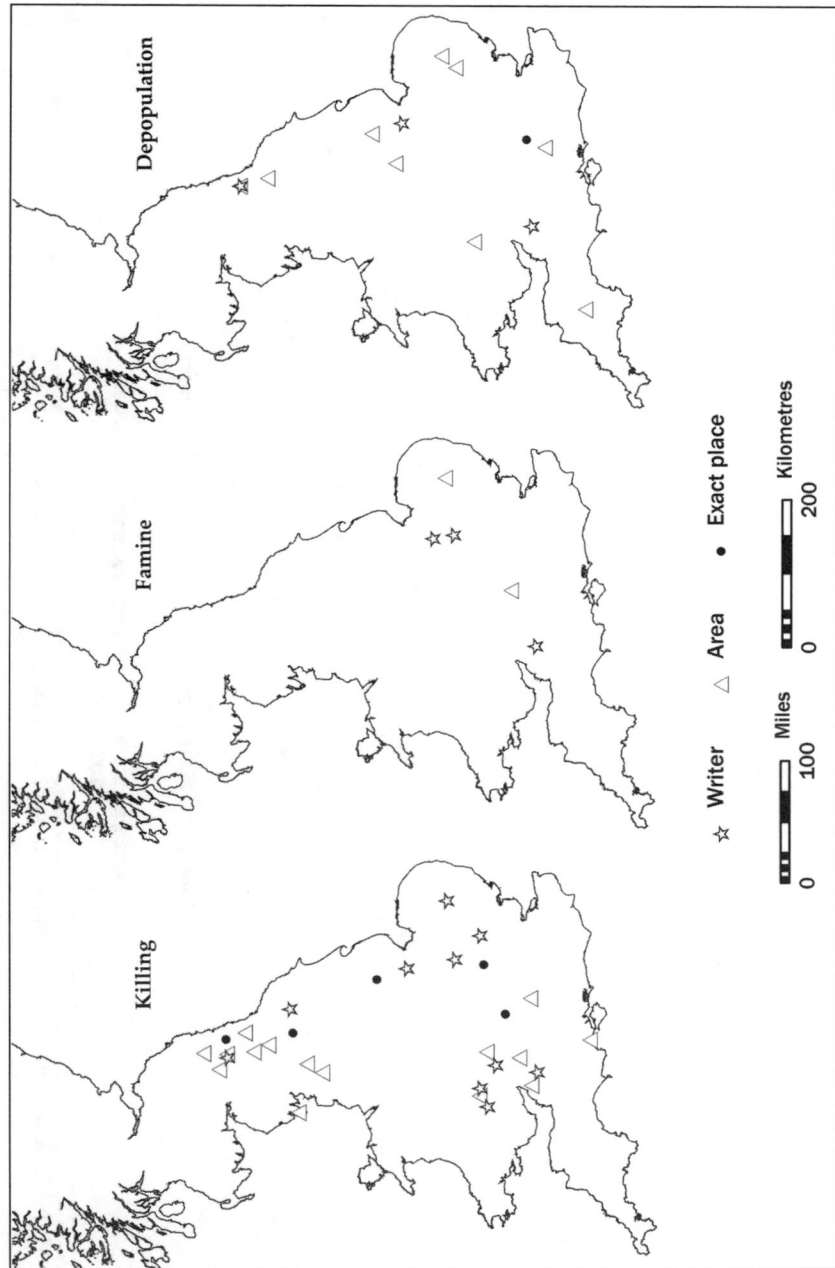

Map 11. Killing, famine, and depopulation in Stephen's reign

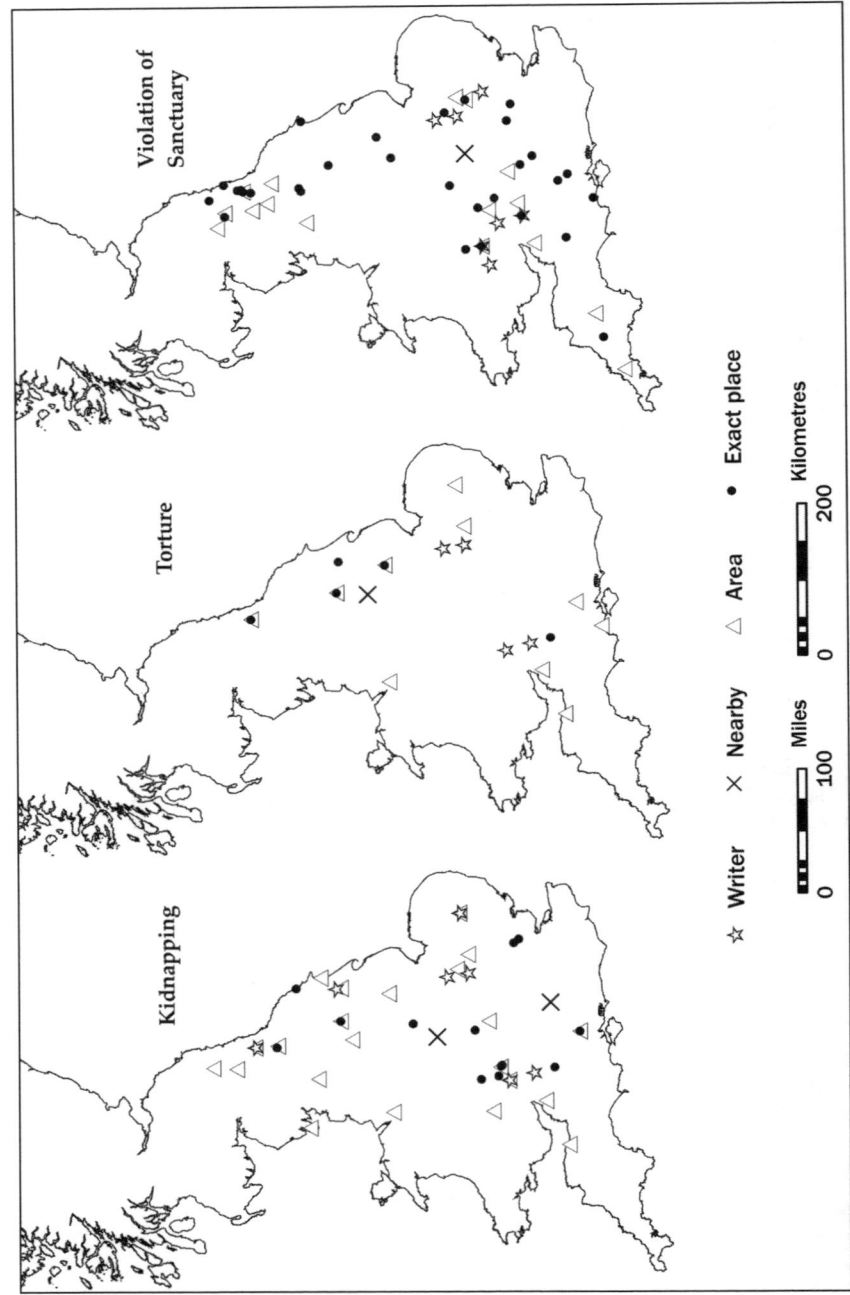

Map 12. Kidnapping, torture and violation of sanctuary in Stephen's reign

9

The Lure of Stephen's England:
Tenserie, Flemings, and
a Crisis of Circumstance

T. N. BISSON

To the memory of Pierre Bonnassie

A FEW YEARS after the 'sedition between King Stephen and Duke Henry for acquiring the kingdom', as he called it, a monk of Abingdon recalled that a constable of Wallingford, having promised to protect the monks in return for a payment by Abbot Ingulf (1130–58), had reneged and plundered the monastic vill of Culham. When the Abbot humbly sought restitution, he was rebuffed, and it was only when the constable was mortally wounded and needed release from ecclesiastical anathema that his brother promised to return the plunder – and in the end that promise, too, was compromised.[1]

This sort of 'protection-money' had its own name – *tenseria* – during the reign of Stephen. Although this term itself is lacking in the Abingdon account, John Horace Round rightly cited this case in his brief study of 'Tenserie' published more than a century ago.[2] For indeed, when allusions to coercive payments and intimidation are added to the comparatively few mentions of *tenseria* as such, the implications of a form of violence with its own vocabulary are considerably enlarged. They open two perspectives of research: that of the nature and origin of *tenseria*, and that of the nature of violence in a society often described as suffering from 'anarchy'. The first and smaller of these perspectives is what chiefly concerns me in these pages, but I wish to say at once that nothing in what follows is meant to argue that anarchy prevailed under King Stephen. That contemporaries thought it did was well argued by Edmund King a decade ago; yet the passionate sense of our chroniclers that constituted powers had failed the

---

1 *Historia Ecclesie Abbendonensis: The History of the Church of Abingdon*, ed. J. Hudson, 2 vols. (Oxford, 2002–7), ii, 314–15.
2 J. H. Round, *Geoffrey de Mandeville: A Study of the Anarchy* (London, 1892), 414–16.

people hardly amounted to a charge that derelict authorities had vanished. The real trouble was that they had multiplied. 'We suffer as many kings as the castles that oppress us', wrote Abbot Gilbert Foliot in a weary phrase that made the rounds.[3]

Protection-money was one of their devices, as the story from Abingdon shows. Whether it was a normal device amongst constables, sheriffs, and magnates is another matter, as we shall see. What may be noticed at once is that the levy seems not to have been customary in England before 1135. That it was unheard of seems unlikely, and it could well be concealed in allusions to seizures, demands, and constraints, or in renunciations of 'unjust exactions' and 'bad customs'.[4] But it was conceptually incompatible with the Conqueror's averred modes of demand; moreover, its natural affinity with advocacy over church lands points to an institution that was unknown in Normandy.[5]

So it may not be accidental that exactions labelled *tenseria* (or *tenserie*) are known only from Stephen's day and after. Round cited four examples from the years 1135–54; to these may be added at least four others, not counting an extravagant canon of the Council of Tours (1163) that surely originated with one of the prior English occasions. At once the most famous and most informative of these mentions of *tenseria/tenserie* is found in the Peterborough annal for 1137, which was composed many years later. Of Stephen's ever worsening 'nineteen winters', the very first illustration was the repeated levy of a 'geld' on the villages, '7 clepeden it "tenserie" '. This was an arbitrary tax, for no payment seems to have satisfied the collectors, who ended up as pillagers.[6] The earliest securely dated allusion is found in Empress Matilda's protection-charter for Luffield in early spring 1141: the monks were to be 'in my protection and *tenseria* with all their possessions'.[7] Towards 1144, Abbot Walter of Ramsey felt compelled to pay numerous castellans '*redemptiones* or *tenseriae* for his peasants', and a year or so later Abbot Gilbert of Gloucester was complaining about abusive *tenseriae* in his

---

3   *The Letters and Charters of Gilbert Foliot*, ed. A. Morey and C. N. L. Brooke (Cambridge, 1967), no. 26. See also Reginald of Durham, *Libellus de admirandis beati Cuthberti virtutibus quae novellis patratae sunt temporibus*, ed. J. Raine, Surtees Society, 1 (1835), 134; *Newburgh*, i, 69. On 'anarchy' my only reference here is to E. King, 'Introduction', in King, *Anarchy*. On 'violence,' see below, pp. 177–8.

4   For example, *De iniusta vexacione Willelmi episcopi per Willelmum regem filium Willelmi magni regis*, ed. H. S. Offler, in *Camden Miscellany XXXIV*, Camden Society, 5th ser., 10 (1997), 89; *Select Charters and Other Illustrations of English Constitutional History*, ed. W. Stubbs, 9th edn rev. H. W. C. Davis (Oxford, 1913), 117–19.

5   See generally Jean Yver, 'Autour de l'absence d'avouerie en Normandie', *Bulletin de la Société des Antiquaires de Normandie*, 57 (1965), 189–283.

6   *The Peterborough Chronicle, 1070–1154*, ed. C. Clark (2nd edn, Oxford, 1970), 55–6; commentary, 106–7. For a prohibition to pay *censarias* (or *tensarias*) in the Council of Tours (1163), see *Compilatio* II.27.1, ed. E. Friedberg, *Quinque compilationes antiquae* (Leipzig, 1882), 91.

7   *Regesta*, iii, no. 571.

lands.[8] By this time the Holy See had been enlisted, for we learn from a letter of Pope Lucius II (May 1144) that 'some men' in the patrimony of Ely '*sub nomine tenseriarum* [had] pillaged [the priory's] villages and people and they oppress by unjust demands for labour and exactions'; and in 1146 the monks secured from Eugenius III a comparable prohibition against 'tallages, *tenseriae*, also illicit *operationes* and other unjust exactions' levied on their men.[9] This association of *tenseriae* with forced labour (*operationes*) figures likewise in Stephen's undated privilege for Saint John's, Colchester, and in Canon 1 of the Council of London held in March 1151.[10]

What are we to make of this evidence? Few modern scholars have pressed it, perhaps because Round had rounded up most of the documentation and had plausibly identified *tenseria* with protection-money. The editor and two translators of the *Peterborough Chronicle* all rendered *tenserie* as 'protection-money' in their versions of half a century ago.[11] An uncharacteristic dissent came from R. H. C. Davis, who opined in 1966 that *tenserie* may have resulted from scribal confusions of 'c' and 't'. Uncharacteristic, I say, for Davis, himself the editor of the *Gesta Stephani*, had (otherwise) little doubt about the prevailing violence of the 'anarchy.' His was an untenable view, for the verb *tensare* in its substantive forms is massively documented, mostly before 1154.[12] Recently some renewed interest has flickered. In 1984 Edmund King was the first to wonder about the provenance of *tenseria*, and his suggestion that it was an importation into England was exactly right, as we shall see. A decade later, when clarifying Round's stress on violence and distinguishing between the (little known) views of castellans and the tendentious ones of churchmen, King called for more work on foreign influences.[13] The problematic nature of *tenseriae* has lately engaged David Crouch, although not their origin; while in the newest book on Stephen Donald Matthew makes no reference at all to the phenomenon.[14]

When these allusions to *tenseria* (and *tenserie*) are read together, three points of interest stand out. First, it looks as if the experience of an exaction so called was widespread in southern England. It extends from Dorset to Suffolk, with

---

8   *Chronicon Abbatiae Rameseiensis*, ed. W. Dunn MacRay (RS, 1886), 334; *Letters of Foliot*, no. 27.

9   *Papsturkunden in England*, ed. W. Holtzmann, 3 vols. (Berlin and Göttingen, 1930–52) [hereafter *PUE*], ii, no. 36; iii, no. 58.

10   *Regesta*, iii, no. 233; *Councils & Synods*, ii, no. 150.

11   *Peterborough Chronicle*, 56, 107; *English Historical Documents ii*, ed. D. C. Douglas and G. W. Greenaway (2nd edn, London, 1981), 210; *The Anglo-Saxon Chronicle*, trans. G. N. Garmonsway (London, 1953), 264.

12   Davis, *King Stephen*, 80 note. Cf. J. F. Niermeyer, *Mediae latinitatis lexicon minus* (Leiden 1976), 1019–20; *Select Pleas of the Crown. I. A.D. 1200–1225*, ed. F. W. Maitland, Selden Society, 1 (1888), no. 43; and below, p. 174.

13   E. King, 'The Anarchy of King Stephen's Reign', *TRHS*, 5th ser., 34 (1984), 137; King, 'Introduction', 30–1 and note 113.

14   Crouch, *Reign of Stephen*, 335, who speaks of *tenserie* as taxation; and Matthew, *King Stephen*.

conspicuous points or clusters at Sherborne, Gloucestershire, the Fenlands of Ramsey and Ely (and Geoffrey de Mandeville), and the patrimony of St John's, Colchester. Much as northern shires were similarly afflicted, they were seemingly exempt from *tenseriae*.[15] Second, while all our texts appear to equate *tenseria* with 'protection-money', they also tend to associate it with other impositions, notably tallage. This is why Round dwelt on one notable case of protection-money *not* called *tenseria*; but it also explains why subsequent studies have sometimes lost sight of *tenseria* in quest of evidence for (or against) anarchy. What matters to all such views is that in England *tenseria* could not be exercised, let alone defended, as distinct from arbitrary taxation, seizures, and forced labour. That is why *tenseria* is, indeed, critical to the assessment of 'anarchy', why its provenance matters historically. Third, and most telling of all, no fewer than four of the eight texts here in question affirm, or imply, that *tenseria/tenserie* was a novel or problematic concept in the 1140s. 'Ransoms or *tenseriae*', wrote the chronicler of Ramsey; 'under the name of *tenseriae*' were the words of Pope Lucius; 'which are commonly spoken of as *tenseriae* or tallages', said the bishops assembled in London; 'and they called it *tenserie*', wrote the monk of Peterborough.[16] What this suggests is that the impositions so designated were defended by their perpetrators as functional or even utilitarian taxes, unlike novel exactions. This appearance, when coupled with the certainty that monastic lands everywhere were said to be afflicted, strongly supports Edmund King's conjecture that *tenseriae* appeared in England as a pretence of advocacy over church lands.[17]

Where but from French-speaking lands could it have come from? England, to be sure, was such a land. But neither advocacy nor *tenseria* were English. Writing of the imposition with palpable disdain, the monk of Peterborough had no native word for it; on the contrary his phrase '7 clepeden it "tenserie" ' appears to convey a French singular form rather than the Latin plural. Could this have been a word voiced by masses of foreign knights pouring into England? Two issues arise from this question: first, the imposition itself in lands across the Channel; second, the likelihood of its export from France. Once again, as formerly with the Norman Conquest, it may help to view English history from the mainland.

With respect to *tenseria* the first point to notice is that this term does not appear in France. Its nearest analogues would seem to be *tessara*, which is renounced in a judgment of Prince Louis (1100–08) relating to lands of Saint-Vaast (Arras), and *tensura*, which figures in Flemish charters of the 1120s.[18] These are the terms of

---

[15] Citations in R. Bartlett, *England under the Norman and Angevin Kings, 1075–1225* (Oxford, 2000), 284–5.

[16] *Peterborough Chronicle*, 56; *Chronicon Rameseiensis*, 334; *PUE*, ii, no. 36; *Councils & Synods*, ii, no. 150.

[17] King, 'Anarchy', 137.

[18] *Recueil des actes de Louis VI, roi de France*, ed. J. Dufour, 4 vols., Chartes et Diplômes relatifs à l'Histoire de France (Paris, 1992), i, no. 16 (line 29), but I do not share the editor's

rights or claims, not levies; yet they bear something like the same meaning as in England. Conceivably, the vernacular substantive of *tensare* crossed the Channel with Flemish knights in these or some such forms, for no other continental words conform so nearly with *tenserie*. And it follows from this, and not only from this, that the Latin *tenseria* has the looks of an English coinage of the years 1135–45; that is, of a usage arguably derived from the spoken word *tenserie*. In records pertaining to England the spelling is almost always *tenseria(e)*, although from the primal verb *tensare* one might expect *tensaria*.[19]

In any case, the usual word for protection-money in provincial France was *tensamentum*. This is attested in regions extending from the Chartrain through the Ile-de-France to its borders with Champagne. When King Louis VI reserved his right to *tensamentum* on his peasants at Bagneux in 1117, he specified an annual customary payment in produce to his agent in this domain. When an advocate of Saint-Denis in the Soissonais got into trouble with Abbot Suger a few years later, the same king reserved the advocate's *tensamentum* in coin and kind while restricting his wider claims to lordship.[20] These cases point to a traditional Frankish practice associated with public justice and defence. The greater lords possessed of *tensamenta* clung to them, like Louis VI. These impositions multiplied under Philip Augustus, who clearly viewed the protections he was reviving as a fiscal resource to be exploited.[21] Whereas the *salvamentum*, found in Burgundy and elsewhere, evoked the *salvatio* of asylum and the peace, the *tensamentum* marked the conceptual persistence of distinctly regalian protection.[22]

So described, however, the *tensamentum* yields less than we need of it. To say that it was a correct and justifiable imposition in France, often the rightful remuneration of advocates, is only to say what is known in writing. The whole truth is surely bigger. Luckily, we happen to know what went on in a newly settled domain of the monks of Morigny towards 1100. There a courageous manager named Baldwin took it upon himself to resist 'impious men' who, seeing the place prosper, were bent on imposing new customs of lordship over free peasants. Among these was a demand for (the price of) 'protection [*tutamentum*], which is

---

view (27, note 2) that *tessara* corresponds to *tenseria*, which is not attested in France (cf. C. du Fresne Du Cange, *Glossarium mediae et infinae latinitatis*, new edn, 10 vols. (Niort, 1883–7) vi, 542); *Actes des comtes de Flandre, 1071–1128*, ed. F. Vercauteren, Commission royale d'Histoire, Académie royale de Belgique (Brussels, 1938), no. 115 (lines 22–3); Niermeyer, *Lexicon*, 1020. See also P. Duparc, 'Le tensement', *Revue historique de Droit français et étranger*, 4th ser., 40 (1962), 46.

19 Citations above, notes 6–10. For the variant in manuscripts of *Compilatio* II see above, note 6.
20 *Recueil des actes de Louis VI*, i, no. 124; ii, no. 409.
21 For example, *Recueil des actes de Philippe Auguste, roi de France*, ed. H.-Fr. Delaborde et al., 4 vols., Chartes et Diplômes relatifs à l'Histoire de France (Paris, 1916–79), i, nos. 196, 232, 332; iii, nos. 1018, 1087, 1092; and see generally Duparc, 'Le tensement', 54–7.
22 H. Sée, *Les classes rurales et le régime domanial en France au Moyen Age* (Paris, 1901), 479–80.

popularly called *tensamentum*'. The very words of the tormentors, characteristi-
cally self-serving, are evoked in an affectionate memoir of a good and faithful
servant.[23]

If the history of protection-levies in France is hardly less problematic than in
England, it is because they arose undocumented with the new coercive lordships
they typically disguised. That advocacy and its price are not attested in Normandy
cannot mean that the ducal protectorate of churches was absolute, although it may
help to explain the denunciations of Flemings.[24] What is well nigh unique about
the tale of Morigny is that someone – most likely the would-be lords themselves –
had presumed to dignify their seizures as earned rewards. Of those who got away
with this no records were made. Yet once *tensamentum* is plucked, this story
becomes one of many about wicked men turning arbitrary seizures into the
customs of domination. What is more, there was nothing to prevent the advocates,
whose office rendered legitimate the very concept of paid-up protection, from
multiplying their demands of helpless people. Had not Abbo of Fleury long since
seen through those prepared to admit they were not so much advocates as lords?
In the 1160s one could refer to 'our advocate, yea our pillager'. And as denunciations of advocates multiplied from Flanders to Lombardy, the easy prosperity of
these functionaries became a spectacle for all to witness.[25]

And not least for landless French-speaking knights who could see that the
protectorate of clerical lands – so why not call it *tensura* or *tenserie*? – was a prof-
itable offer to make. They had a notorious forerunner in such licensed pillage: the
huckster monk Henry who had bluffed his way to the abbacy of Peterborough in
1127 and managed to loot it thoroughly before being ousted.[26] To be sure, not all
the knights who went to England could expect to secure lordships, yet they were
armed *déracinés* in the service of chieftains, such as William of Ypres,[27] whose
interest in the concept of *tenserie* was to render their oppressive demands for
service and money as palatable as they could.

That armed men from the lands or borderlands of *tensamentum* and *tensura*
flocked to England with Stephen of Blois or in his wake is beyond doubt.

---

[23] *La chronique de Morigny (1095–1152)*, ed. L. Mirot, 2nd edn, Collection de Textes pour
servir à l'Etude et à l'Enseignement de l'Histoire (Paris, 1912), 5–6.

[24] See C. H. Haskins, *Norman Institutions* (Cambridge, Mass., 1918), 35–9, 63–4; and Yver,
'Autour de l'absence d'avouerie en Normandie', 265–70, where it is well shown how later
Norman records accord with a developing canon law to redefine protection in relation to
presentation.

[25] Abbo of Fleury, *Collectio canonum* ii, in *PL*, cxxxix, 477; letter of 1162–80 in *Recueil des
historiens des Gaules et de la France*, ed. M. Bouquet et al., 24 vols. (Paris, 1738–1904),
xvi, 170 (no. 500). The records of abrasive advocacy are too numerous to cite; see generally
J. Flach, *Les origines de l'ancienne France*, 4 vols. (Paris, 1886–1917), i, 437–44; Sée,
Classes rurales, 474–6; *Fourth Lateran Council* c. 12, ed. J. Alberigo et al., *Conciliorum
oecumenicorum decreta* (3rd edn, Bologna, 1973), 241.

[26] *Peterborough Chronicle*, 48–54; C. Clark, ' "This ecclesiastical adventurer": Henry of
Saint-Jean d'Angély', *EHR*, 84 (1969), 548–60.

[27] *Historia Novella*, 38, 62 note, 104, 106 note, 116; Crouch, *Reign of Stephen*, 26, 66–7 note.

Virtually all the chroniclers say so, emphatically. Once in possession of King Henry's treasure, wrote William of Malmesbury, Stephen was beset by 'knights of all sorts' including

> men who served in light harness, especially from Flanders and Brittany. They were a class of men full of greed and violence, who cared nothing for breaking into cemeteries and pillaging churches; moreover, they not only rode down men of religious orders, but even dragged them into captivity; nor was it only foreign knights, but also native ones, who had hated King Henry's peace which had so diminished their prosperity.[28]

Writing later of the 'brutality of war' in 1140, William spoke of 'castles multiplying all over England, each defending its own district or, to be more truthful, plundering it'. He goes on to detail the violence perpetrated by 'knights from [these] castles', citing specifics of pillage, ransom, and torture that nearly coincide with the recitation of horrors in the retrospective Peterborough annal; and concludes with a distinction of stunning plausibility: 'Under King Henry many aliens, displaced by troubles in their native land, sailed to England and lived in peaceable leisure under his wings. Under Stephen many from Flanders and Brittany, who were used to living by plunder, swarmed to England in the hope of great booty.'[29]

Not all is to be blamed on the Flemings. The *Gesta Stephani* tells only of 'a savage multitude of foreigners who had flocked to England to serve as mercenaries', men who were violent by nature and who, when the barons who had summoned them could no longer pay or retain them, had lapsed into vile cruelties including (specifically, here again) forced labour and payments.[30] But 'Fleming' was more than simply a metaphor in these heated recollections. It happens that the very men cited by Gilbert Foliot as imposing *tenseriae* in Gloucestershire are named as Flemings in the *Gesta Stephani*. And then some! Henry de Caldret and his brother Ralph, we read, were 'bellicose men' and abrasive, 'who had left Flanders for England to serve as soldiers'. And amongst their outrages, here detailed in an extended portrait, were the very demands for labour and tribute that were identified as *tenseriae* in other sources and that Abbot Gilbert, using that very word, surely had in mind as well.[31] The danger perceived by contemporaries should not be minimised. The very first measure of Henry II, announced in his coronation assembly of December 1154, was the expulsion of Flemish mercenaries from England.[32]

That expulsion cannot have happened overnight. But one thing is certain: as a bad custom *tenseriae* faded fast in England. It is mentioned together with *prisae* in the

---

[28] *Historia Novella*, 32–3.
[29] Ibid., 70–2.
[30] *Gesta Stephani*, 152–4. See also 104; *Waltham*, 76–82; *Orderic*, vi, 482, 536.
[31] *Letters of Foliot*, no. 27; *Gesta Stephani*, 188, 190.
[32] W. L. Warren, *Henry II* (London 1973), 59.

iter (1194) of Richard I; while the verb *tensare* could be attached to an alleged seizure from shippers in Lincolnshire as late as 1202.[33] In France *tensamentum* persisted as a commuted or justified payment for protection, as we have seen. What has vanished is the evidence of protection-money as a common and abrasive experience in English societies, which is what we should expect of a land where arbitrary distraints were coming to be limited by new procedural remedies. And when prevailing orders of power under King Stephen are viewed in the wider perspectives of time and space, it becomes arguable that the lure of England for fighting men in search of lordships resembled that of an opportune and rewarding frontier.

Yet it would be wrong to suppose that Flemish (or foreign) knights alone were tempted. Orderic Vitalis, like William of Malmesbury, makes clear that the contingency was structural: that Anglo-Norman magnates had found Henry I a repressive keeper of an order at variance with their own.[34] Robert of Gloucester was said to have created a regal domination centred on the captured castle of Sherborne, a *dominium* of 'laws and commands' of 'peace and tranquillity' such as only a regime of multiplied castles built with forced labour and generating oppressive impositions could produce. By his own confession Earl William of Chichester had done much the same, if on a lesser scale, in the diocese of Chichester; and while not all the brutality charged against Geoffrey de Mandeville can be viewed as constructive of lordship as distinct from vengeance, he too was in quest of power.[35] To dismiss such pretensions as unrealistic is easier for us to do than it would have been for contemporaries. For penurious knights to offer their services to partisan magnates was in the nature of an investment in possibility.

And it is this convergence of baronial ambitions and lesser knightly temptations that reduces this crisis of Stephen's reign to the status of an incident in a bigger and longer history. *Tenserie* in England – itself an element in a syndrome of coercive demands aimed at creating lordships of constraint – corresponded to *tensamentum* of precisely the same description in France. The difference is that in the Ile-de-France and borderlands extending north and east that levy remained akin to legitimate as well as to pretentious protectorates, and survived as the former in unwritten custom; whilst other terms (*comandisia, tallia*) became the more common pointers to lordships on the make. Already in the early eleventh-century customal of Vendôme *tensamentum* and *comandisia* appear as distinct exactions, which according to Dominique Barthélemy persist as virtually synonymous.[36] They need not have been coercive, and must surely have been justified in

---

33 *Select Charters*, 256; *Select Pleas*, no. 43.
34 *Orderic*, vi, 328–32, 444.
35 King, 'Anarchy', 133–4, citing *Gesta Stephani*, 148, 150, from which I quote; Crouch, *Reign of Stephen*, 209–12.
36 *Vie de Bouchard le Vénérable*, ed. C. Bourel de la Roncière, Collection de Textes pour servir à l'Etude et à l'Enseignement de l'Histoire (Paris, 1892), 36. See also D. Barthélemy, *La société dans le comté de Vendôme de l'an mil au XIVe siècle* (Paris, 1993), 328–9, 736.

realities undocumented; they were clearly manifestations of new and expanded lordships in growing domains.

The late lamented Pierre Bonnassie, in a remarkable study published in 1980, projected a historical dynamic for the spread and implantation of coercive lordships in west Mediterranean lands. He showed irrefutably that public structures of justice and command in the eastern Pyrenees, still virtually intact past 1010, were swept away in a paroxysm of castle-building in the years 1020 to 1060. He found the same tendency less destructively paced in Occitania; and it is a remarkable result of recent research that not even the disentangling of familial dynamics in a more complicated history of the Midi has much altered Bonnassie's chronology. So too in Spain, where the constraints of a perilous frontier preserved the cohesion of an old public monarchy, until it collapsed after the death of Alfonso VI (1065–1109). Strong lord-kingship was a reality in this world, not least where it was lacking.[37] What happened along the pilgrims' road under Queen Urraca (1109–26) and Alfonso the Battler (1104–34) uncannily prefigured the disorder under Stephen and Matilda in its lure to foreign knights clustering about insurgent lordships. And when one looks beyond Bonnassie's modestly cautious range, what is striking is the very generality of such crises down to 1150: protracted challenges to old orders from new or usurping claimants in multiplying castles in the Lazio, Tuscany, Lombardy, and Lotharingia in scattered spurts from 975 to past 1100; more disruptive ones, possibly in Poland in the 1030s, and certainly in Saxony after 1075, and Flanders in 1127.[38]

It is not my contention that a sweeping 'feudal revolution' reached England only with the death of Henry I. But similar challenges to old public order were experienced in almost every land of Latin Europe from about 975 to 1150, resulting in successive crises of growth, competition, and power. For special reasons the relatively disciplined lord-kingship of the Normans impeded the consequences of structural crisis; the new baronial lordships, ever threatening royalist order from the 1070s to 1106, burst forth anew after 1127, to be suppressed only under Henry II. Need anyone be reminded that virtually the same scenario, differently timed, played out under Louis VI of France and Henry V in Germany? What links England with these continental trajectories of power is the still incompletely known history of castles and the virtually unknown – perhaps unknowable? – history of needy knights in precariously endowed castles and baronial retinues. It is in this perspective that Stephen's England looks like a welcome new frontier for panoramic ambitions doomed finally to fail.

The evidence for this perspective has not, to my knowledge, been challenged, still less refuted.[39] Yet it has been questioned in other ways that bear directly on

---

37 'From the Rhône to Galicia: Origins and Modalities of the Feudal Order', reprinted in *From Slavery to Feudalism in South-Western Europe*, trans. J. Birrell (Cambridge, 1991), 104–31.

38 To be argued and documented in a book in progress.

39 It was sketched in T. N. Bisson, 'The "Feudal Revolution" ', *Past and Present*, 142 (1994), 29–39, pages that were little addressed in the 'Debate' that ensued.

the troubles under Stephen. According to some critics England cannot then have been so troubled or so violent, nor the Ile-de-France under Louis VI, as the sources make out. Those sources, they contend, are partisan as well as exaggerated. Petitions and narratives overstate not only the destruction but also the disruption of royal power. Moreover, the violence attributed to magnates, castellans, and knights (often Flemish) in the English accounts is thought to be suspect because it misrepresents the motives of aggrieved plaintiffs while making too much of damages. By one estimate barely ten per cent of religious houses were damaged in Stephen's reign, a circumstance quite at variance with the claims of massively generalised distress in the chronicles. A more recent account not only rejects the clerical evidence as a whole, but discredits the rhetorical lamentations of widespread disorder in particular. A further objection related to this scepticism is that those inclined to accept contemporary accounts of violence and disorder are misreading the preconceptions of societies in which rectitude and legitimacy have little relation to public order, and in which vengeance and moral outrage seem often in inscrutable conflict.[40]

These arguments relate to a wider and longer history than is needed here. Whatever their merits, they do little to explain what we surely know of Stephen's reign. It is clear enough that Flemish knights did not go to England to fight other people's feuds. They came to secure or to share in the rewards of lordship. *Tenserie* in England was a device to that end. That being so, it seems more than likely that the constraints associated with it in the generalised lamentations – the outrages of humiliation as well as forced works on castles – were likewise, at least primarily, symptomatic of coercive efforts to establish customary lordships of affective superiority. As everywhere else, those efforts were the usual reason for beating or demeaning peasants.

That the violence so described was as widespread in England as claimed seems unlikely; that it occurred is beyond reasonable doubt. Not only are the rhetorical lamentations borne out by specific and localized incidents, not only was the suffering of the 1140s long remembered, but the evidence of these accounts corresponds in chilling detail to that of independent accounts from France and León in the 1110s and from Catalonia during the same years as in England.[41] Moreover, in all these places as in England, the violence was conceptualized as violation, as disruptive of peaceful order. And because this happens to be the only 'order' represented in the sources cannot be a reason for rejecting the implication that for

---

40 See generally, Crouch, *Reign of Stephen*, ch. 16, who cites (336) Thomas Callahan Jr's study minimizing damages to clerical patrimonies, *Albion*, 6 (1974), 218–32, but not C. W. Hollister's rebuttal, ibid., 233–9; also Matthew, *King Stephen*, ch. 6, and 149, 162–9; and on France D. Barthélemy, 'Quelques réflexions sur Louis VI, Suger et la chevalerie', *Liber largitorius. Etudes d'histoire médiévale offertes à Pierre Toubert par ses élèves*, ed. D. Barthélemy and J.-M. Martin, Ecole pratique des Hautes Etudes. Sciences historiques et philologiques (Geneva, 2003), 435–53.

41 See, for example, *Crónicas anónimas de Sahagún*, ed. A. Ubieto Arteta, Textos Medievales, 75 (Zaragoza, 1987), 53–81, and T. N. Bisson, *Tormented Voices: Power, Crisis, and Humanity in Rural Catalonia, 1140–1200* (Cambridge, Mass., 1998).

the masses of working people as well as for the monks of Ely and Peterborough this violated regalian order was disorder. Nor would this inference be to privilege our problematic sources. It is merely to recognize that the equally effectual yet wholly undocumented culture of knightly ambition – a conflicting order of power in itself – was not the only imperative driving attitudes and events in the 1140s. The craving for patrimony and status must have been quite as powerful a motive as vengeance in this age, and it was countered by an unwavering conceptual persistence of public order. Many thought – surely the voiceless peasants as well as the monks, no less truthfully than tendentiously – that this was the order that had been violated.

Tenserie has the looks of a minor incident of disorder in Stephen's England. Yet the allusions to it that we have, when taken with other known circumstances, help to illuminate the underside of elite conflict in a crisis of conflicting ambitions and loyalties. The power to protect, once fumbled by the lord-king and his adversaries, allies, and sheriffs, must swiftly have become the talk of the castles. That is, of magnates in need of knights, and of knights in need of castles and patrimonial rewards. Theirs was the crisis of these years, for their victims, this time not wholly ignored, must have grasped what was happening. And of the knights in need, many came from lands familiar with protection-money. From their plight it was but an easy lapse into the brigandage that would become a scourge in the next generation.

10

Legal Treatises as Perceptions of
Law in Stephen's Reign

BRUCE R. O'BRIEN

J. H. ROUND's account of the burial of Geoffrey de Mandeville provides us with a point of departure for a discussion of law and its recorders in the reign of King Stephen. Geoffrey's body, Round tells us, was, according to one account, wrapped in lead and hung from a fruit tree in the Old Temple's burial ground, where it dangled for twenty years until the earl was allowed a Christian burial. Round underlined the irony of Geoffrey's gravesite: 'around the nameless resting-place of the great champion of anarchy, there was destined to rise, in later days, the home of English law'.[1] Here we see the perfect counterpoint – disorder and law; the one giving birth to the other; their symbiotic relationship symbolized by body and gravesite. Both ends of Round's irony are based on misperceptions. English law did not begin at the Temple, nor was Geoffrey so typical of the violent and lawless barons of the Anarchy. English law – the written tradition recording it – had begun with the first Anglo-Saxon kings to convert to Christianity in the early seventh century. Rebellious barons may have rejected royal authority as had Geoffrey de Mandeville, but when called upon to govern their territories, did so at times with remarkably royal best practices.

The irony, nevertheless, appeared clearer to Round than to us because, although a critical reader of charters of Stephen's reign, he was an uncritical user of the chronicles, and so without filter repeated their prejudices and distortions. To cite only one of countless instances, consider Round's description of Geoffrey's actions at Ramsey and Ely in 1144. His prose mostly consists of unmarked (though referenced) verbatim translations and paraphrases of passages from the *Liber Eliensis*, *Liber de Fundatione Cenobii de Waledena*, the Ramsey Chronicle, *Gesta Stephani*, and William of Newburgh's and Henry of Huntingdon's histories.[2] Round even repeats, without hint of disbelief in his prose, Gervase of Canterbury's comment that when Geoffrey rested on his way to the

---

[1]   J. H. Round, *Geoffrey de Mandeville: A Study of the Anarchy* (London, 1892), 226.
[2]   Ibid., 207–19.

siege of Burwell, in Round's words 'the very grass withered away beneath the touch of his unhallowed form!'[3] Nowadays, no one would read the Anglo-Saxon Chronicle's account or any other as anything other than the dark glass through which we perceive the events of Stephen's reign.

Round thought Earl Geoffrey characterized the period of violence and rebellion that marred most of King Stephen's reign, and Round was not alone in his belief. His teacher, William Stubbs, had already cast this position in concrete in his monumental *Constitutional History* in 1874.[4] Round's credulousness with chronicles may be due to Stubbs's reliance on these records in the construction of his own portrait of the age. Despite the *Select Charters*, Stubbs was a chronicle man.[5] For the better part of a century from the days of Stubbs and Round, few historians have desired or tried to shift this interpretation. Only since H. A. Cronne's work in 1970 has there been any sustained attempt to overturn or amend it, work joined by a number of scholars in the later years of the twentieth century, including, most notably, Edmund King.[6] The most recent additions to this revisionist tradition are the study by Graeme White of the aftermath of Stephen's reign, which includes a lengthy prelude covering the administration of justice under Stephen, and David Crouch's recent biography of the king.[7]

There is no need at present, consequently, for another consideration of the functioning of justice during Stephen's (and Matilda's and Count Henry's) reign. I think that work has been done and done well. I want to consider, nevertheless, a part of the legal territory rarely explored, but which I think will shed some light on the times. What I will be talking about is law, not justice. I will be looking at law when it was self-consciously conceived of as law, and at, albeit briefly, the perception of order and disorder that inevitably inform our interpretation of the normative statements that make up the law.

Historians who study law are usually less concerned with the development of legal principles, and more interested in their application. For that reason, they have studied the administration of justice much more than they have law, or

---

3   Ibid., 220, citing and quoting in full in the note Gervase of Canterbury's *Chronica: The Historical Works of Gervase of Canterbury*, ed. W. Stubbs, 2 vols. (RS, 1879–80), i, 128.

4   1874 was the date of the first edition; for his final relatively unchanged word, see W. Stubbs, *The Constitutional History of England*, 3 vols. (6th edn, Oxford, 1897), i, 353–4. See also H. W. C. Davis, 'The Anarchy of Stephen's Reign', *EHR*, 18 (1903), 630–41.

5   Such a dependence on chronicles is why Stubbs sets up the interpretative frame for each reign by arranging select passages from the chronicles before providing the documentary records: *Select Charters and Other Illustrations of English Constitutional History*, ed. W. Stubbs, 9th edn rev. H. W. C. Davis (Oxford, 1913), 134–44. The first edition came in 1870. In the 9th edition, William of Malmesbury dominates, with Henry of Huntingdon and the worst slice of the 1137 annal from the Peterborough Chronicle making up most of the rest.

6   H. A. Cronne, *The Reign of Stephen 1135–54: Anarchy in England* (London, 1970), 245–82; E. King, 'The Anarchy of King Stephen's Reign', *TRHS*, 5th ser., 34 (1984), 133–54.

7   G. J. White, *Restoration and Reform, 1153–1165: Recovery from Civil War in England* (Cambridge, 2000), 12–69; Crouch, *Reign of Stephen*.

rather, statements of black letter law, as a modern law student would put it. In fact, the last half century of anthropologically driven scholarship in customary law, dispute settlement and feud has left such statements, when they occur, in an evidentiary limbo – cited, but often avoided as unauthorized or unrepresentative, passed over in favour of what purport to be records of actual cases.[8] Some scholars act as if the records of disputes are themselves transparent and thus unproblematic. That they are anything but this is clear. So before the creation and survival of routine government records like pipe and plea rolls, scholars have only two types of non-anecdotal sources available: charters and law codes or treatises.[9]

This chapter will discuss law in Stephen's reign by considering contemporary statements in legal treatises of what the law was supposed to be. Such a focus inevitably changes the shape of how we understand and describe what we study. Justice, for instance, is about governing and control, not norms, in medieval contexts. And if we ask about government and governing, we are, for England during Stephen's reign, evaluating Stephen's rule. By looking at law through this lens, we implicitly accept law as king-centred – even if we plead that this is a limitation of our evidence.[10] Law, on the other hand, is a bigger thing, though often less evidenced in written records. It is the totality of rules concerning right and wrong, reinforced by strong censure or coercive force, and includes also the beliefs behind those rules. It includes what people wrote about law, believed the law to be, and what the law actually was. It is the unspoken and spoken norms that governed conduct. It is the personnel as well as the policies of law makers and judicial administrators. And it is always in flux.

So if we ask about law during Stephen's reign, we are not principally evaluating Stephen as a judicial administrator. We are asking instead about the norms governing conduct, the customs in the localities, their application, interpretation, enforcement, sometimes as performed by the king, sometimes done by someone else.[11] The sources that help answer these questions are many. One type that has not been much explored for Stephen's reign is, as mentioned, written statements of what the law was, or was supposed to be. The difference here between what was and what should be, between the ideal and reality, is immaterial, as all medieval statements of the law are normative, not descriptive. There are reasons to take another look at such sources since they may be able to offer a fresh

---

8   One work that does not do this and gives the codes serious attention is P. Hyams, *Rancor and Reconciliation in Medieval England* (Ithaca, NY, 2003).

9   Royal writs and charters, however, provide a sounder base for general kingdom-wide perceptions of royal justice as working, since subjects sought out its remedies: White, *Restoration*, 22–36. By treatise, I mean any legal text that is not official or authoritative in its origin – for example, a text that describes the kingdom's laws and is attributed to a king, but is not that king's nor necessarily a description of the kingdom's law.

10 Almost all works dealing with law during the Anarchy have this as their goal.

11 Consider White, *Restoration*, 36–69, who analyses the rule by the empress, her son Henry, and the magnates (including the church).

perspective for thinking about law, norms, and the administration of justice under Stephen.

There is a good case to be made that two twelfth-century legal treatises were written during Stephen's reign. These works were privately composed, selective in their coverage, and, for the most part, original – i.e., not derived from specific texts. The first, and perhaps the earlier of the two, is the *Leges Edwardi Confessoris* in versions one and two.[12] This treatise is framed as a royal code that recorded a council held in 1070, where men 'learned in the law' swore to the *laga Edwardi*, the laws that had held force before the Conquest. After hearing these customs, King William I is said to have confirmed them and authorized the collection. Version 1 consists of thirty-four chapters which are divided between three concerns of the author: the first (chapters 1–11) treats the laws and customs of the church; the second (chapters 12–19) covers the king's peace, or royal rights; and lastly, chapters 20–33 describe how the law was to be administered and both church's and king's peace ensured. Seen through this scheme, the list of topics appears less miscellaneous: (part one) peace of the church, the judicial liberty of ecclesiastical courts, sanctuary, tithes, ordeals, Peter's Pence, exemption from danegeld; (part two) the king's peace, assault, homicide, treasure trove, murder fines, pardons, culpability of wives of murderers and traitors; (part three) frankpledge, suretyship of lords who have sake and soke, culpability through hospitality, publicizing discovery of stray animals, protection of the Jews, court of the *decanus*, hundred and wapentake courts, trithings and shire courts, reeves, and small hundreds and their fines.

The legal contents of the *Leges* are derived from no known Old English legal sources, or, with few exceptions, any texts for that matter.[13] This is particularly striking given the trend of legislative composition from 1066 to the 1130s, where all but one legal treatise were either translations of older English laws or principally derived from those old laws.[14] The one exception, in fact, may be in origin not a private treatise like the rest, but a version of original legislation of William I.[15] The contents of the *Leges Edwardi* show a remarkable similarity not to Old English law codes but to the kinds of things found in charters and writs, and which one would, as a holder of privileges, be asked to know about or administer. If it was derived from any texts, it was derived from an actual collection of charters and writs, to which it stood as a commentary to explain the various rights, exemptions, and procedures.

This origin helps narrow the number of places where the treatise might have been composed. Since the *Leges* covers those points of law that would govern

---

[12] For much of the following, see B. R. O'Brien, *God's Peace and King's Peace: The Laws of Edward the Confessor* (Philadelphia, 1999), chs. 3 and 4.

[13] The exceptions are c. 2, which comes from a continental text of the Peace of God, and c. 5 on sanctuary, which derives in part from the *Capitulare legibus additum* of 803.

[14] See below, 191.

[15] The so-called Ten Articles of William: see P. Wormald, *The Making of English Law: King Alfred to the Twelfth Century. Volume I: Legislation and its Limits* (Oxford, 1999), 402–3.

contact between clerics and the outside world (royal or otherwise), and does not mention monks, it likely originated in an episcopal household.[16] If it was indeed a commentary based on the archival records of the see, then it would best fit with the charters and writs of Lincoln and Coventry, with Norwich, York, and Worcester also possible. Because the treatise is interested in the customs of the Danelaw, and in particular its curious small hundreds, Lincoln provides the best circumstantial fit.[17] Among the household of Lincoln (or any of the other cathedral communities), many might have had the time, skill, and inclination to produce the treatise. The archdeacons are possible authors, as well as the deans and household clerks. The most likely suspect in Lincoln, however, was the lay steward of the bishop – either Goslin or Walter de Amundeville. Their duties would be most closely aligned with the contents of the treatise.

A strong case can be made for a date of composition early in Stephen's reign. The most likely period was in the year or two after 1136, since it looks like the treatise is a response to King Stephen's general charter of that year at Oxford. Neither the physical evidence of the manuscripts, nor the contents, disagree with this date, and the later development of the text in the last years of Stephen's reign or early under Henry II argues for it.[18] And although King Stephen at the start of his reign invoked the *laga Edwardi* as his legal benchmark, the legal minds of the day appear already to have shifted to the first half of the twelfth century as their measure of good law, choosing to compose new treatises rather than translate the old. After Henry II's accession, there are no more references to a restoration of the laws of King Edward in coronation charters.

The text grew during Stephen's reign, adding five new chapters. The original text was also revised slightly. These revisions and additions may have occurred in two stages, though the sole manuscript witness to the intermediate stage might just as easily show contamination of the original by a copy of the second version, or vice versa. Nevertheless, the reviser – whether or not the same person as the author – added items that may tell us where and how the treatise was being used. Ignoring for the moment chapter 35, which is a rhetorical continuation of the original version's chapter 34, four legal chapters were added. Chapter 36 is about what to do when someone was executed for theft, but was believed by some to be innocent. Chapter 37 prohibits usury and recounts Edward the Confessor had banned it. Chapter 38 prohibits the buying or selling of animals without good witnesses; 39 is a qualification of 38, because the butchers from the cities and boroughs claimed the right to slaughter buy and sell animals every day, and the citizens and burghers claimed 'as their own customs that around the feast of St Martin they used to purchase animals without pledges in order to do their butchering in preparation for Christmas'. The king agreed the citizens could keep their custom.

---

16 O'Brien, *God's Peace*, 49.

17 Ibid., 53–60.

18 Ibid., 47–8, 106. The third version was finished by 1170, based on manuscript evidence, but may have been done significantly earlier.

Where might these chapters have been added? Or rather, to where had the treatise travelled? A case can be made for London. Here we should be cautious. London is a magnet for sources. Nevertheless, London may have been where the *Leges* was in the late 1130s or 1140s. Let me revisit an old theory of mine.[19] The revision and enlargement of the *Leges* may be evidenced by one manuscript witness, BL MS Cotton Cleopatra A.xvi, which ends at chapter 37 on usury. In the 1130s, Osbert of Clare, prior of Westminster, had first reported Edward the Confessor's dislike of usury in his *Vita sancti Edwardi*, written to support the unsuccessful bid at that time to have Edward canonized.[20] Earlier works on Edward do not mention usury. The full second version of the *Leges* adds titles that are distinctly urban – they only make sense in a market town or city where the slaughter of animals could be regulated. Lincoln of course fits the bill, but so do many English towns, especially London. It is the story of the Confessor, however, that provides an extra reason for seeing the *Leges* in its later version as a London text.

If the text were in London by the late 1130s, it may have played a role in the soured relationship between the Londoners and the Empress Matilda. One source from the period may hint at this. The Gloucester continuator of the *Chronicle* of John of Worcester, discussed in Edmund King's contribution to this volume, tells us about Matilda's difficulties in London. This continuation provides unique details explaining why the relationship between the Londoners and the empress soured. The crucial line relevant to the *Leges* is the following: 'The lady was asked by the Londoners that they might be allowed to live under the excellent laws of King Edward, and not the oppressive ones of her father, Henry.[21] She did not listen to good advice but harshly rejected their petition, and there was great disorder in the city'.[22]

What if the Londoners had used this basic text as a statement of the *laga Edwardi*, and had added to it a few items of local importance. And what if when they approached Matilda in 1141 to ask for confirmation of the *laga*, it was this text they presented to her, rather than a simple oral plea for the good old law? Her rejection of it may be because the Londoners trashed her father's laws as *graues*. It might also be because the *leges optime* were credited to Edward and William I, rather than to Henry I, whom the Angevins made their legal benchmark. It is impossible to know whether or not the Londoners had a text in hand. Despite the

---

19 Ibid., 39.
20 Osbert de Clare, *Vita Beati Edwardi Regis Anglorum*, c. 1, in M. Bloch, ed., 'La vie de s. Édouard le Confesseur par Osbert de Clare', *Analecta Bollandiana*, 41 (1923), 67.
21 Note the similar scene in the *Leges Edwardi Confessoris* (hereafter ECF), c. 34–34.1a, where the barons of England (here Englishmen who were learned in the law) objected to foreign laws (which were familiar to William's nobles) and asked for King William I to confirm the laws of King Edward. Their objection is based on the fact that Edward's laws were traditional and familiar, while Norwegian law (which William had praised) was new and unfamiliar. William, unlike Matilda, acquiesced. This chapter of the *Leges Edwardi* appears to belong to the earliest recension, and not to the later additions.
22 *John of Worcester*, iii, 296–7.

abundance of London texts of the *Leges Edwardi* used in this way in the thirteenth and fourteenth centuries, earlier citations of the laws of Edward the Confessor appear often to be general labels for the good old law, in or out of texts.[23] But if they did have the text, which is at least a possibility, then this would be the entrance of the *Leges Edwardi* into the realm of national politics, a place it was certainly to hold near the time of Magna Carta, if not earlier, a topic to which I will return at the end of the article.

While the Londoners in 1141 are conjectured users, other eyes and hands are certain. The second version of the *Leges*, as mentioned earlier, attracted a reviser sometime after the 1140s, but before 1170. This reviser improved the style of the treatise overall and enlarged it slightly. The legal contents change hardly at all. Another reader, the reviser of the fifth edition of Henry of Huntingdon's *Historia Anglorum* had the text in hand as early as 1149. He inserted a copy of the *Tripartita*, a frequently found grouping of the Ten Articles of William I, the *Leges* in its third version, and a Norman genealogy, into Henry's text as an illustration perhaps of the general tenor of William I's governance of England as well as of his legitimacy.[24] Both of these users may, in fact, postdate Stephen's reign; the manuscript witnesses to the revision of the treatise and to its incorporation in Henry's history are, while rough, the only certain dates we have. They would place the revision no later than *c*. 1175 and its insertion into Henry's text no later than *c*. 1190.[25]

What is as interesting for our purposes here is what is not in the treatise. First, there is no occurrence of *violentia* as commonly understood by either the proponents of England's place in the 'feudal revolution' – the exercise of power by castle-dwelling lords and their retinues, not restrainable by law – or in the more general or common meaning of acts that cause harm. Despite the church fussing about diminished tithes and lost exemptions from some taxes, there are no *malae consuetudines* in what is a treatise on customs. When tithes are withheld, for example, it was not bad lords who were at fault, but the Devil – which is a typical

---

23   W. Ullmann, 'On the Influence of Geoffrey of Monmouth in English History', in *Speculum Historiale: Geschichte im Spiegel von Geschichtsschreibung und Geschichtsdeutung Johannes Spörl dargebracht,* ed. C. Bauer, L. Böhn, and M. Miiller (Freiburg, 1965), 257–76; J. C. Holt, *Magna Carta* (2nd edn, Cambridge, 1992), 93–5, 115–20, and idem, 'The Origins of the Constitutional Tradition in England', in *Magna Carta and Medieval Government* (London, 1985), 1–22; J. Catto, 'Andrew Horn: Law and History in Fourteenth-Century England', in *The Writing of History in the Middle Ages: Essays Presented to Richard William Southern*, ed. R. H. C. Davis and J. M. Wallace-Hadrill (Oxford, 1981), 370–2, 387.

24   *Huntingdon*, clii–clv. The intention to illustrate a royal reign by inserting a law code is clearer in version 5B, where the *Instituta Cnuti* has been inserted at the end of Cnut's reign, immediately before his death.

25   The earliest copy of the third version is in Paris, BN fons lat. 4771, datable to the third quarter of the twelfth century: Liebermann placed it *c*. 1160; I would date it slightly later, *c*. 1175: see B. R. O'Brien, 'The *Instituta Cnuti* and the Translation of English Law', *ANS*, 25 (2003) 184 and note 40. The earliest copy of Henry of Huntingdon's version 5A is London Lambeth Palace MS 118, copied at the end of the twelfth century: *Huntingdon*, cxxxiv–v.

Anglo-Saxon response to bad events and was inherited by some of the Anglo-Norman historians writing under Stephen.[26] This attitude resembles that of Wulfstan's early eleventh-century sermons on the Viking invasions and destruction they wrought – these disasters were all a result of sin and thus constituted God's punishment of the Christians.[27] Wulfstan was no forgotten homilist in the mid-twelfth century: his sermons were still being copied and read.[28] While then there was no *violentia* committed by renegade lords and their followers, there were still problems in the world of the author. Men and women stole, committed assaults, and murdered one another. But the author assumes that the bishop is usually the person to take care of things legally and by himself, and that one went to the king only as a last resort for enforcement with contumacious folk.[29] There is no hint that such a final appeal would go unanswered.

Again, it is likely during Stephen's reign that a second legal treatise was composed. This one, the *Leis Willelme*, the first legal treatise or code to appear in French anywhere in Francophone Europe, combines chapters that appear for the most part to be original with translated selections from Cnut's laws.[30] It is difficult to date. Like the *Leges Edwardi*, it acknowledges Edward the Confessor and William I as its authorizing kings; it does not speak of Henry I at all.[31] This, I think, places it earlier than 1154, when Henry I became the standard legal benchmark. It is interesting to note about both of these texts, that their attributions to older kings reduces any partisan response to them – these are not the *Leges Henrici I* (for which we have no early copies – only one is twelfth-century) or the *Leges Stephani Magni*.[32]

The *Leis Willelme* is similar in many ways to the contents of the *Leges Edwardi*, covering the kinds of issues an ecclesiastical body (whether regular canons or bishop's household) might have encountered. It starts with the

---

26 ECf 8.3a; Henry of Huntingdon, for one, saw the operation of God's judgment in the events of his world, *Huntingdon*, lix, and, for example, the prologue to book v.

27 Wulfstan, 'Sermo Lupi ad Anglos', in *The Homilies of Wulfstan*, ed. D. Bethurum (Oxford, 1957), 255–75 (no. XX); M. Godden, 'Apocalypse and Invasion in Late Anglo-Saxon England', in *From Anglo-Saxon to Early Middle English: Studies Presented to E. G. Stanley*, ed. M. Godden, D. Gray, and T. Hoad (Oxford, 1994), 130–62.

28 *Homilies of Wulfstan*, 2 (MS Bar), 5 (MS H), and 7 (MS V). See also the works in M. Swan and E. Treharne, *Rewriting Old English in the Twelfth Century* (Cambridge, 2000).

29 For example, ECf 6, 8.2

30 Wormald, *Making*, 407–9; O'Brien, *God's Peace*, 28–9; J. Wüest, *Die 'Leis Willelme': Untersuchungen zur ältesten Gesetzbuch in französischer Sprache, Romanica Helvetica*, 79 (Bern, 1969). Still useful is F. Liebermann, 'Über die Leis Willelme', *Archiv für das Studium der neueren Sprachen und Literatur*, 106 (1901), 113–38.

31 Leis Wl prol.

32 The author of the *Leges Henrici Primi* composed introductory sections to his *Quadripartitus* that were meant to cover both books. These sections comment directly on the contemporary legal scene as seen from the position of a writer seeking royal patronage: see Richard Sharpe's analysis and translation in 'The Prefaces of "Quadripartitus" ', in *Law and Government in Medieval England and Normandy: Essays in Honour of Sir James Holt*, ed. G. Garnett and J. Hudson (Cambridge, 1994), 148–72.

inviolability of church sanctuary. This is followed by the king's peace (including the accountability of royal officials and barons); the obligations of suretyship of those accused of robbery or larceny; obligation to raise hue and cry against thieves and to exhibit strayed livestock; procedure for paying wergeld; wounding; false judgment and compurgation; breaking into churches and homes, breach of the archbishop's protection, Peter's Pence; rape; attachment of alleg-edly stolen livestock; murder fine; modes of proof in select cases; crimes on the four highways; forfeiture of thieves' goods; guarding the roads; and heriots.[33] Certain elements of this list should sound familiar. They read like the litany of complaints by chroniclers and ecclesiastics about aristocratic misbehaviour under King Stephen.[34] The last item in the list, heriots, highlights one of the sources of danger during this time; heriots would have been a matter of concern to what David Crouch has called affinities – nobles and their retinues tied under pressure of war to greater lords in larger coalitions.[35] Following this original section of the *Leis*, there is a hodgepodge of five chapters,[36] a collection of rules and a couple of odd case scenarios taken, it appears, from Roman law, and then a translation of much of II Cnut.[37] Considering the whole, the relationship of lords and men figure more prominently here than in any other post-Conquest legal treatise. Is this a reflection on the increasing pressure such relationships were under in the twelfth century, especially when the large affinities identified by Crouch were taking shape?

So, circumstantially, the text makes most sense written not so early in Stephen's reign, when there was no civil war in England, but later, perhaps broadly 1139–1150, or after the cataclysms of 1141. But a circumstantial case can easily be driven by wishful thinking. There is really very little to go on to help tie this treatise down chronologically. Both of these datings – of the *Leges Edwardi* and *Leis Willelme* – are best cases, not only or certain cases. Dating either text as I have depends on my assumption that the author was rational, honest, and responding to events. Too often this is the unspoken bedrock of our interpretation of anonymous texts; only sometimes can it be independently confirmed.

Stephen's reign, then, likely saw the composition of two legal treatises, both pretending to be royal, which neither is. Both seem to show us law in some locality – the *Leis* in old Mercia and the *Leges* in the Danelaw.[38] Both focus on the administrative ground level of law and provide some comment on its reasoning

---

33 Leis Wl 1–28.2, though note that in the earliest manuscript, BL Additional MS 49366, c. 20, on heriots, is placed after c. 28.

34 For example, the less shrilly anecdotal, more generalizing section of the 1137 entry in *The Peterborough Chronicle, 1070–1154*, ed. C. Clark (2nd edn, Oxford, 1970), 56.

35 Crouch, *Reign of Stephen*, 153–5. Both the *Leis Willelme* and the *Instituta Cnuti* amend Cnut's law on heriots, strengthening the case that this was of more than passing interest to contemporaries; *Quadripartitus* and the *Consiliatio Cnuti* do not amend the law.

36 Leis Wl 29–36, covering the tenurial security of farmers and obligations of peasants; and feudal rights.

37 Leis Wl 33–8; Wormald, *Making*, 409.

38 Leis Wl 2 and 3; ECf 12.3–4, 18.3a, 20, 27.1–2, 30–1, 33 and 34.

and enforcement. Both are primarily original texts, having no known textual sources. For comparison, in Henry I's reign, the *Quadripartitus-Leges Henrici Primi* author was at work – though there is no sign that anyone read the contemporary description in the *Leges Henrici* until the thirteenth century (it may have been too big to justify the time and materials copying it).[39] There may also have been two other translators at work – the *Instituta Cnuti* was done by 1123, and the *Consiliatio* may have been done under Henry (or possibly Stephen). So for all the attention Henry I receives as a lion of justice, the legal works of his reign are almost wholly derivative of Old English legal texts.[40] A large proportion of the *Leges Henrici* is a translation.[41] But in Stephen's reign, we have the first original treatises describing English law since the Norman Conquest.

Was the production of these texts, with their focus on peace and destructive crimes, inspired or provoked by the war and violence of Stephen's reign? Were these treatises insistent restatements of the norms in the face of the behaviour of now unrestrained lords? Are they a plea for good governance that is now lost, a call back to earlier kings who administered justice, a sign that bad times encourage hard thinking about law?[42] This was how the extensively doctored fourth (or London) version of the *Leges Edwardi* was used in the early thirteenth century.[43] Or are these treatises evidence of functioning government, trust in royal law and its administration, a sign that less of a breakdown occurred than some contemporary observers claimed? It all depends on how we read the Anarchy. Do we trust the Peterborough chronicler's account of endless tortures between 1139 and 1154, or the *Gesta Stephani*'s implication that all that occurred were the misdeeds here and there of a few traitors? And for our related purpose, then, there is the linked question of how significant it is that these two legal treatises were likely composed in a period of some disorder. How are we at this

---

[39] H. G. Richardson and G. O. Sayles, *Law and Legislation from Æthelberht to Magna Carta* (Edinburgh, 1966), 45. The *Quadripartitus*, on the other hand, was read and copied: see P. Wormald, 'Quadripartitus', in *Law and Government in Medieval England*, 111–47.

[40] *Quadripartitus* and *Leges Henrici Primi* are a translation of Old English laws and a statement of current law (*c.* 1115) that drew heavily on Old English texts; the *Instituta Cnuti*, completed by 1123, is a revision and translation of Cnut's laws and other Old English laws; the *Consiliatio Cnuti* is likely to have been created around the same time, though its dating probably needs to be revisited. It consists of a translation of Cnut's laws along with a few other titles from older kings. As mentioned above, the one exception to this trend is the so-called *Willelmi articuli decem*, which looks like a compilation made from legislative writs. On all of these, see Wormald, *Making*, 402–6, 411–14; O'Brien, *God's Peace*, 27–9; O'Brien, 'The *Instituta Cnuti*', 177–8, 184–6.

[41] For example, Hn 41.9, on the procedure for a lord to clear himself of complicity in the flight of one of his men after an accusation, is a close translation of Cn 31.1a – note that this is almost verbatim how the author had translated the same passage in Cnut for his *Quadripartitus*: *Die Gesetze der Angelsachsen*, ed. F. Liebermann, 3 vols. (Halle, 1903–16), i, 336–7; *Leges Henrici Primi*, ed. L. J. Downer (Oxford, 1970), 148–9, 350.

[42] Cf. Holt, *Magna Carta*, 93–6.

[43] O'Brien, *God's Peace*, 118–19; F. Liebermann, *Über die Leges Anglorum saeculo xiii ineunte Londoniis collectae* (Halle, 1894).

remove to measure twelfth-century disorder, which is larger than the issues in this paper and has captured the attentions of generations of historians, not just medieval but for all periods?[44] The core of the problem is what to label as violence, as signs of disorder. In the scholarly contributions to this issue, there has been one I think glaring absence from the calculations. Here I only wish to offer some observations on this issue, since it does colour our interpretation of the legal treatises, before turning back to interpreting the context of the legal treatises.

Consider the murky relationship between justice, authority, and violence or disorder. If medieval justice worked, and we accepted that its results were fair – meaning, you go after a thief and catch one (and not someone else) – then the fact that Henry I is praised for enforcement of a judicial peace in his kingdom would stand in stark contrast to Stephen's failures. This understanding of medieval justice is the basis for many of the harsh judgements by Stephen's contemporaries. It is also implicit in many modern analyses. If on the other hand, you may have some doubts about the fairness of a system of justice that makes Texas look enlightened, where many of the accused (by later records) fled out of fear of justice rather than have their day in court, where proofs like the ordeal, while anthropologically understandable, would not likely lead to the truth of an event and therefore a fair verdict, what do you do to measure the level and consequences of state-inflicted violence? Is the hanging of a convicted thief an act of violence even if the thief was guilty and death was the penalty? How would the execution be perceived by onlookers in the man's village?[45] What if the man had been seized during a time of famine, and the theft was of the lord's food rents? Can we assume that most people executed were innocent (consider the state of Illinois's 2003 admission that the majority of its death row inmates were likely innocent)? Round attributed the rebellions of Stephen's reign to Henry I's tough justice.[46] Ignoring the jingoistic rhetoric of how safe Henry made England for wandering widows and merchants, one could see him as a violent tyrant, abrogating rights, arbitrarily imprisoning and fining, and lashing out at invisible foes with the power of his state, rather than as a due process king interested in treating every man fairly.[47] Round would not disagree with this negative appraisal of

---

44 This has been an issue for some time; consider the following attempts: A. MacFarlane, *The Justice and the Mare's Ale: Law and Disorder in Seventeenth-Century England* (Oxford, 1981); L. Stone, 'Interpersonal Violence in English Society, 1300–1980', *Past and Present*, 101 (1983), 22–33; J. A. Sharpe, 'The History of Violence in England: Some Observations', *Past and Present*, 108 (1985), 206–15; J. S. Cockburn, 'Patterns of Violence in English Society: Homicide in Kent, 1560–1985', *Past and Present*, 130 (1991), 70–106; and the debate between Thomas Bisson and Dominique Barthélemy, Stephen White, Timothy Reuter, and Chris Wickham in *Past and Present* between 1994 and 1997.

45 Andrew Reynolds's archaeological work makes clear how visible a hanging would be to the local communities: *Later Anglo-Saxon England: Life and Landscape* (Stroud, 1999), 105–10 and fig. 37.

46 Round, *Geoffrey de Mandeville*, 35.

47 Cronne recognized this back in 1970: *Reign of Stephen*, 247–8.

Henry I.[48] What would this perspective do to comparisons of the violence during the two reigns? Perhaps our expectations for justice under Henry I are too high, our perception of its diminution under Stephen too extreme. But we should at least recognize that by any modern standard – ideal or real – both kings likely failed to provide anything like justice the majority of times it was called for. For those on the receiving end, royal justice was hardly distinguishable from the violence of a cavalcade.

Violence and disorder are in the eye of the beholder and the receiver. Violence is, after all, a relative experience that varies not only by time and location, but also by class and education. Thus the lack of many complaints about violence before Stephen and their increase thereafter should not make us think that life for peasants and the church was not already violent before. Rather, what was probably a violent world became even more violent. The change was visible to observers; its true scope, based on a fair comparison with what had gone on before, was not what they aimed to understand. Yet I do not think the change was so easily perceptible to those living through it in 1139 or in 1150. It was not so much of kind as of geographic spread, and in an age where travel and writing were not so easily indulged in, it would take some time before enterprising historians (for the most part) heard from enough sources and produced their evaluations of the reign. It is worrying that these mostly took place after the reign was over, during the triumphant days of Henry II.[49] Perhaps the best comparison is with the downfall of the Lancastrians and their replacement by the Tudors, whose propaganda machine effectively controlled historical views of the fifteenth century for long ages to come.[50]

So why did a number of contemporary observers describe the actions of England's nobles in a way that could not avoid reminding readers of continental nobles out on cavalcades? They described England as awash with noble violence

---

[48] See Round, *Geoffrey de Mandeville*, 28.

[49] The sixth version of Henry of Huntingdon's *Historia*, which introduced the most strident criticisms of Stephen's rule, was produced after the 1153 Treaty of Westminster or the accession of Henry II in 1154: *Huntingdon*, lxxvi, lxi (citing a *c.* 1155 copy of version 6). The hypercritical passages in the *Peterborough Chronicle* were composed in a single block sometime 'in or after 1155' according to Dorothy Whitelock and Cecily Clark: *The Anglo-Saxon Chronicle: A Revised Translation*, ed. D. Whitelock (New Brunswick, NJ, 1961), xvi, and *The Peterborough Chronicle*, xxv. William of Malmesbury was from the start a client of the empress's party: *Historia Novella*, 1 (pref. to Robert of Gloucester). Orderic, writing mostly from 1136 on, avoided political commitment, no doubt because of the vulnerable position of St Evroul on the Norman frontier with Anjou: *Orderic*, vi, xviii, xxv. John of Worcester, compiling his last version between 1140 and 1143, found it wise only at that date to insert an account of the council of London where Henry I had his barons swear fealty to his daughter (*John of Worcester*, iii, xxxii, 166–7). Note that the Gloucester version puts this in different text in 1128: ibid., 176–83.

[50] M. McKisack, *Medieval History in the Tudor Age* (Oxford, 1971). The success of the Angevin story can be read in almost all of the chronicles produced after 1154: for example, the Battle Abbey Chronicle, where the official line is starkly repeated: *The Chronicle of Battle Abbey*, ed. E. Searle (Oxford, 1980), 210–13.

because that is how they framed their world. Such a social ordering is where their metaphors and *topoi* came from – the language generated by the breakdown of the Carolingian world and its replacement by something less clean.[51] They also acted out of innocent ignorance: they could not have known that the Old English state inherited by the Normans had deep roots and greater recent continuity of power and stability than other states of Europe, including Francia or any of its parts, which had long been independent by the mid-twelfth century.

Our legal writers probably would have moved in these circles, but they show no similar bias. They describe their law without obvious connection to the allegedly lawless world in which they lived. There are at least three reasons for this. First, one should remember that disorder was localized and of limited duration in England's Anarchy.[52] The composition of a legal treatise that aimed to explain local law might have perceived no significance in the rare and often distant political or criminal actions on a description of law. Second, these writers chose a frame that, while retrospective, was aimed at a different target than that of the contemporary chroniclers. While their chronicling contemporaries took the post-1154 agenda of the victor back into the balance of events under Stephen, the legal writers took the law of their own day and projected it back on the Norman Conquest. Here were Edward the Confessor's laws confirmed by William I, his heir.[53] And no one could really say otherwise. The third reason why the legal writers show no political bias is that they were governed by England's long tradition of written royal laws (and their private recording), which created the mould into which they poured their contemporary observations.[54] In a different but related way, the traditions of churchmen lamenting the nasty ways of lay lords created a narrow language of description for chroniclers of the woes of Stephen's reign.

Law does not so easily respond to our prodding. Is the production of an orderly structured view of the world that is implicit in most medieval law codes a sign of disorder? Are they inversely related? Or is the treatises' existence a reflection of business as usual? One can't say based on two texts potentially composed at the time, and neither of which is transparent about the intention or purpose of the author. But two things we can say about where they came from and where they

---

51 E. Magnou-Nortier, 'Les mauvaises coutumes en Auvergne, Bourgogne méridionale, Languedoc et Provence au XIe siècle: un moyen d'analyse social', *Structures féodales et féodalisme dans l'Occident méditerranéen, X–XIIIe siècles: bilan et perspectives de recherches* (Rome, 1980), 135–72; J.-P. Poly and E. Bournazel, *La mutation féodale, Xe–XIIe siècles* (2nd edn, Paris, 1991).
52 A perusal of any of the primary sources conveys this impression.
53 ECf 34.1; Leis Wl prol.
54 In contrast to the French world, where Carolingian precedents and practices must have seemed distant by the twelfth century and in any case, though still read and copied, sparked no contemporary secular imitation. See O'Brien, *God's Peace*, 19–21; consider the evidence of late eleventh- and twelfth-century manuscripts of Carolingian laws described in the catalogue of H. Mordek, *Bibliotheca capitulorum regum Francorum manuscripta*, MGH Hilfsmittel, 15 (Munich, 1995).

were going. First, the survival of the tradition of written law codes, attributed to kings regardless of whether they deigned to actually make law, is a testament to the power and resilience of the Old English state. Its habits had a momentum that carried them past 1066 and deep into the twelfth century: the recording of royal law was only one of these.[55] Second, we can say that this legal activity during Stephen's reign, embracing not only the composition of new treatises, but the copying of old, and their spread in further copies in the third quarter of the twelfth century, prepared the way for the course the Becket conflict took.[56] It is to these laws that bishops had recourse during the dispute, and whose existence in the anti-royalist arsenal likely inspired *Glanvill*'s canard that English law was unwritten.

[55] J. Campbell, 'The Late Anglo-Saxon State: A Maximum View', *Proceedings of the British Academy*, 87 (1994), 39–65; Wormald, *Making*, 398–415, 481–3.
[56] B. O'Brien, 'The Becket Conflict and the Invention of the Myth of *Lex Non Scripta*', in *Learning the Law: Teaching and the Transmission of Law in England, 1150–1900*, ed. J. A. Bush and A. Wijffels (London, 1999), 1–16.

Index of Names and Places